ONE STOP
ONE LIFE

ONE STOP ONE LIFE

From market stall to 1,000 shops in 25 years

KEVIN THRELFALL

ICON BOOKS

Published in the UK in 2014 by
Icon Books Ltd, Omnibus Business Centre,
39–41 North Road, London N7 9DP
email: info@iconbooks.net
www.iconbooks.net

Sold in the UK, Europe, South Africa and Asia
by Faber & Faber Ltd, Bloomsbury House,
74–77 Great Russell Street, London WC1B 3DA

Distributed in the UK, Europe, South Africa and Asia
by TBS Ltd, TBS Distribution Centre, Colchester Road,
Frating Green, Colchester CO7 7DW

Distributed in Australia and New Zealand
by Allen & Unwin Pty Ltd,
PO Box 8500, 83 Alexander Street,
Crows Nest, NSW 2065

Distributed in Canada by
Publishers Group Canada,
76 Stafford Street, Unit 300
Toronto, Ontario M6J 2S1

Distributed in South Africa by
Jonathan Ball, Office B4, The District,
41 Sir Lowry Road, Woodstock 7925

Distributed in India by Penguin Books India,
7th Floor, Infinity Tower – C, DLF Cyber City,
Gurgaon 122002, Haryana

ISBN: 978-184831-858-8

Printed and bound in Europe by Latitude Press

– CONTENTS –

List of Illustrations		6
Acknowledgements		8
Foreword		9
Introduction		11
Monetary Values		13
1	Born in a Bucket	15
2	Lord of the Flies	25
3	Barrow Boy	43
4	Gypsies, Tramps and Thieves	59
5	Moving Up the Food Chain	71
6	Chain Smoking	93
7	90p Pete and the Stock Exchange	103
8	What Next?	123
9	Marriage of Convenience	135
10	Following a Paper Chain	151
11	1,000 Stores	161
12	Non-Stop then One-Stop	179
13	Working Day & Nite	193
14	Over and Out	207
15	Up the Creek Without a Paddle	223
16	Jack in the Box	235
17	Well Done, Beef!	249
18	Going Back to School	261
19	Stick to Your Knitting	273
20	Life After Death	283
Appendix		303
Index		315

– LIST OF ILLUSTRATIONS –

Foreword: Sir Terry Leahy

1. My first school: Elston Hall Primary.
2. Moreton Country Club.
3. Inspection day, Denstone College, 1967.
4. The all-conquering rugby side of 1966/67.
5. Shrewsbury House, Denstone College.
6. Cannock market stall, 1971.
7. Celebrating record takings, Cannock market, 1969.
8. The famous dog food delivery van.
9. Outside of Lo-Cost Wolverhampton, 1972.
10. Before the grand opening, Lo-Cost Wolverhampton, 1972.
11. First cigarette kiosk, Wolverhampton market, 1975.
12. St Michael's Church, Tettenhall, 5 March 1977.
13. The happy couple.
14. Established Lo-Cost fascia for all stores.
15. High street fascia with familiar advertising.
16. Playing golf with the 'Great White Shark'.
17. The T&S board celebrating the opening of our 100th store.
18. A bit of R&R with the boys, Jersey 1988.
19. Announcement of the Preedy/Dillons purchase, May 1989.
20. Meeting Princess Anne at the NEC.
21. The famous Fantasia range of pick and mix confectionery.
22. Acquisition of Mac's convenience stores.
23. Press announcement of our takeover of M&W plc.
24. Willie Thorne opens our 1,000th store in Poole.
25. T&S board photo, 1998.
26. A corporate golf day with 'Monty' and Jimmy Tarbuck.
27. Convenience stores rebranded to the One-Stop fascia.
28. Expanding up north with the Day & Nite acquisition.
29. Breaking through the £1 billion turnover figure.
30. Front-page news in the *Financial Times*.
31. Receiving Entrepreneur of the Year Award.
32. Business partner and lifelong friend Dave.
33. Dave, Lorraine, Gill and I.
34. Welcome to the Wolves board from Sir Jack Hayward.
35. Announcing that Steve Morgan has bought the Wolves.
36. Father dies, February 1991.
37. Receiving the 'Monkey Classic' golf trophy from Ian Botham.
38. Ian Botham opens Fordhouses Cricket Club, 2013.
39. My office above the garage in Wolverhampton.
40. The opening of the Threlfall Library at Denstone College.
41. The Horns at Boningale.
42. The team that saved my life.
43. The 'Threlfall' boardroom at One-Stop Brownhills.
44. At Compton Abbas with my Trinidad TB20.
45. Grandkids Jack, Mia, Sam and Oliver with our dogs.
46. Yet another holiday – Gill and I cruising in 2011.

This book is dedicated to Martin Knowles, Steve Woodward,
the Ambulance Service and the Air Ambulance Service.
Without their combined skills and quick thinking I would
not have survived on 23 April 2014.

– ACKNOWLEDGEMENTS –

My thanks go out to my wife Gill for her
constant encouragement and the endless cups
of coffee ferried across to my study. Particular
thanks also go to the David Peters Photography
Studio for all their time and effort in making
sense of some very old and tatty photographs.

– FOREWORD –

Kevin Threlfall can claim to be one of the pioneers of the modern convenience store. Today, in villages, high streets, council estates, city centres and university campuses, bright, shiny convenience stores play an important role in people's busy lives. In a sense, Kevin has changed the face of Britain, and for the better. This lively book tells the story of a great retailer.

Sir Terry Leahy

– INTRODUCTION –

I never really felt comfortable about writing my own book for two reasons. Firstly I doubted my ability to put pen to paper, and secondly I worried that the content might not interest enough people to make the venture worthwhile.

I certainly had no intention of writing an autobiography before I was drawing my old age pension. Too many people write their life story before they have reached the point when they can look back properly and analyse all the years; the good ones and the bad ones.

I eventually succumbed to my wife's badgering because she desperately wanted the story to be told, if not for me, for our grandchildren.

I cannot claim to be a natural storyteller but I have thoroughly enjoyed trawling through my memory vaults and recalling events that were long forgotten in my normal day-to-day life.

Most of my life has been spent in retail, which for me has been hugely rewarding because it is a career that involves the interaction of people. Developing the skill to understand your customers as well as your suppliers takes time, and to succeed in business necessitates building teams that can work together to achieve a common goal.

The book took six months to write and it was nearing completion when I dropped down dead on the golf course. As you will read, I was incredibly lucky to survive and every day now is a bonus that I never take for granted.

Like most children, when I walked through the gates of my primary school at the tender age of five, I had no idea where my life would take me. Fleetingly, with my interest in nature, I thought about becoming a doctor – but retail was not only in my blood, it was in my bones.

The journey has been amazing, full of mistakes, full of wrong turnings but always eventful and always enjoyable.

I worked with some incredible people, not all of whom are mentioned in this book, and I apologise to those not named personally.

Between us we built a wonderful business of over 1,000 shops.

It is a legacy that endures to this day, and One-Stop continues to prosper and grow under the massive Tesco umbrella.

I feel very humble to have been part of the story, which I hope you enjoy reading.

Money and its value is always a problem when writing about a period that stretches over a number of years, particularly when parts of that period have included some years of very high inflation. Furthermore, establishing a yardstick for measuring the change in the value of money is not easy either. Do we take the external value of the pound or what it will buy in the average (whatever that may be) weekly shopping basket? Do we relate it to the average manual wage? As we know, while prices in general might rise, and have done so in this country every year since the Second World War, the prices of certain products might fall. However, we are writing about a business, and money and its value crop up on almost every page. We therefore have to make some judgements. We can only generalise, and I think the best yardstick is probably the average working wage.

Taking this as the benchmark, here is a measure of the pound sterling relative to its value in 2014.

Apart from wartime, prices were stable for 250 years, but began to rise in the run-up to the First World War.

1665–1900 multiply by 120
1900–1914 multiply by 110
1918–39 multiply by 60
1945–50 multiply by 35
1950–60 multiply by 30
1960–70 multiply by 25

1970–74 multiply by 20
1975–77 multiply by 15
1978–80 multiply by 8
1980–87 multiply by 5
1987–91 multiply by 2.5
1991–97 multiply by 1.5

Since 1997, the rate of inflation has been very low by the standards of most of the 20th century, averaging until very recently less than the government's originally stated aim of 2.5 per cent (since reduced to 2 per cent). Some things – such as telephone charges and many items made in the Far East, notably China – have gone down in price while others, such as houses, moved up very sharply from 1997 to 2008 before falling back in the financial crisis. In 2011, on the back of sharply rising commodity and food prices, inflation accelerated again to reach 5 per cent per annum. However, as commodity prices fell back and much of the world suffered very low growth, the rate of inflation began to subside again in 2012 and 2013. By 2014 the industrial nations were starting to worry about deflation.

CHAPTER 1

Born in a Bucket

I t was a typical December morning, chucking it down with rain, blowy and very cold. As usual it was impossible to park in the surgery car park and I had to drive a couple of hundred yards to find a spot. I jogged back and, as I registered, was glad to see that the doctor was only running ten minutes late. I took my seat in the waiting room and crossed my fingers.

The doctor opened the door and beckoned me into his room. He fixed me with a somewhat sympathetic stare and took a breath:

I am sorry to say, Kevin, that the results are not good. The tumour appears to have grown, but more worryingly the cancer appears to have spread to your liver and also your pancreas.

I could feel a drop of sweat forming on my brow as I asked him how long I had got. Without hesitation he replied:

I am afraid to say weeks, not months.

I shot bolt upright in bed, my heart thumping as it slowly dawned on me that I had been having the same repetitive dream once again. For two years since my lifelong friend and business partner had died of throat cancer, I had experienced this same dream every couple of weeks. Dave had suffered for ten long years and I guess that deep down I was frightened of going the same way. My life had been wonderful and I hoped for a few more years yet.

That life had started back on 29 September 1948 in the Queen Victoria and Albert hospital in Wolverhampton. According to my mother I had been born into a bucket; why a bucket, she had never actually told me.

I remember very little of childhood up until my first day at school aged five. My sister Sharron, who was two years older than me, had walked me through the gates for my first day at Elston Hall Primary School. It was one of the largest primary schools in the West Midlands, with over 600 pupils and average class sizes of 42.

I hated it, cried all day long and would not play in the sand tray with all the other boys and girls. Things only got worse when at the age of six I developed a squint, which meant that I could only really see out of one eye. So there I was sitting in a classroom of 42 with my pink National Health specs, unable to read much on the blackboard. It was not a great start to my academic career.

I lived in an area of Wolverhampton called Low Hill, which was one of the largest council house areas in the Midlands. My mother was one of eleven children, her father having developed a local painting and decorating business. My father was a Lancastrian whose family background was very much coal mining and weaving. Dad worked in a cotton mill for three years from the age of fifteen. In later life it was to come back to haunt him as he suffered quite badly from emphysema.

Dad moved down to the Midlands for a job as a sales representative and my mother was one of the people he interviewed for promotional

My first school: Elston Hall Primary, Stafford Road, Wolverhampton.

work. Needless to say she not only got the job, she also got the boss because within two years they were married.

My parents were early entrepreneurs; they were determined to get on the housing ladder and my father used to go around the pubs in the town selling hot dogs, which my mother had made in the kitchen of their one-bedroomed flat. Mom quickly realised that if she cut the ends off the hot dogs, every sixth hot dog could be made out of all the end bits. At a stroke she had improved the gross margin by 20 per cent and the profits started to roll in.

Within a couple of years they had made enough money to put a deposit down on a small semi-detached house on the edge of the council estate in Low Hill.

Central heating and refrigerators were still only for posh people but we did have an inside loo, so I guess we were semi-posh. In the winter, frost would accumulate on the inside of the windows and I used to drive my sister mad by scratching my fingernails across the glass. With open fires being the only source of heat, the real fun was making the fire up with paper twists, sticks and coal. Sometimes the chimney would catch fire and I would run out into the cul-de-sac to watch the flames bursting out into the night sky.

The other really good game in town was to watch the chimney sweeps' brushes protrude out of the top of the chimneys while they were being cleaned. Now that really is an industry that has disappeared for good.

Life at school started to improve after I had an operation on my left eye to correct the squint. As an eight-year-old, I was terrified when they wheeled me down to the operating theatre and I can still remember the green gown of the surgeon as he told me that I would soon be going to sleep.

I woke up with both my eyes bandaged and unable to see a thing. In literally blind panic, I tried to rip off the bandages because I was convinced that I was now blind. Can you believe that nobody had told me that for a couple of days after the operation, I would not be able to see? To this day I cannot sleep in a completely darkened room; if I do, I wake in the same traumatised state and have to switch on a light.

Now I was old enough to wander beyond the confines of our cul-de-sac I became a little more interested in what was going on around me. The main railway line was only a couple of hundred yards away and within months I was completely hooked on trainspotting.

It became my life's ambition to become a train driver, and all my spare time was spent standing by the bridge with my Ian Allan trainspotting book hoping to see one of the glorious steam trains of the day.

The best times for us as a family were summer weekends. My father was captain of our local cricket club and from April onwards we spent most Saturdays and Sundays at the ground. My sister would help my mother with the teas and I would make a general nuisance of myself, either by climbing trees or by running across the nearby field to get the number of another passing train. I never went anywhere without my precious trainspotting book and it lived with me day and night.

Most of the players hated me, because just before the game was about to start I would pinch the brand new match ball and hide it under the pavilion. I would then refuse to give it back until they had all given me a penny so that I could buy some sweets. They regularly gave me money to go and play on the railway lines; I could never understand why!

I often got a swift backhander from my mother when she caught me stealing the cakes that had been put out for the players' tea.

But they were great family days and I would be immensely proud of my father if he scored 50 runs or more. He opened the batting for the first team and when he was eventually out, I would run on to the pitch to congratulate him. From a really early age he became my hero.

In those days there were no drink-driving laws and Sharron and I would be allowed to stay up late while Mom and Dad enjoyed a tipple or two with their friends and the players from the visiting team. I could never understand why they were always so happy when we were driving home and we would all sing songs at the top of our voices. They would rush us off to bed and bet that they could get to sleep before us – I don't think so!

I was now growing up fast and doing better at school as I could finally read what was on the blackboard. My father had started his own grocery wholesale business and was now earning enough money to educate Sharron and me privately, so just before I was to take my eleven-plus exam I left Elston Hall and started a new life at Birchfield Preparatory School.

That move was to change my life forever.

The first shock was that the teachers had difficulty in understanding my broad Wolverhampton accent and I was sent for elocution lessons. I didn't realise it at the time but most of my fellow pupils came from a completely different social background to mine. Back in the late 1950s the only people who could afford private education were professionals such as doctors, dentists and lawyers. Arriving at school in my dad's van did little for my street cred and because of this it was hard to make friends. I think the other parents thought we were gypsies.

As time went on I did make some good friends because parents may be snobbish, but children rarely are. I was amazed at the size of some of their houses, and the gardens were enormous. Where I lived all the houses were the same, with almost identical postage-stamp lawns. I think the first seeds of ambition were sown when I realised what could be bought with money.

The class sizes were much smaller than I had been used to, and it was strange to sit among only 16 pupils having been used to 40 or more. Some of the teachers were very scary. Our Latin teacher, Mr Ratray, used to pick at the skin around his fingernails, so much so that they were permanently bleeding. He was a stickler for using correct English. One day I asked him if I could go to the toilet.

'You certainly can, Threlfall,' he boomed across the classroom.

I got to the door and he shouted, 'Boy, where do you think you are going?'

'To the toilet, sir. You said I could go.'

'I said you could go to the toilet. In other words you are physically able to go to the toilet. The correct question should have been: "May I go to the toilet?"'

'OK, sir, may I go to the toilet?'

'No, you may not. Go and sit down, you horrible little child!'

Another teacher, called Mr Carver, had a fearful temper and it didn't take much to wind him up. In those days the blackboard rubbers were about 20cm long and made out of solid wood. In one fit of temper he hurled it as hard as he could at a boy at the back of the class who wasn't paying attention; missing his head by a whisker, it hit the wall and a great big chunk of plasterboard fell to the floor. If it had hit him I am sure it would have killed him instantly.

My parents were paying good money for this!

The teachers generally were very strict and misbehaviour was just not tolerated. The punishments included detention, standing facing the wall or, the most ludicrous of all, changing practice. This involved changing from school clothes into sportswear, including putting on and lacing up your football boots. You then had to report to the master and then change back again. The normal punishment was to do this five times but sometimes it was ten.

Unfortunately I didn't like the headmaster and he didn't like me so I was not picked for any of the school teams, although he knew I was good enough to play in them.

With my father's business doing well, we had moved house a couple of miles into the Fordhouses suburb to be close to some garages where he could store his stock. We were now within a stone's throw of the cricket club, but unfortunately for me nowhere near a railway line. I was slowly becoming a real anorak!

However, every cloud has a silver lining and I soon made friends with a boy from across the road whose mother owned the Moreton Country Club. In the 1960s there were a lot of privately owned country clubs, which were only open to members, and the attraction of them was late drinking (pubs in those days closed at 10.30pm) and gambling.

Lee was the same age as me and in the school holidays I spent most of my time over at the club, either playing football or just larking about. However, the real benefit of the friendship was the food. In the evenings I would watch the television with Lee and we would order all manner of fantastic meals from the kitchen. The restaurant was never too busy, so the chef was happy to cook us the most amazing dishes you have ever seen. We were growing lads and used to order the biggest mixed grills you could imagine, followed by treacle sponge and custard. We even had a waitress bring the food up to us, which I have to say I am embarrassed to admit to. Needless to say my mother was delighted, as it was one less mouth to feed. The waitress, Anne, had a daughter named Christine who became my first girlfriend and, all in all, I really had landed on my feet.

I had to catch two buses to get to school, one into town and then another out to Tettenhall. The benefit of this was that the twenty or so boarders at the school could ask me to stop off in town and pop into the Models and Hobbies shop for things they needed. This presented me with my first business opportunity as I quickly became one of the shop's best customers. With the boarders spending most evenings making models, I was constantly being asked to pick up balsa wood, thinners, glue, etc. After a few weeks I asked the shop owner if I could have a 10 per cent discount for orders that came to more than £10. He agreed to let me have a rolling credit and in no time at all, he owed me enough that I was able to buy a wonderful model of an American fighter/bomber called an NA39. Everyone was happy; the boarders got what they wanted on a regular basis, the shop owner got the bulk buys but more importantly, I got to be the middleman.

I worked hard and did well at Birchfield. I even managed to come top of the class in every subject one term and I still have the school report to prove it. I wasn't clever; it was just that I was incredibly competitive and hated being beaten.

All that wonderful food at the Moreton Country Club.

I was only at Birchfield for three years and at the age of thirteen I sat the Common Entrance exam for senior school. It was decided (I certainly do not remember being involved in the decision-making process) that I would be sent to a boarding school and Denstone College just outside Uttoxeter became the hot favourite. If you were clever the options tended to be Shrewsbury, Oundle or Repton. If you were average then Bromsgrove, Wrekin, Denstone or Ellesmere were the obvious choices. Denstone had a great reputation for sport, and as a pal of my father had been there it became the natural choice. I loved all sports and couldn't wait to go and visit the school where I would be spending the next five years of my life.

– CHAPTER 2 –

Lord of the Flies

It was in the spring of 1962 that I started at Denstone College near Uttoxeter. Back then it was an all-boys boarding school with 365 pupils and fairly full. There were nine different houses in all, with about 40 boys in each house. All the houses except one were located in the main building, in either the north or the south wing.

I had never been away from home before and I didn't know a soul, so to say that my stomach was churning when we drove in through the gates was an understatement. I felt physically sick.

My parents and I were ushered to the library where I met my housemaster, Mr Brear. He and my father got on like a house on fire as they both had an interest in cricket and I relaxed a little. Mom put on a brave face as we said goodbye, and I wandered off to the common room to meet the other new boys.

The dormitory had 21 beds on either side of a long corridor and your belongings had to fit into a cabinet about one metre wide by two metres tall. Lights-out was at 9.30pm and, as I drifted off to sleep, I wondered what on earth I had done. I was already missing my pal Lee, my first girlfriend Christine, my nice warm bed but, most of all, those wonderful mixed grills!

I was woken in the morning by the loudest bell I had ever heard. It was a nightmare getting ready, as I had to learn how to put a collar and stud on to my shirt. In this way you saved on laundry as the collars were washed regularly but the shirts only twice a week.

It was a mad dash down to breakfast and, if you didn't make it for 7.45am, you were in big trouble. A first-termer was called a 'Sprog' and you had to sit at the end of the table known as 'The Arse'. It was your responsibility to clear away all the plates and leftovers as they winged their way down the table to you. Anyone who has been to boarding school learns to eat quickly; otherwise there is not enough time to do all the jobs. In addition to this there were always any number of hungry jackals waiting to steal your food.

Breakfast was horrendous, with thick porridge being the staple diet, followed by fried eggs which came on a tray covered in grease. The eggs used to slide around and were accompanied by deep-fried bread, baked beans and, depending upon the day, either sausage or bacon. It was not exactly a Jamie Oliver-type school meal but I have to say that the taste of baked beans on fried bread still brings back great memories. There was never really enough food to fill you up and most of the time you felt hungry.

After breakfast you had to rush upstairs to make your bed and have it inspected by a dormitory prefect before dashing off to go to the loo. The toilet block was outdoors and absolutely terrible. Six 'traps' were designated to each house and you had to secure one of these before the older boys came along and kicked you out. Because the traps were only fitted with half-doors, in the winter months the snow would blow under the doors and around your ankles. The only benefit of this was that you really didn't want to hang about.

Then it was off to chapel for a quick morning assembly, a race back to the house common room to collect your books, and then off to lessons, which started at 9.10am sharp.

Lunch wasn't much better than breakfast and I struggle to remember what we were actually given. It really was cheap and cheerful food washed down with a glass of water.

In the winter months we played rugby in the afternoons and then lessons followed, but in the summer months we had lessons after lunch followed by cricket or athletics later on.

Tea was around 6.00pm followed by two hours of prep and then bed. Every day was the same routine and apart from the sport it was bloody awful. Those first few weeks seemed to pass like months and my mother must have done something right because I became very homesick. Why had I been sent to this horrible cold gulag on top of a hill when I had been so happy at home? Because I couldn't settle, I also got into a lot of trouble with the prefects. At my prep school, I had been a top dog in my final year and very popular with the boarders but now I was a nobody. Everyone was older than me, no one seemed to like me and I became desperately unhappy. I used to walk out to the phone box in the village and beg my mother to take me out of this hellhole and let me come home. I would inevitably end up in tears when she kept telling me to give it time as I would eventually settle.

I didn't settle and they had to drag me back to Denstone to start the winter term of 1963, which was to be one of the coldest winters on record. The rugby pitches were frozen and the fields were thick with snow, so no cross-country running; the food had got no better, the prefects were vile and my work started to suffer badly. On top of this, two weeks into that third term, Christine wrote to tell me she had met someone else and it was all over. I looked down into the quadrangle from our second-floor dormitory and seriously thought about ending it all.

After what seemed like twelve years, the twelve-week term finally ended and I was able to go home from prison for a few weeks before the second year started. My parents knew I was desperately unhappy but I agreed to give it two more terms. The Lent term would be followed by summer, when I would be able to play cricket and at least it would be a little more bearable.

I somehow got through that first year and had made a few friends. We were all in the same boat; some boys were bullied more than others, with cold baths a regular occurrence. Because I was in the school teams and could be vicious, the bullies tended to pick on weaker members of the house.

With me being away from home and my sister Sharron now working as a junior hairdresser, my mother had joined the family business. She was a fantastic saleswoman and soon had the orders rolling in from new accounts. My father had also taken on a Saturday stall on Wellington market, selling cut-price groceries to supplement his wholesale business.

Changes in the law relating to competition in retail had created new opportunities for entrepreneurs like my father.

The most significant concerned resale price maintenance. This was the practice whereby a manufacturer and its distributors agreed that the distributors would sell the product at certain prices (resale price maintenance), at or above a price floor (minimum resale price maintenance) or at or below a price ceiling (maximum resale price maintenance).

Some manufacturers defended resale price maintenance by saying it ensured fair returns, both for manufacturer and reseller, and that governments did not have the right to interfere with freedom to make contracts without a very good reason.

However, in 1955 the UK government recommended that resale price maintenance when collectively enforced by manufacturers should be made illegal, but that individual manufacturers should be allowed to continue the practice. And in 1964, the Resale Price Act ruled all forms of resale price maintenance to be against the public interest, unless it could be proved otherwise.

Effectively the floodgates were now open and heralded a new era for cut-price operators. My father was one of the first people in the Midlands to sell cut-price groceries. He knocked a penny off the price of a packet of Typhoo tea and had a queue of people twenty yards long waiting to be served. He restricted their purchases to a maximum of four packets, but if they wanted more they invariably just got back in the queue for a second time.

He increased the range of cut-price products he was selling and also took a stall on Thursday as well as Saturday. He was now working very hard but for the first time in his life making very decent money. Instead of playing football with Lee, school holidays became all about helping my parents on the market and also earning some pocket money for myself. But of course, he didn't have things all his own way for long; throughout the mid-1960s supermarkets such as Tesco, Sainsbury's and Fine Fare started to spring up all over the country.

Jack Cohen, the son of Jewish immigrants, founded Tesco in 1919 as a series of market stalls. The name Tesco was first used in 1924 when Cohen bought a shipment of tea from T.E. Stockwell and combined these initials with the first two letters of his own name. The first Tesco store opened in Burnt Oak, Middlesex, in 1929. By 1939 there were 100 stores. The company was floated on the London Stock Exchange in 1947. During the 1950s and 1960s Tesco grew both organically and through acquisition so that by the end of the 1960s there were 800 stores. The first self-service store opened in St Albans in 1956 and the first supermarket in Maldon in the same year. Jack Cohen's motto was 'Pile it high and sell it cheap'. He also had a motto for his staff – YCDBSOYA – or 'You can't do business sitting on your arse'.

The Sainsbury's chain, a partnership between John James Sainsbury and his wife, started as a single shop in Drury Lane in 1869. It expanded under the heading 'Quality Perfect, Prices Lower' and, in 1922, when it was the largest grocery group in the UK, incorporated itself as J. Sainsbury Limited. When John James Sainsbury died in 1928 there were 128 shops. In the 1950s and 1960s the company pioneered self-service supermarkets.

Fine Fare opened as a single shop in Brighton in 1956, and by 1962 there were 200 outlets. It was acquired by Associated British Foods in 1963.

The queues stopped forming at our market stall in 1965 when Fine Fare opened in Wellington High Street. Dad still had a good business because he could still undercut them on a lot of products, but the days of easy money were over.

I was good at mental arithmetic, which helped enormously, as our till was an old OXO tin.

Having decided to stay at Denstone after all, the second year improved a little as I got over my homesickness and made friends with a couple of boys who could not have been more different. Jim Davies loved soccer, trainspotting and larking about, whereas Bob loved rugby and was quite serious and very religious. He also happened to be one of the best sportsmen that ever passed through Denstone. He ended up as first-team captain of rugby, cricket and fives and at the age of sixteen was scoring centuries for the first XI cricket team. He was also an outstanding centre at rugby and pretty much unbeatable on the fives court.

Jim was from Leicester, and we had an ongoing banter as to whether Wolves were a better footballing side than Leicester.

I was in my last year of 'fagging', which involved doing any odd jobs that were required by the house prefects. This could be cleaning their army boots, cleaning their shoes or just running errands from one end of the school to the other. The reward for doing this was the occasional piece of toast or, if you were really lucky, beans on toast.

I got into the under-15 rugby, cricket and cross-country running teams and although we never played other schools at soccer, I did introduce it into the school as a Friday afternoon activity.

Inter-house rivalry was almost tribal and depending upon which term we were in, there were matches played between houses to find an eventual overall school winner. There was a flag each for the major sports of athletics, rugby, cricket and fives and these were hung above the winning house's three tables in the dining room. The minor cups for other things were arranged on the window shelf above the tables.

It was fantastic to be involved in these inter-house matches and if you won it was celebrated by 'dormitory singing'. When we were all in bed the house captain would bring through the trophy and we would all sing our hearts out. The prefects would bring in hot chocolate and toast, and for that one night of celebration we were all friends together.

The juniors would be made to stand on top of their cabinets and sing a song. If you had a reasonable voice you were fine but if not you would be battered with pillows and eventually knocked off, hopefully onto your bed.

After the first year we were allowed home more than twice a term and my sister would come to chapel on a Sunday morning. She was not religious so I can only think that, being a mini-skirted blonde, she enjoyed the attention.

In my second year, I received what was known as a sixth-form beating. I had sworn at one of the prefects for picking on me and rather than apologising to him, I was prepared to take a beating. This involved standing in the middle of the prefects' common room, leaning on a chair, with my trousers and pants down by my ankles and being beaten in front of all eighteen school prefects. I found out where the prefect lived and for a couple of years, I was going to go round to his house in the holidays and get my own back. Fortunately, I didn't and now I can't even remember his name.

The other unfortunate incident that happened to me that year involved me ending up in hospital. I was playing in an under-15s rugby team against Bromsgrove and dived on the ball just as the opposition forward decided to kick it. Unfortunately he ended up kicking my head instead of the ball. This resulted in me losing my two front teeth and badly breaking my nose. I was rushed off to Derby hospital and spent the next week there while they tried to patch me up. What was never a pretty face in the first place was now considerably worse and for the next fifteen years of my life, I had to put up with a partial plate with two false teeth. At least I did look fearsome when I took it out.

As I moved up the pecking order life improved term by term and I was delighted when we got a new housemaster, who was not only much more lenient but was also married. Mike Swales was an Old Denstonian himself, who had gone to Cambridge and then returned to Denstone to teach biology. His lovely wife, Elizabeth, taught art but also had a never-ending supply of biscuits. It was really through Mike that I became interested in all aspects of nature and I was lucky enough to study both botany and zoology at A level.

He was a fantastic teacher who had the knack of being able to hold your attention. The 40-minute lessons seemed to fly by and I always looked forward to his classes. Unfortunately, I had chosen chemistry as my other A level and that bored me to death.

I was now in my penultimate year at Denstone and had been made a house prefect, but my best pal Jim had unfortunately been expelled. At the age of sixteen he had met an attractive blonde in the nearby village of Alton (of Alton Towers fame) and was seeing her at every opportunity. Unfortunately this started to extend to evening trysts and, as Deanne could drive, they started to meet more regularly.

Instead of being in prep, Jim would cross the fields and meet her in the nearby village. This all worked perfectly well until one evening, when they were enjoying a meal in a nearby restaurant, one of the masters happened to walk in with his wife. The sight of Jim drinking a pint of beer and smoking a cigarette must have blown his mind!

Needless to say, Jim was expelled and banished to Canada by his father to get over his youthful lust. The happy ending to this romance was that a few years later Jim returned to England and subsequently married Deanne. My wife Gill and I have kept in touch with them and the four of us regularly go away on holiday together. Jim and I helped each other get through those difficult first few terms at Denstone and we have remained close friends ever since.

Although I thoroughly enjoyed studying botany and zoology, I knew by now that university was not for me. I was becoming far more interested in selling cut-price groceries than dissecting earthworms or collecting fungi.

However, I was determined to finish my time at Denstone and my love of sport made me decide to stay on for the last year. Like Jim, I had become a bit of a rebel and had started smoking to relieve some of the boredom. It was difficult to find places that were safe as there were regular checks by the housemasters. The pigsties, however, were never checked and became a great place to go to after prep. The sleeping pigs slowly accepted my nightly visits and they became quite comfortable with my presence. Another secret smoking place was in the sluice area down by the kitchens. It was a horrible place that I never thought would be discovered, but one night, as I was coming out, a master happened to see me. He told me to empty my pockets and my packet of ten Gold Leaf fell on the floor.

This episode led to my second beating but this time by the headmaster. Even with eight sides of blotting paper down my trousers he still managed to cut me with the ultra-thin stick that he used.

Today I could have probably taken him to the court of human rights but in those days you just grinned and bore it. As it was a very serious offence, I was told that if I were ever caught again I would be expelled. However, it didn't stop me smoking; it just meant more trips to the pigsties!

I dreaded my end-of-term reports, which were generally not very good because I was always in trouble. I used to read them before my father could get hold of them and, where possible, try to change a few words. I remember my Latin teacher stating that I tried hard but in class I was the 'ace interrupter'. With careful modification I managed to change it to the 'ace interpreter' and what was bad now became good!

However, Denstone in the mid-1960s was starting to become a little more civilised. Fagging had been abolished and we were allowed to grow our hair a little longer. In the 'outside world', The Beatles were at number one in the hit parade and Carnaby Street fashions were becoming more and more outrageous.

Sport was compulsory on Mondays, Wednesdays and Thursdays, but Tuesdays were reserved for CCF (Combined Cadet Force) activities. We could choose to be in either the Army, Navy or Air Force section. We had to dress up in full uniform and march around the quadrangle pretending to be the real deal. As we had to do it, I became quite involved and went on a couple of courses with the Army in the school holidays. I even changed for one term to the Air Force so that I could go on a trip to RAF Wattisham to see the Lightnings in operation. I then reverted back to the Army section and headed up the advanced infantry section. I finally made Company Sergeant Major, in charge of the whole school Army section. As a reward for this, I was made a school prefect and was probably the only boy in Denstone's history to be beaten by the headmaster for smoking and subsequently made a school prefect.

On Friday afternoons we were allowed to do other activities such

Inspection day, C.S.M. Army section, Denstone College, 1967.

as canoeing, mountaineering or a non-mainstream sport such as fencing. I chose to do 'old age help', which involved doing housework, gardening and errands for older people who lived in the nearby village of Rocester. However, I was somewhat lucky in that the old dear I was assigned to really just wanted some company as she lived on her own and was very lonely. She made the most wonderful cakes and she also let me smoke, so I did absolutely no work at all and just sat there in her armchair filling my face with cakes, puffing away and listening to the same life story for two hours every week. We became good friends and I was sad when she eventually had to move into sheltered accommodation.

Back in Wolverhampton my friend Lee said that he had met a girl called Heather and they were going out together but as I was away at boarding school, he would let me take her out in the school holidays. I thought 'What a proper chap,' but when I got home Heather didn't seem too keen on the idea – so he finished with her so he could knock around with me instead. I told you he was a proper chap!

After a great summer break of thirteen weeks, I returned to Denstone for my final year and for the first time ever, I was actually looking forward to it. I was in a study with my pal Bob Short. He was head of house, I was deputy head of house and we were both school prefects. Bob also happened to be school captain of rugby, cricket and fives.

I was in the school second VIII cross-country running team and on the fringe of the first XV rugby team. I was now over six feet tall and my main job in the team was to catch the ball in the lineout and add weight as second row in the scrum. We had an awesome amount of talent and were tipped to be one of the best school teams in the country. I was desperate to get my place in the team but unfortunately there was a better player than me already well installed, whose name was Andy Seymour. As you can imagine, the inter-school rivalry was immense and every year fourteen matches were played over two terms. We played against the top rugby-playing schools of the time, travelling long distances to compete with schools such as Stonyhurst, St Peters of York, Ampleforth and Bromsgrove. The last two matches were played on a tour of London when we came up against the formidable opponents of Whitgift and Blundell's.

Dating back to 1868, Denstone had never won all fourteen fixtures in the same year and there was a feeling that this could just possibly be the year to do it. We easily won the first five matches but the team was devastated when right at the end of the fifth match, Andy broke his arm, ruling him out for the rest of the year. Sometimes to achieve your dreams in life you need a little luck, and I stepped into his position as the natural replacement. My first match in the team was at home against Ellesmere College and I was as nervous as a kitten as we jogged on to the first-team pitch to the applause of some 350 boys (the whole school had to watch first-team rugby matches) and as many as 50 parents and teachers. It was bitterly cold, windy and muddy as the ref blew the whistle for the start of the match. After about ten minutes one of the Ellesmere players broke through our back line and as he was now heading for the corner flag, I was the last line of defence. With all the speed I could muster I threw myself headlong at his waist and made perfect contact, taking him into touch and, as we both slid through the mud, about ten yards into the crowd. I had prevented him from scoring a try and also justified my place in the team.

We won the match and also the last two of the term, making it eight straight victories on the bounce. The dream of winning all fourteen matches became a genuine reality as we returned to school for the 1967 Lent term. We trained really hard and prayed that none of the fixtures would be called off due to bad weather. We beat Wrekin College at home and then murdered Worksop away 27–0. It was now ten down and four to go.

The training got even harder as all of us started to realise the enormity of what could be. It has to be understood that rugby success was just as important to the schoolmasters as it was to the pupils. Most of the teachers were confirmed bachelors and came from sporting backgrounds. As they didn't have children themselves, in a funny sort of way we became their family.

The weather held and so did our next two results. It was now down to the final two matches to be played against two of the top schools, Whitgift and Blundell's. We knew that Whitgift had a star player but also had about 300 more boys in the school to choose from than we had. They rarely lost a match away from home, and for them to lose at home was unthinkable.

The all-conquering rugby side of 1966/67.

We went through all our plans again and again as we made the long journey from the West Midlands down to London. After spending so much time together we had all become great friends, and we also knew how much this meant to us all. None of us could eat a thing before the meal and the butterflies in my stomach felt more like birds.

Finally the game began and all the nervous energy went in the first few minutes as we ripped into them and started to control the game. We were fast, fit and completely focused on what we had to do. By half-time we were leading 3–0, which was just one score in a rugby match. They didn't know what had hit them, but they came back at us in the second half and we were hanging on for dear life. The minutes ticked away and although by now we were completely exhausted, we somehow managed to hang on and at the final whistle we sank to our knees. We had achieved the impossible. Teams didn't come to Whitgift to win, but we had.

After the euphoria of our victory, we had to regroup as there was one more match to play the following day, but deep down we all knew that nothing was going to stop us from winning it. And so we did and the dream was achieved.

On the evening of the final victory we were treated to the finest steaks at the Aberdeen Angus Steak House in Trafalgar Square. Our rugby masters, 'Nipper' (Nigel) Green and Lynton Stocks, joined in the celebrations and turned a blind eye to the beer we were taking back to the hotel. We sang our heads off into the early hours of the morning but as the booze, exhaustion and utter relief finally sank in, our bodies gave way to sleep and to the end of the greatest day of our lives.

Normally in a school year, full school colours were awarded to a handful of talented sportsmen who were over-achievers. The following term the headmaster stood up in front of the whole school and announced that in view of our unique achievement, every member of the team was to receive their full school colours and the flashy green jacket that went with them. The whole school cheered; it was a truly great moment for all of us.

Five years before, as a homesick new boy, I had watched these seemingly massive specimens throwing themselves around the rugby pitch, knowing that I would never be big enough or good enough to represent my school at the top level. I had hero-worshipped the few who were awarded their green jacket and now I was in this elite club.

Very few people could ever know what that achievement meant to me at the time. What it did was make me realise that with hard work, dedication and team spirit anything was possible. That philosophy was to guide me through my business career. No one is ever too small or too insignificant to achieve their own goals in life providing they believe in themselves.

Before I returned to Denstone for my final term and A level

exams, I knew it was all a bit of a waste of time. My father's business had grown to such an extent that the year before he had taken on a partner called John Latham, who ran the recently acquired Cannock market stall. Unfortunately John had the opportunity to open a supermarket in Birmingham and announced that he was leaving in July, which just happened to coincide with the date I was leaving school. Dad suggested that I join the family business but I was very reluctant, as I knew that most father/son business relationships ended in disaster. However, I did realise that it was a fantastic opportunity to get into business.

I had served my apprenticeship for the last five years and knew that I could make money from selling groceries. I suggested to my

Shrewsbury House, Denstone College, final year.

Dad that if I ran Cannock as my own separate business it could work. He agreed and from that point on being at school seemed a little pointless. But as the last term was summer it also meant that I could play a lot of cricket. Unfortunately I did not enjoy the same success in cricket as I had in rugby and although I opened the bowling for the first XI once, there were better players around than me and I was duly relegated to opening the bowling for the second team. A level exams came and went and, apart from botany, I knew the results would not be good.

And so my final day at Denstone duly arrived. I swapped telephone numbers and addresses with my pals and we all made promises to keep in touch. We all filed into chapel for one last time. As the headmaster addressed us I looked back on my time with very mixed feelings. The first two years had been the worst years of my life but the last two had been the best. I had changed from a homesick wimp to a confident eighteen-year-old, and the rugby achievement and the friends I had made meant more to me than any string of successful exam results. As we sang our school song, 'Jerusalem', together for the last time I had a tear in my eye. I had, after all, survived Denstone and if I could do that nothing that happened in the future was going to frighten me.

This had been my home for five years but it was now time to start a new chapter for which I was more than ready. My pal Bob Short had been offered a place at Cambridge because of his outstanding sporting ability but we decided to go abroad for a month and travel a little around Europe. Bob was a devout Christian and wanted to become a missionary after studying agriculture at university. He was very different from the rest of my rugby pals; he never swore and hardly ever had a bad word to say about anyone. He was quite a calming influence on me and although we were very different people, we somehow got on really well. We decided that part of the trip would be spent helping out at a home for unwanted children in a village called Gallneukirchen, just outside Linz in Austria.

Most of the children had Down's syndrome but a few had learning disabilities and some suffered from severe epileptic fits. When we arrived we were horrified at what we saw. There were about 24 boys from the age of three to twelve being looked after by four people!

These poor children had been dumped by their parents because they were misfits or difficult to look after or both. The hours were long and it didn't help that we could only speak pidgin German. It was possible to organise some of the older boys into doing basic duties such as washing up or taking younger boys to the toilet, but by and large it was a nightmare just to get through the day and then get them to bed. We stayed a few weeks and we both felt terribly guilty for leaving. It made us realise how lucky we were.

After returning home with a beaten-up Triumph Herald and no money, it was time to start work on the markets and, for the first time in my life, be in charge of my own destiny.

– CHAPTER 3 –

Barrow Boy

Market days were Tuesday, Friday and Saturday and buying days were Monday and Wednesday, with Sunday morning reserved for ordering.

As I had effectively taken over from my dad's partner, I was straight into work after returning from the trip around Europe. This involved driving to Birmingham early on a Monday morning to buy goods from the two Cash & Carrys situated only a couple of miles apart. I had asked my next-door neighbour, Andy Hawthorne, to join me in the venture and as he had just left school aged sixteen and was looking for a job, he readily agreed. Andy and I had been pals for over six years and as we got on really well, I knew we would be able to work together. We agreed on a salary of £20 (£500 in today's money) per week each.

The range of products that we sold was a strange combination. We had no refrigeration and therefore could not sell chilled and fresh-and-frozen products. This in turn meant that we would only ever be the type of outlet where people would buy special offers or just do top-up shopping, rather like a convenience store today. In the mid-1960s there were far more canned and packaged products sold than today and also a lot more processed foods.

It must be remembered that back then not everyone owned a fridge/freezer and those who did only had limited space. Bread and milk was delivered to most houses on a daily basis, the local butcher sold meat and the greengrocer sold fruit and veg. Bottles of beer were bought from the outdoor section of the nearest pub and in some locations delivered door to door. The sale of wine for home consumption was practically non-existent.

The fledgling supermarkets had very poor reputations for their meat, and stand-alone butchers were far more popular, as were national chains such as Dewhurst (Dewhurst the Butchers chain was built up in the post-Second World War era by the Vestey Group). Fresh fish was still relatively cheap and sold by local merchants, but again there was also a national chain of fresh fish shops called Mac Fisheries (founded by William Lever, later Lord Leverhulme, who built up Lever Brothers, which merged with a Dutch company to become Unilever). People's lifestyles were also very different from today, with most married women spending their time looking after the home and children rather than going out to work. Few women had cars and so most of the grocery shopping was done locally and on a daily basis.

Most women would catch the bus into town once or twice a week to shop for bargains in places such as Woolworths or to buy clothes and household goods from department stores. F.W. Woolworth, founded in the USA in 1878 by Frank Winfield Woolworth as Woolworth's Great Five Cent Store, expanded into a huge chain of stores and moved into the UK, where eventually every town of any significance had a store.

All shops, with the exception of newsagents and a few chemists, were closed on Sundays and trade was also very slow on Mondays as, for most women, Mondays were washdays. Washing machines and tumble driers were very few and far between and provided it wasn't raining, clothes would be pegged out to dry on washing lines in people's back gardens all around the country. Ironing day would be Tuesday or Wednesday and so for most housewives there was a daily routine, which very rarely changed from one week to another. This was the reason why market days in towns were rarely more than two or three times a week – there was work to de done at home!

Because our market stall at Cannock was small (four metres long by three metres deep) we could not afford to carry the whole range of products in a particular group. For example the best-selling jams were blackcurrant, strawberry and raspberry in that order. We would not, therefore, carry the whole range found in most supermarkets, which might include apricot, bramble seedless and raspberry seedless. However, we did carry the full range of washing powders. The reason for this was simple. Almost every housewife had to buy a packet of soap powder every week and we decided that because it was a 'must-buy item' we would undercut the supermarkets on it, sometimes making as little as 1p per packet, to attract customers to us. We made a list of all these 'must-buy items', and undercut the supermarkets on all of them. The list included Blue Band margarine, Lurpak butter, Heinz beans, Heinz soups, OXO cubes, Camay soap, Fray Bentos corned beef, John West salmon and many, many more well-known products that people bought week in, week out. Various phrases have been coined over the years to describe this approach to retailing, such as 'a sprat to catch a mackerel'. 'Loss leaders' was another. But even if it was only a penny profit, we never sold anything at a loss.

In being the cheapest on KVIs (known-value items) we had a marketing edge on all the competition. People knew that we were the cheapest on everyday necessities and they assumed, therefore, that we were the cheapest on everything else. But of course that was not true.

We had another list!

The second list included all items that women needed on a daily basis and would not want to be out of stock. This list included toilet rolls, tins of peas, biscuits, paper kitchen towels, bin liners, and Kit Kats for the kiddies' lunch box.

So the conversation might go something like this: 'Good morning, madam, how can I help you today?' They might reply with a request for, say, a packet of Daz, two tins of Heinz beans, a tin of salmon and 1lb of Lurpak. Now we would make very little out of this order: maybe 10p.

Then bang, we would move in with the sales pitch: 'Now are you sure you haven't forgotten anything? Are you OK for toilet rolls, peas, biscuits, kitchen roll, bin liners or Kit Kats for the kiddies' lunch box?'

This patter never failed. There was always something we could tempt them with, and sometimes it would be the lot.

And, of course, the items we sold to them carried a much higher profit margin than the products they had originally ordered. What started as a profit of 10p on their order turned into 30p by the time we had finished with them.

So although our range of products looked on the face of it like a very random selection, it was in fact a very sophisticated range with a wonderful balance of necessity and temptation.

Andy and I would arrive at our first port of call early on Monday morning in order to avoid the traffic queues into Birmingham. Before 1960 nearly all groceries were delivered to shops by wholesalers and there was very little price competition. But after the abolition of resale price maintenance, grocers started to search around for the best prices and the phrase 'Cash & Carry' was soon coined. It meant specifically that you picked up your own goods, paid for them there and then (no credit given) and you were on your way.

J&F Cash & Carry had started life as a wholesaler and was one of the first to change to the Cash & Carry format. Ralph Feeney was the owner and, born and raised in Birmingham, had built up a reputation as being a really smart trader. He understood market trading and was not frightened to buy in huge quantities provided the price was right. He would negotiate a deal for ten lorry loads of a product and then say to the manufacturer, 'OK, knock me off another 10p a case and I will double the order.'

We had a twin-wheel-based Ford Transit van that we had acquired on hire purchase. It was perfect to start with as it was great for heavy loads, but we very quickly had to supplement it with the addition of a much larger 'box' van as sales started to increase. Andy and I scoured the Cash & Carry for the best deals and then moved up the road to Ruston Cash & Carry to buy any of their special offers or products that Ralph happened not to have in stock. We would then drive to our lock-up stall on Cannock market to unload all the goods we had bought. The following day was a quiet trading day and we used the spare time when not serving customers to dress the stall as shown in the photo below.

Because of the lack of space, it was essential that everything be put away in exactly the same location every time. Obviously we kept product groups together as much as possible and did not keep products like detergents and soaps next to the biscuits. The takings at Cannock had averaged about £250 per week before Andy and I took over and while that doesn't seem a lot, it must be remembered that in 2014 money, it represents about 25 times that amount or £6,250. It also means that while our salary of £20 per week sounds quite paltry, it was actually equivalent to £500 per week today – not a bad sum for an unqualified eighteen-year-old.

Turnover slowly started to increase as we got to grips with what special offers attracted customers the most and our reputation started to grow. Andy had a great sense of humour, was a good-looking lad and had a twinkle in his eye. I started to notice that

Cannock market stall, 1971.

he was serving far more of the younger housewives than I was!

As our first Christmas approached takings had increased to £400 per week and we were flying. We had found another unique selling opportunity that gave us an advantage over the supermarkets.

Most manufacturers from time to time would try to tempt the housewife with a money-off coupon on the tin or the packet to ensure that she repeated the purchase the following week. If, for example, the coupon value was 10p then we would offer to cash the coupon there and then providing we shared half the value. They were more than happy to do this because first, they did not have to make another purchase and second, they did not have to remember to bring the coupon back the following week.

It was a fantastic way of making money because it increased our gross profit margin substantially. The only downside was that quite often the whole label would fall off the tin and the customer didn't know what was in it. I think a lot of children in Cannock ended up getting rice pudding when they thought they were getting tomato soup. We remedied the problem by writing on the can what was inside with a felt tip marker.

The word was starting to get around about our stall.

Andy and I started to scour all the Cash & Carrys to find products with money-off coupons attached and from that point on never had decent thumbnails. We also found out that the Cash & Carrys were not too fussy about checking whether the coupons we cashed in actually matched the products we were buying. I will explain.

In the 1960s there were a lot of new products coming on to the market and the manufacturers needed to promote them. This would be done with money-off coupons in daily newspapers, magazines or sometimes in booklets composed entirely of coupons. Quite often we did not sell the product for which the coupon was offered, but as the Cash & Carry didn't seem to bother, neither did we. We started to tell our customers to collect as many money-off coupons as they could and we would offer them half the value and just simply knock the cash off their bill.

Sometimes a customer would bring £1 worth of coupons and we would give them 50p off their bill, making 50p ourselves. We were now making money from coupons in general, coupons on the tins and, oh yes, a little bit of profit on the product. Our overall profit margin was going through the roof.

The word was now well and truly getting round about Andy & Kev's, as it was becoming affectionately known. We were really excited by Christmas because it meant that we could sell additional products that everyone needed.

We made another list!

This list included jars of mincemeat, cooking foil, stuffing, dried fruit, tinned ham, mince pies, tinned salmon and Christmas crackers. So from the beginning of December our normal patter of reminding customers what they may have forgotten changed to the Christmas list. We made little profit on most of the Christmas products because obviously they had to be keenly priced to match the competition. However, the exception to this was Christmas crackers.

We had bought a van load of crackers at a cracking price (please excuse the pun) but obviously taken a risk, because if any were not sold by 1 January they would have to be stored for another year. The other problem was that they were extremely bulky and we couldn't physically get them into our market stall until Saturday. I decided the best way to sell them was to 'pitch them'. This involved getting a crowd around the stall by shouting to them. The patter went something like this:

Ladies, gentlemen gather round quickly because I have something to sell you that is so cheap you won't believe it. These Christmas crackers [I would now pass round a few boxes] were on their way to be sold at Harrods but unfortunately fell off the back of the lorry. [Laughter from the crowd and shouts of 'Oh yes, I bet.']

No, no seriously, all kosher folks, do I look the sort of chap who would get involved in dodgy dealing? Now these crackers retail for £1. They are stuffed with hats, caps, snaps, novelties and mottoes; there is no better box of crackers on the market. Now I am not asking for 90p, 80p, 70p, 60p, or even half price at 50p. I must be mad but I know money is tight at Christmas so Andy and I want to give you a Christmas present from us. We are prepared to offer these crackers to you at 30p a box on the basis that nobody has more than one box each. Oh all right then, seeing as it is Christmas, two boxes each.

Within minutes we had sold 50 boxes and made a profit of 10p per box, or £5. As our market stall rent was only £20 per week, it was great business. After the crowds had dispersed and moved on, we would repeat the exercise every half an hour throughout the afternoon. Needless to say we sold the complete van load by Christmas, but more importantly word was getting round.

We averaged over £500 (£12,500 in today's money) per week during December, which was double what we were turning over at the start. The problem was that we hadn't a clue what profit we were making per week. We made it up as we went along, selling things cheaply if we had to but making good money when we could. The profit we were making from the coupons also muddied the water somewhat. There was no business plan like there might be today, we just worked on the basis that if the bank balance was increasing, things must be going well. Obviously we kept books, but really our business had very few costs apart from our wages, the market stall rent, our vehicle costs and the couple of garages we had rented to store surplus stock.

By the end of the year we had paid back my father for the stock we had taken over at the outset and paid off the balance we owed on our two vans, so I guess we must have been doing something right.

Meanwhile, what was Britain, Great Britain or even the United Kingdom doing in the 1960s? It was doing three things. Socially, it was breaking out from the class and age straitjacket of the 1950s or even, if you like, of the Victorian era. Politically, it was about to try a new form of government, having grown tired of the old Conservative regime, which it saw as increasingly incompetent and complacent. Economically, it was waking up to the fact that the world was suddenly a competitive place.

Socially and culturally, nothing sums up the shift in British life like The Beatles and the transformation that they represented. From the Cavern in Liverpool, a wonderful city in the nineteenth century but not yet greatly admired by the 1960s, The Beatles broke on to the national, and indeed the international, stage in 1963.

Politically, it was the turn of the Labour Party to govern the country. Labour won the 1964 general election, defeating a tired Tory party led by Sir Alec Douglas-Home, who frightened many voters by admitting that he tackled economic questions by counting matches in his hand. With his estate in Scotland he certainly reminded voters of his privileged background far removed from the housing estates in which most of them lived.

My early career in business coincided with the peak of the exciting early career of John Bloom, who became nationally known as the man who gave many English housewives the chance to buy washing machines at reasonable prices. Buying from a Dutch manufacturer, he sold direct twin-tub machines with a washer and separate spin-dryer at 39 guineas (£40.90, or just over £1,000 in today's money). This was about half the price of the machines in the shops. In the early 1960s he was selling 500 machines a week. He became a household name

Celebrating record
Christmas takings,
Cannock market, 1969.

and a TV personality, appearing on *That Was the Week That Was* and
getting the better of Bernard Levin. In 1962 he even had lunch with
Her Majesty the Queen. His company, Rolls Razor, floated on the
London Stock Exchange and he entertained celebrities such as The
Beatles and Shirley Bassey from his flat in Park Lane. Unfortunately,
the washing machine manufacturers and retailers hit back with their
own price cuts and drove his company into liquidation.

Throughout the following year our sales continued to increase and we had found another niche market to exploit in pet food. For some reason the supermarkets were never too competitive on their prices and because we were, sales started to rocket. As most customers bought at least six or seven cans of food a week, plus ancillary mixer biscuits such as Bonio and Winalot, it was a lucrative trade. However, the major problem with pet food was the weight of the cans. Most housewives came to Cannock on the bus from the surrounding mining areas such as Hednesford and Chasewater and it was a real drag that, in addition to their groceries, they had to carry home heavy tins of dog food.

We came up with an idea. If they bought a case load (normally 24 tins), we would deliver it free of charge. We posted a big banner on the front of the stall advertising free delivery of all pet food. The idea took off and our Wednesdays were soon taken up with delivering orders taken at the stall. We even introduced a telephone number to phone in the evening. As I still lived at my parents' house, my mother was not too pleased if the phone rang late at night when I was out!

I became really excited by the idea of the pet food delivery service and couldn't see why it would not work anywhere. I decided to go door-to-door selling and see how many people were interested. I carried a board with me and the patter went something like this: 'Good morning, madam, sorry to trouble you but I am doing a survey in the area on how many people own pets. Do you own a pet?'

If the answer was no, I moved on but if the answer was yes, I asked how many tins of food they were likely to buy a week. If for example they only had a small cat, then it would not be cost-effective to deliver, but if they had two big dogs, bingo!

The next question would be, 'Do you get fed up with having to carry all the heavy pet food back from the shops?'

'You bet,' would come the reply.

'So if you could buy the pet food cheaper than the shops and have it delivered for free you would be interested?'

I carried a price list of all the different products and tried to get the order on the spot. I learnt very quickly to get a commitment there and then from the customer, never to let them think about it overnight.

Every Wednesday for three months I canvassed the area around where I lived. It was boring work, which resulted in about one success every twenty houses, but slowly I built up a round that was worthwhile.

My pals were always asking me whether there were any side benefits to being a door-to-door salesman, such as those related in the film *Confessions of a Window Cleaner*. The only time I came close was when an old biddy with missing teeth answered the door in a short negligee and asked me what I wanted. When I asked her whether she had any pets, she replied that she had a wonderful pussy and would I like to see it! I was off like a shot.

Including what we sold from the market stall and the door-to-door deliveries, we were soon selling about 200 cases a week. This allowed us to open accounts with the manufacturers and get better prices than we were paying at the Cash & Carrys. There were only two major players in the pet food market. The massive Mars Corporation, better known for confectionery, owned Pedigree Petfoods, which sold well-known brands such as Chum, Lassie, Chappie and Kit-E-Kat. The other big player was Spillers, which sold such famous brands as Kennomeat and Winalot.

As sales increased we were able to get the manufacturers' best terms providing we could take a lorry load of stock. We rented another four garages next to our existing six so that we could take advantage of the better terms.

The garages were at the back of the petrol station, exactly three doors up from where I lived, so we were close to what was effectively our warehouse. We were fortunate that we could also park our vans there. There was a brook, however, that ran very close and just behind the garages we were using, and this was to cause a problem that could never have been foreseen.

One of the biggest sellers in the pet food market was a biscuit product called Winalot, which was mixed in with the tinned dog food to bulk up the meal. It was supplied in 7lb bags with a handle on the top. In order to keep the bags off the damp garage floor, we placed them on wooden trays that had been previously used for the delivery of cakes. Our first order of Winalot was so cheap that we bought hundreds of bags and started filling the garage down the whole of one side. We had bought two months' supply in one go, but what we hadn't realised was that the garage door did not fit flush with the ground and there was a small gap under which mice would be able to get through.

As you can imagine, with the running water from the brook, a never-ending supply of food and a ready-made bungalow under the bags, we had created a five-star residence for the mice. To start with we noticed nothing untoward, but as we worked through the supply we began to notice that the mice had nibbled some of the bags.

The further we got down the garage wall the worse it got and we started to get paranoid about how many mice were living there. Eventually we had no choice but to confront the problem and move all the bags one by one to see the extent of the damage. To start with we only saw a few mice but as we got further down a few mice became a few dozen and as we dragged the last bags from the back of the wall, there were dozens of families running everywhere in blind panic. It was like a scene from an Alfred Hitchcock movie.

Andy and I were in complete shock and ran screaming from the garage, holding our trousers so that the little blighters couldn't run up our legs. The garage was now empty apart from the wooden cake trays that lay on the ground. We had no idea how many mice were living under the trays so we closed the doors and went to pick up our two dogs from home. One dog was a border collie and the other an Afghan hound. No doubt they had never seen mice before and we were uncertain how they would react when they started running around.

We finally plucked up the courage to lift the trays and, as we did so, the full horror story emerged as dozens of mice emerged from underneath. They had made perfect nests from the Winalot bag paper and the number of families was growing like Topsy. The dogs did their job and killed most of the mice, but we were amazed that some of them even managed to escape by running up the walls and escaping through the vent holes in the bricks and back to the safety of the brook.

We learnt a very expensive lesson, as about 20 per cent of the bags had to be destroyed and all the benefit of having a bulk delivery was lost. We never again stored any product in the garages that could be nibbled at by hungry rodents.

Around this time, a shop became vacant on Cannock High Street, which was an ideal size and location from which to sell pet food. This time I did draw up a business plan. But, in whatever way I crunched the numbers, it still worked out that we would be working to pay the landlord until Saturday afternoon. The weekly rent was ten times that of the market stall and we decided it was just too big a risk.

To this day it is one of the few business regrets I have as, with hindsight, I am sure it would have worked and set me off on a completely different retail path. At the time regrets about the past didn't outnumber dreams for the future. The pet food market has continued to grow in size and complexity since the late 1960s and specialist shops have benefited from an explosion of product range in both food and accessories. One of the specialists, Pets At Home, has 350 stores in the UK and joined the stock market in 2014 with a valuation of around £1.5 billion.

Back at the market, sales continued to increase and, in the week before Christmas 1969, we finally took £1,000 for the first time. In today's money that is equivalent to about £15,000, and from a stall measuring four by three metres was no mean feat. In just 30 months we had quadrupled our turnover.

As we entered a new decade I had turned 21 and life was good. I loved the cut and thrust of market life, I was my own boss and making sufficient money to drive around in a second-hand Jaguar E type. Life was very busy and the pet food business had grown to such an extent that we now had to deliver on a Tuesday evening. I was still drinking in the Moreton Country Club with my pal Lee, and had also met someone else with whom I shared the same ambitions and energy levels.

The famous dog food delivery van.

– CHAPTER 4 –

Gypsies, Tramps and Thieves

Dave Smith was a couple of years older than me and ran a car body repair business in Wolverhampton which he had inherited when his father died after a long illness, aged 64.

We spent hours at the bar talking about how we were ever going to make any real money. We were very comfortable for lads of our age but we were determined to build a substantial business.

One day we happened to see an old touring caravan, which was for sale for £100. Dave suggested that if we resprayed it and fitted a new carpet, it would look brand new. He happened to have a top-quality paint shop and all the facilities to do the necessary work. We promptly bought the caravan for a negotiated £90, had a tow bar fitted to my twin-wheel-based Transit van and set to work one evening to transform our new purchase. For two hours we rubbed down the existing paintwork to get it to a standard Dave was happy with and then resprayed it.

The result was absolutely fantastic and by the time we had fitted the new carpet, it looked to all intents and purposes like a new caravan. In four hours' work we had changed an ugly duckling into a swan. The problem was: how and where were we going to sell it?

My mother Edna was a brilliant saleswoman and agreed to try to sell it for us. We parked it on our drive at home, put an advert in the local paper advertising 'good as new Cresta caravan for sale, £250' and it sold the first night!

We could have sold it ten times over, and quickly realised we were onto something good.

Flushed with success, we decided to do some research and found that the best-selling touring caravans were the Sprite Musketeer, the smaller Sprite 400 and the larger Sprite Major. We scoured the local papers and snapped up as many second-hand models as we could. Dave's mother Dot agreed to sell them from her house as well and suddenly supply was the problem, not demand.

When Dave and I bought the first few caravans, we were desperately short of capital. My father kindly lent us £250 but each time we sold a caravan, we bought another one and we didn't get around to repaying the loan. Dad kept asking me when I was going to repay the money and I got annoyed. I eventually managed to get the £250 together and threw it on the table towards him. He looked up from his half-rim glasses and calmly said, 'You weren't given it like that. I hoped you would return it with some gratitude.'

I felt as big as a chip and it taught me a lesson I have never forgotten. Needless to say I apologised immediately.

One evening we had just bought a beaten-up old Sprite Musketeer and were driving back to Dave's body repair business, towing the caravan with the twin-wheel-based Transit van. As we approached a set of traffic lights, I indicated and moved over to the right-hand lane. It was starting to get dark so I turned the lights on, but unbeknown to me they were not working on the caravan.

As I waited for the lights to change there was a knock on my driver's door and when I opened the window, this chap boomed at the top of his voice, 'Hey, Gypo, your lights ain't workin'.'

I was completely taken aback but immediately saw the funny side when I realised what a Transit van pulling an old caravan would look like. 'Excuse me,' I replied, 'I'll have you know I am not a gypsy and in fact I went to public school.'

'Yeah, and my mother's the Queen,' he retorted.

We were managing to acquire about one caravan a week and so I was now working every day except Sunday; Tuesday evening I was delivering pet food and Wednesday evening helping with the caravans. Dave and I then had another brainwave to make money and I was to get even busier.

With the rise in popularity of music during the 1960s, discotheques had come into fashion to such an extent that they were springing up everywhere. They were easy to organise; you just needed a large room, a good 'disc jockey' and a venue that was on a bus route.

One of the pubs that we regularly visited fitted the bill perfectly and we offered the landlord £20 (£500 in today's money), employed a local disc jockey for £20 and we were up and running. We charged £1 entrance fee and all Dave and I had to do was sit at the top of the stairs and take the money. We also got to see which of the girls were single and which ones were with boyfriends. The first night we took £80, which for a Monday night was excellent, and as we had all made £20 each, everyone was happy.

We talked Lee's mother into allowing us to do the same thing on a Wednesday night at the Country Club and managed to secure our third venue in a local village pub for Friday night. I then had the idea of advertising membership of all three venues at a discounted rate, calling it the 'Triangle Club'. I put an expensive advert in the paper and got three replies! This was another lesson learned: just because people are able to fork out £1 for an evening's entertainment, they may not have sufficient money to join a club.

My life was now getting ridiculously busy and I was working six days a week and five evenings.

I had discovered another small wholesaler in Wolverhampton, called GBL Wholesale after the initials of the owners, who for some reason were able to sell luxury goods cheaper than all the major Cash & Carrys. It was a very small business run by two men in their seventies but had been established before the Second World War. The premises were like a rabbit warren and they sold all manner of household goods, toys and toiletries but in a very small way. The prices were all fairly expensive except for luxury items. This absolutely intrigued me until they explained the reason.

Purchase tax had been introduced into Britain in October 1940 to raise funds for the war effort. The initial rate was 33.3 per cent and was levied on non-essential goods. Companies that existed at the time of the introduction were granted what was known as a 'purchase tax number' and they were allowed to buy direct from the manufacturer and apply the rate of purchase tax on the sale of the goods rather than when they bought them. As time went on the number of businesses that held these so-called 'tax numbers' started to dwindle and eventually the manufacturers started to invoice their goods including the purchase tax. But providing you still had a business that had started before purchase tax was introduced, you could still insist on being invoiced free of purchase tax.

The implications of this situation are difficult to explain, but it was of monumental significance.

By the early 1970s there were three rates of purchase tax in existence and the top rate of 55 per cent was levied on luxury items. A good example of this was a product called Radox bath salts, that sold really well. The non-purchase tax cost from the manufacturer for a case of six packets was £3. To this was added the 55 per cent, making a total invoice cost of £4.65. If you bought a lorry load of the product you could also get a 50p bonus, reducing your overall cost to £4.15 per case.

Now because GBL Wholesale still held a purchase tax number it was allowed to buy a lorry load net of purchase tax, so it paid £3 less the 50p bonus, making a total invoice cost of £2.50 per case.

Obviously the 55 per cent rate of tax had to be applied when the goods were sold and depending on the mark-up you used, would always make the product more expensive than the price at which the manufacturer could sell.

But I then had a eureka moment that made me feel I had won the lottery. I realised that if you sold the product on with a minimum uplift of, say, 10p per case you could end up selling it cheaper than the manufacturer could!

This is how it worked: Having the purchase tax number allowed you to buy it at £2.50 per case. Adding a profit margin of only 10p per case meant that you were now selling it at £2.60. On top of this you added the mandatory 55 per cent purchase tax and the total came to £4.03, which meant that you would now be selling the product 12p per case cheaper than the manufacturer!

As there were 1,500 cases on a lorry load, I realised that I could make £150 per delivery and the wholesaler would also save £180 per delivery. Within two weeks I had bought their business and started selling in bulk to the large Cash & Carrys.

I made an appointment to see Ralph Feeney, the owner of J&F Cash & Carry in Birmingham, and we started to work more closely together. As one of his biggest market customers I had got to know him fairly well over the previous couple of years and we seemed to have a lot in common.

He represented everything I wanted to achieve in business, as he had been incredibly successful in building up a small Birmingham wholesale company into one of the largest and most successful Cash

& Carrys in the country. He drove a Jensen FF sports car and lived in
a beautiful house in Lady Byron Lane, Solihull, one of the premier
addresses in the West Midlands. The only problem with Ralph
was that he supported Aston Villa football club and I supported
Wolverhampton Wanderers.

After decimalisation in February 1971, inflation really started to
take off in Britain and prices were rising weekly. This gave us another
opportunity to make money and our garages became full as we
started to purchase goods ahead of price increases.

The price of John West tinned salmon had increased substantially
but Ralph had missed a trick and was still selling at the old price.
I bought all his stock of 150 cases and promptly sold it the same
day to his competitor down the road, making £150 profit. He was
not amused but I think I won a few Brownie points for seeing the
opportunity.

It was now 1971 and I had been my own boss for just over three
years. My business interests included market trading, a pet food
delivery service, renovating caravans, running discotheques and most
recently the wholesale business.

I realised that I had not had a holiday since leaving school. More
importantly, I couldn't see how I could ever take one with business
life being so hectic.

We had acquired the stall next to us at Cannock market and as
sales continued to climb, Andy and I were having to make extra trips
to the Cash & Carrys during the week. It was impossible for one of us
to cope with all the work alone and I honestly do not know what would
have happened if either of us had fallen ill. We now employed two
assistants on Friday and Saturday to cope with the increase in trade.

As inflation took hold but wage increases failed to match rising
prices, money was not going as far as it had and people were
becoming far more cost-conscious.

A company called Kwik Save Discount had opened in Wales with prices way below what the supermarkets were charging. Their retail formula, like most good things, was very simple.

Founded as Value Foods by Welsh entrepreneur Albert Gubay, the first shop opened in Rhyl in north Wales in July 1959. In 1964, Gubay visited the USA and learnt about the 'baby shark' method of retailing. Combined with ideas taken from the West German retailer Aldi, the business model was based on buying a limited range of lines on favourable payment terms, distributing and selling them at below cost before the payment fell due, and using the interest on the favourable cash flow to fund the business.

First, they reduced labour requirements by displaying the products in cases rather than individually. They then adopted what is known as 'Pareto's principle' or the 80/20 rule. This basically means that 80 per cent of all sales are achieved through 20 per cent of the product range. Instead of selling the normal 3,000 products that were to be found in the average supermarket, they reduced their range to 600 products. The real benefit of having a reduced product range was that the cashiers were able to remember all the prices and there was, therefore, no need to price everything individually. This saved an enormous amount of money in labelling costs.

Their business model was brilliant and I drove to Wales to see one of the shops. I couldn't believe how much cheaper they were compared with the supermarkets and realised that this was the way forward.

While the market stall was making good money, I was a prisoner of its needs and couldn't see how I could ever escape from the day-to-day running of it or indeed ever take on another market stall. I was far too busy at the coalface to look up and take the opportunities open to me.

I became obsessed with opening my own discount store.

For weeks I scoured all the local towns around Wolverhampton, desperately searching for premises that could be a potential discount store, and then I had the most amazing stroke of luck that would have been impossible to imagine.

A factory unit near Wolverhampton market and right opposite a large car park had caught my eye as a potential site. It was the perfect size at around 5,000 square feet, had adequate car parking and was very close to the market, which of course attracted cost-conscious customers.

It had also been vacant for a number of years but did not appear to be for sale. To my absolute astonishment I found out that it was owned by my girlfriend's father! He had been hanging onto it with a view to selling it when he needed some cash. I asked him whether he would be prepared to lease it to me if I could get change of use from industrial to retail. If I could, it would also enhance the value of the freehold.

Change of use ended up being no trouble at all but as I had nowhere near the amount of capital that would be necessary to convert the factory into a retail unit, how was I going to fund it?

I phoned Ralph from J&F Wholesale and he came over from Birmingham with an architect to view it with me. As it happened the premises were ideal for conversion except that it was going to be touch and go whether the lane at the back of the store was wide enough for an articulated lorry to deliver goods. A 30ft delivery van was sent over to test it and by the narrowest of margins just about managed to reverse up to the back of the store and into the loading bay. My luck was holding.

Ralph and I then went out to dinner to discuss the financial details of how we were going to proceed. His accountant had prepared some figures that showed the venture was going to cost around £50,000 and if I wanted half, I would have to advance

Outside of Lo-Cost Wolverhampton, March 1972.

£25,000. It was out of the question as it was like asking me for about £250,000 in today's money.

I hadn't really got much more than £1,000. In the end he loaned me £5,000, which the bank then matched and I ended up with 20 per cent of the business. It remains to this day one of the most generous gestures I have ever known. I felt incredibly humbled that here was a very wealthy man who was prepared to invest a large sum of money in a 23-year-old market trader whom he hardly knew. I have never forgotten his generosity and we remain great friends to this day.

At the age of 22, I had dropped a bombshell by telling my parents that I was getting married. Dad went absolutely cuckoo and said I was stark raving mad. Not because he disliked my fiancée but because, he said, I was too young. I obviously didn't want to upset my future father-in-law, especially as he was going to be my future landlord as well, but as time moved on I could see my father was right. I had only gone out with a few girls before leaving Denstone and was far too young and immature to make a lifetime commitment.

The night before the grand opening, Lo-Cost Wolverhampton, 1972.

Fortunately my fiancée started to go off the idea of marriage at around the same time, so we sort of drifted apart and became good friends instead.

The world really was my oyster now and I couldn't sleep at night for excitement, thinking about what the future held. There was to be at least six months' building work to be done before we could open the store and I was involved in every small detail. As this was going to be my life from now on, I had to tidy up my other business affairs. The caravan business folded when Dave decided to go to Marbella to open a bar with another friend of ours. In total we had sold, or more correctly our mothers had sold, over 70 caravans. As time moved on it became more and more difficult to find the models we wanted as we had cornered the market. We had to travel further and further afield to buy anything worth having and in truth the idea had run its course. It didn't help either when one night a caravan was stolen from the front of Dave's drive.

The disco business collapsed after fights started breaking out and we sold the pet food delivery service to a friend of ours called Mike Ross. This only left the market stall business that Andy continued to run for the next couple of years. It eventually ran out of steam as competition in Cannock increased significantly with the opening of two new stores. Andy pulled down the shutters on our stall and moved on into a completely new career.

We had worked together for almost five years, shared some great moments and also had a lot of fun. We both still look back on those years with fond memories and I learnt more about business from market trading than I have from anything else in my life.

I had decided to call the store Lo-Cost Discount, which Ralph thought was a great name. And even before I had opened the first store, I was beginning to wonder whether Lo-Cost could become another chain like Tesco.

As the fireworks lit up the night to welcome the year 1972, I looked up into the sky and privately drank a toast to the future of my new baby, Lo-Cost Discount Stores.

The grand opening was to be in March and I couldn't wait.

CHAPTER 5

Moving Up the Food Chain

Ralph had an interest in another company called Buy-Wise Supermarkets Ltd. It was jointly owned with Ray Ridgley, who had also started on the markets and built up his grocery business over a number of years in the Birmingham area. The company was trading from four stores and I decided to meet Ray and take him to see the Kwik Save store in Wales. Although he was almost twenty years older than I was, we immediately got on well.

After visiting Kwik Save, we both agreed that the discount model was the way forward and we would tailor our product range accordingly. As my store was opening in March, it was important that we were both buying from the same product range. Ralph had employed a bright young accountant called Derek Bennett, who was a friend of Ray's and also a shareholder in Buy-Wise. He came over to see me in Wolverhampton and help set up all the bookwork for the forthcoming opening. He frightened me to death with the amount of complexity that had to be introduced in order to keep control of the business. I had absolutely no idea of bookwork; I had used an old OXO tin on the market for loose change and put all the notes in my back pocket. We had never bothered entering daily figures into a control record and I didn't know how a cash machine worked.

Derek explained to me that I needed to employ someone who would be in charge of the six checkout cashiers, going to the bank to collect change for the tills and organising rotas for tea and lunch breaks. When he showed me the cashing-up book, I nearly fainted. For each till an opening and closing reading had to be entered to ensure that the total money in the till agreed with the takings. There was a column for this, a column for that and then all takings for the tills had to be transferred to one final column. From this, expenses and wages had to be deducted to give a final banking figure. It was all a bit different from the OXO tin and back pocket!

We placed adverts in the local paper for shelf-stackers, cashiers and an assistant manager and, as the building work came to an end, deliveries started to arrive from Ralph's warehouse. The butchery and greengrocery sections had been franchised to specialists, with a cut-price cigarette kiosk completing the retail offer. Bread and cakes were the only deliveries we would receive on a daily basis, with all other goods coming from Ralph's warehouse two or three times a week depending on turnover. Each 30ft lorry load contained a maximum of 40 roll-on, roll-off cages, the beauty of which was that a delivery would take minutes to unload, with all the cages then stored in the back area until being wheeled onto the shop floor for unpacking. It was certainly a lot easier than the markets, where everything had to be handled individually.

With all the staff selected, we set an opening date of Friday, 3 March 1972 and placed a two-page advert in the local paper with some great opening offers.

Needless to say I didn't sleep much the night before the opening, and got to the store at 7.00am to open up for the butchers, who needed two hours' preparation time for their displays. We were opening at 9.00am, and from 8.00am I kept looking out of the window to see if a crowd was forming – it wasn't.

At 8.30am there were still no people outside and I was beginning to panic. I went into the staffroom for a cup of tea with the cashiers and wished them well for the first day. The girls had learned all the prices off by heart and I kept testing them on different products to ensure they had got it right. The wonderful thing about having six checkout operators in a line was that they could ask each other the price of a particular item if they were unsure and one of them would always know.

I came out of the staffroom at 8.45am and forced myself to peep out of the window. I could not believe it. There was a queue stretching down nearly to the end of the road.

'Get ready girls!' I shouted, 'It's about to happen.'

I opened the doors to another chapter of my life at exactly 9.00am and was nearly knocked off my feet as the crowd surged in. By 9.15am all the aisles were rammed and the six tills were in full swing. I stood and listened to the sound of the machines all clattering in unison. Forget Mozart, Beethoven and even The Beatles, this was the sweetest music I had ever heard.

The first problem occurred around about 9.30am when the cashier manager informed me that we were running out of change. I thought we couldn't be as we had bought a load from the bank the day before. But no one had foreseen the problem with the new type of till we had installed. To speed up the operation, we had bought a brand new machine that incorporated a dispenser, which automatically distributed change to the customer. This was supposed to speed up the till operation as it saved the cashier fiddling around selecting the correct amount of change to be given.

The problem was that if the bill came to, say, £35.01 and the customer offered £36, the dispenser automatically distributed 99p in change. Normally the cashier would ask the customer if they had the 1p and all the change would be saved. It meant that the change machines had to be constantly topped up, which was far too labour-intensive and time-consuming. In addition, we had to make too many trips to the bank to collect all the change. After a couple of weeks, we changed back to the normal style of till and gave up with the experiment. The speed of the checkout operation was actually all down to the speed of the operator. It must be remembered that checkout scanning and debit card transactions did not exist back in 1972.

One of our opening offers was a packet of shortcake biscuits for 5p. We sold 100 cases in the first hour, and the 500 cases that we had hoped would last a whole week had disappeared by lunchtime on the second day.

The first full week's trading was twice what we expected and from the very start we were making money. Derek's strict financial controls were vital in understanding what gross profit margin we were making and also what costs we had to bear.

Wolverhampton had a large West Indian community that was attracted to our low prices and word soon got around that we offered great value for money. Because our store was so close to the main market and opposite a large car park, it turned out to be a great location. I decided to build on the Caribbean shopping experience by introducing a West Indian section that catered for their tastes, which were often for sweet things. We introduced products such as Nutrament (a sweet-flavoured milk drink), ackees (the national fruit of Jamaica) and coconut milk.

We also started selling different types of rice such as pre-fluffed and long grain, ensuring that our prices were always below those of the competition. Within a few months we were selling a lorry load of West Indian products a week and the takings continued to rise.

In August, Ray Ridgley was about to open his fifth store at

Burntwood, just outside Cannock, and came over to Wolverhampton to have a look around my store, which had now been open for nearly six months. We went out to lunch and I noticed that he was coughing quite badly. He said he had been to the doctor's three times but each time was told there was nothing to worry about. At my suggestion he had his chest X-rayed, and lo and behold discovered that he had contracted tuberculosis. It got worse when he found out both his children had the disease as well. They were all rushed off into a hospital isolation ward, which meant that Ray would be out of action for at least three months while he and the family recovered.

Ralph, Derek, Ray and I held an emergency meeting to plan a way ahead. I suggested that as I only had one store to look after, why not merge the two businesses and I would become stores and sales director, with Ray becoming managing director upon his return to work. We would also name all the stores Lo-Cost as everyone agreed it was the best name.

The shareholding was split in such a way that Ralph ended up with 51 per cent, Ray 22 per cent, me 17 per cent and Derek 10 per cent. As far as I was concerned, it was a great deal as not only was I now part of a much bigger team with five stores and another one about to open, but I also had a new partner who was not only a great guy to work with but also a very shrewd retailer.

Ray was back at work before Christmas and in April 1973 we opened our largest store to date, a 10,000-square foot store in the Kings Heath area of Birmingham. We then opened our eighth store in July of that year, again in a suburb of Birmingham, known as Rubery.

Throughout the 1970s inflation became a major problem for household budgets as the increase in prices started to overtake the increase in wages. By the end of the decade inflation had averaged 8 per cent a year.

It is worth comparing some everyday prices in the 40-year period just after decimalisation in 1971 to those in 2011:

Mars bar	1971: £0.02	2011: £0.60
First class stamp	1971: £0.03	2011: £0.44
Pint of milk	1971: £0.06	2011: £0.49
Loaf of bread	1971: £0.09	2011: £1.10
Pint of bitter	1971: £0.11	2011: £3.05
Bunch of bananas	1971: £0.18	2011: £0.65
Packet of twenty cigarettes	1971: £0.27	2011: £7
Gallon of petrol	1971: £0.33	2011: £6
Ticket to Wembley Cup Final	1971: £2	2011: £115

Life was not easy in the early and mid-1970s.

Indeed, the 1970s was a difficult decade for economies across the world, not least the UK's. The rate of inflation had started to accelerate in the 1960s as successive governments set about achieving full employment. Determined to avoid a return to the high unemployment levels of the 1930s, successive governments (both Labour and Conservative) implemented Keynesian policies to keep demand high, using public money to prime the economic pump. The result, in a Britain with some archaic industrial management and workforce practices, was the creation of greater demand than supply – the classic cause of inflation.

However, this was just a foretaste of what was to come in the 1970s. Anthony Barber, the chancellor of the exchequer in Heath's government, pumped money into the economy as never before in 1971 and 1972 following the news that unemployment had broken through the 1 million barrier, a shocking total following 30 years of full employment. Unfortunately, Britain's expansion coincided with a world boom, sparked by the decision in the United States to print money rather than raise taxes, in order to pay for the increasingly expensive involvement in Vietnam. In 1971 the US turned from being an exporter of oil into a net importer; and on 6 October 1973, Yom Kippur (the Day of Atonement in the Jewish calendar), Egypt and Syria attacked Israel. Within 24 hours major Arab oil-exporting nations had announced plans to reduce oil production. Ten days later they announced an oil embargo against the USA in response to its support of Israel, and increased the price of petroleum by no less than 70 per cent.

The Yom Kippur War ended with an Egypt/Israel ceasefire on 25 October but Arab frustration at Western nations' support for Israel continued and on 23 December the oil-producing nations agreed on a further increase in the price of oil. The price had doubled since the beginning of 1973. This was a great shock to the developed nations of the world which had enjoyed decades of cheap oil. In 1955 a barrel of Saudi light crude had cost $1.93 and in January 1973 it was still only $2.18. Now the price quadrupled in less than twelve months.

The effect on world trade was little short of disastrous. Both industry and consumers had become extremely profligate in their use of oil, which had been getting cheaper and cheaper in real terms over the previous decade. As panic buying and speculation took hold, the price rocketed. Tens of billions of pounds, dollars, deutschmarks, francs and lira were taken out of the world economy and put in the Arabian desert. Until they could be recycled into the system, the world was going to suffer.

And suffer it did, as Britain with its continuing structural weakness suffered more than most. The 'Barber boom' had not worked. British manufacturers had not invested as much as had been hoped, and the two main results of the expansion in credit had been an explosion in property prices and a rapid increase in inflation. Resentment grew among workers, who benefited little from the rising property and stock market prices but felt the impact of rising prices in the shops.

In an attempt to choke inflation, Heath's government tackled the symptoms – rising prices, dividends and earnings – without tackling the cause: too much money. In the autumn of 1973, just before the oil crisis, the government had introduced stage one of an incomes policy which would allow index-linked rises if inflation rose above 7 per cent. Because of the oil-price hike, inflation rose quickly above that level and the automatic pay rises gave a ratchet effect, pushing it higher and higher.

The National Union of Mineworkers submitted a large claim and imposed an overtime ban on 8 November 1973. Heath panicked and declared a state of emergency on 13 November. A month later he declared a three-day week to preserve fuel, and though negotiations with both Arabs and the miners continued, the only results were the continuation of high oil prices and the reality of a miners' strike rather than just the threat. In the end, and for some people three weeks too late, Heath called an election with the implied platform of: 'Who governs the country, the government or the unions?' The electorate decided it wasn't sure who should govern the country. The Tories had finally shown some signs of standing up to the unions, but Labour might get the miners back to work. Neither party gained an overall majority, but Labour came away with more seats. Heath tried unsuccessfully to negotiate a coalition with the Liberal Democrats, so Harold Wilson formed his third administration.

The Labour government gave in to the NUM and when the rest of the unions followed in the headlong rush, inflation soared to almost 25 per cent. While inflation was soaring and everyone tried to keep pace, financial institutions, and to a lesser extent manufacturing businesses, were suffering severely from the financial squeeze that had finally been imposed in the autumn of 1973. Nearly all the secondary banks went into liquidation or, if it was deemed necessary to maintain confidence, were rescued by the main banks assisted by the Bank of England. If the new chancellor, Denis Healey, had not introduced a corporate tax-saving measure called stock relief, many manufacturing companies would have failed. On the London Stock Exchange, prices fell throughout 1974 and the Financial Times 30-share index reached 147 in early January 1975; it had been over 150 as long ago as 1946.

By 1975 inflation was starting to have a serious effect not only on those who had retired and those without the protection of powerful unions, but on British industry in general.

International confidence in the British government collapsed completely when Labour's 1976 party conference championed the nationalisation of the leading high street banks and the largest insurance companies. In the autumn of 1976 sterling began to fall like a stone.

As prices began to increase in the 1970s, it became obvious to Ray and me that we needed our own warehouse. We had become Ralph's biggest customer by far but were dependent on his buying team to keep in stock everything we sold. Only having 600 product lines meant that we could never afford to be out of stock of our best sellers. Because it could never be predicted accurately what customers at the Cash & Carry would buy from one week to another, the buyers were often caught on the hop and Lo-Cost would suffer. We were fast becoming too dependent on each other and it was also obvious that as we opened more and more stores, eventually the Cash & Carry would not be able to cope with all the deliveries as well as serving its own customers.

The downside, of course, was that if we opened our own warehouse and distribution facility, our costs would increase dramatically. We would need to employ buyers, warehouse staff, lorry drivers and also have our own accounting department. Nevertheless, the more we looked at the figures and considered the pros and cons, the more we thought it was the right move, and we started to look around for suitable premises.

With so many sites in and around Birmingham, it was fairly logical to find somewhere central to our stores and we eventually found the ideal warehouse just outside Oldbury and close to the M5 and M6 motorway complex.

We paused for breath during 1974 and rather than opening any new stores, we improved the ones we had and started to prepare the new 50,000-square-foot warehouse which was to come into operation in 1975.

It was decided that I would become buying director and look after the warehouse side of things and Ray would be in charge of store operations. Vick Cook was a lifelong friend of Ralph's and he joined us as warehouse manager. We also employed a wonderful lady called Miss Homfray as our office manageress working for our newly appointed accountant, a young man called Sean Traves.

As I had received no formal training on buying, it was agreed that I would arrange meetings with the key account managers of the top companies and Ralph would introduce me to them and help with the initial orders. In the event, he came over for one morning and three meetings, then tapped me on the head and said I would be fine. It was like being thrown in at the deep end but right from the start, I enjoyed the cut and thrust of negotiating deals with the suppliers.

I appointed two assistant buyers and we started placing orders in readiness for the changeover, which was to happen in April. Everything went pretty much to plan and the transition was fairly seamless. We were now masters of our own destiny and it was up to me to ensure that the stores were kept well stocked and competitively priced.

Inflation was really starting to cause problems and every time I placed a new order, the cost price seemed to have increased. Out of a range of only 600 products, there would normally be about ten price increases per week. However, as the months ticked by, this increased from ten per week to about 50 per week. This was a major problem because it meant that all the cashiers had to remember the new prices and they became very confused. The upside was that every time we increased the prices there was a profit on the residual stock, both in the shops and in the warehouse. This was a massive help to us in our first year of taking on all the extra costs of the new distribution centre and we still managed to beat our budgeted profit forecast.

Completely out of the blue, Dave Smith, my great friend and partner in the caravan and disco business, returned home from Marbella with his dreams in tatters. He had managed to sell his bar, as he put it, just in time to save him from sinking into a hole with no escape. Many people at the time were tempted to go abroad, either to start a dream business or escape from problems. In reality they rarely achieved either and often ended up returning to the UK, a lot poorer than when they left.

Having sold his body repair business to fund the Marbella adventure, he was stony broke and desperate to find something new to do back home. As is often the case in life, timing is everything and Dave just happened to be in the right place at the right time.

A friend of mine from the local pub had approached me and asked if I was interested in buying his mother's cigarette kiosk in Wolverhampton market, as she was retiring having run it for the previous twenty years. Because of the success we had enjoyed in our cigarette kiosks inside Lo-Cost, I knew that it would be a great site as so many people had to pass it on their way into the market. The cut-price cigarette industry in the mid-1970s was very much in its infancy and most tobacconists and newsagents sold at full retail price.

Because selling cut-price cigarettes took up so little space, it was a natural attraction for cost-conscious customers and a great way of increasing traffic flow through the store.

Ray Ridgley, one of my partners in Lo-Cost, had already cottoned on to the idea that there was a lot of money to be made from cut-price tobacco and confectionery and had already opened a few outlets of his own in the Birmingham area. Until Dave arrived home there was no way I could have found the time to start yet another venture, but suddenly I had a partner I could trust implicitly and a site that provided great potential.

Alfred Preedy & Sons was a chain of tobacconists formed in Dudley in 1868, and by 1975 it was trading from over 150 stores. In addition to the shops it also wholesaled cigarettes to the trade from its warehouse, based at Tipton in the West Midlands. Dave and I approached the manager of the warehouse and asked if they would be prepared to supply us and give us a week's credit into the bargain. Amazingly they agreed, and so we were now in a position to able to buy the kiosk and start up in business yet again. We just couldn't think of a memorable name for our company, so in the end we just called it T&S Tobacco Ltd (Threlfall and Smith) and showed even more imagination by naming our cigarette kiosk Cut Price Cigarettes, which at least did exactly what it said on the tin!

Just after a year after the shutters had come down on a market stall that had spawned a growing chain of discount stores, so the shutters were lifted on another market stall. Little did we realise when we opened for business on 10 October 1975 that this would lead to a much larger venture and that in just over 25 years the company would have 1,280 shops and a turnover of £1 billion per annum.

I had just turned 27 years of age and life had never been better. Lo-Cost was going well, I had just moved into a new flat, my drinking pal and best mate had returned from Marbella and I had another business. But any notions of being the carefree lothario of Wolverhampton had been dashed because I had fallen head over heels in love.

As the lights were coming up at the end of one of the local discos I spotted the most gorgeous girl I had ever seen in my life. She was slim, sexy and dark-haired with piercing light blue eyes but before I could make a move she had gone. The following week I spotted her again and so started the cat-and-mouse game that most of us

First cigarette kiosk, Wolverhampton market, 1975.

go through at some stage in our lives. Gill wasn't interested in me because she was engaged to a lad who worked away during the week in Southampton. I persisted in asking her out but got nowhere. Time, I thought, for the dirty tricks department, so I started suggesting that maybe he wasn't being as faithful to her in Southampton as she was being to him in Wolverhampton. It still didn't work, so one lunchtime, after finding out where she worked, I put on my only suit and tie and went to visit her. I walked into the library, went up to the counter and said in my poshest voice: 'Excuse me, madam, but do you have any books on the sex life of the outer Mongolian water rat?'

Quick as a flash Gill replied, 'No, sir, I am afraid they are all out at the moment but we do have a book that may interest you titled: How to stop being a persistent pest.'

Fortunately, she was impressed that I had made the effort to wear a suit and also take the trouble to find out where she worked. We went out to lunch at the local pub and for the first and only time in my life I fell in love.

Lo-Cost continued to thrive throughout 1976 and we began to see the benefits of having our own warehouse and distribution centre. We opened another four stores, taking our total into double figures, and also embarked on creating a Lo-Cost label range of products. The idea of this was to provide the customer with a cheaper alternative to the product they would normally buy. For example, Robertson's jam, which was the brand leader, would be sold at say 50p per jar. We would then approach another manufacturer of jams, such as Duerr's, and ask them to supply their product to us but with our own Lo-Cost label on the jar. The jam was of comparable quality but sold at a considerably lower price of say 40p. The customer now had the choice of either buying the brand leader at a premium price or a very comparable quality own-label product at a cheaper price.

Customers were more than happy to buy everyday products such as jam, baked beans and canned vegetables at the lower prices and our Lo-Cost label equivalent products were soon outselling the better-known brands.

The logic did not apply to all products because some brands were so well known and respected that customers were more than happy to pay a premium for them. Examples of what are called stand-alone brands are products such as Bovril and OXO cubes, which are difficult to replicate with an own-label equivalent. The classic success story for a company is when the name of a product is actually better known than the product itself. One of the best examples of this is Vaseline, which is actually petroleum jelly, but over time the name has become synonymous with the product and most customers ask for a jar of Vaseline, not a jar of petroleum jelly.

Rising inflation had become a nightmare for shoppers as prices had almost doubled between 1971 and 1976, peaking at just under 25 per cent in 1975. Housewives became incredibly cost-conscious and value for money became more and more important as prices continued to rise. I had ordered ten lorry loads of Nescafé coffee ahead of a large price increase and had been guaranteed both price and delivery, but prices were rising so quickly that the day before it was due to be delivered the sales director phoned me and said it would be cheaper for him to send me a cheque for £5,000 than deliver the coffee. It was getting to the point where we could make more money from just hanging on to stock than from selling it. Discount stores such as Lo-Cost and Kwik Save were stealing business from the more established grocers such as Tesco and Sainsbury's to such an extent that we started to become a real threat to them. Our turnover had increased from £1 million in 1972 to £12 million in 1976, and our profit had increased from £15,000 in 1972 to £300,000 in 1976 (£4.5 million in today's money).

Kwik Save was a much larger company than Lo-Cost and had floated on the stock market in 1970. By 1977 it was opening new stores at the rate of one a week and to our horror had started opening stores in and around Birmingham. Because Kwik Save had far more stores than we did, their purchasing power was far greater and allowed them to sell at prices that were difficult for us to compete with. Because our style of trading was almost identical to theirs, it was obvious which company was going to win in the long term. We had opened our sixteenth and largest store, but we were now extremely vulnerable to their ever-growing presence and realised that the writing was on the wall.

Joint managing directors ran Kwik Save; Ian Howe was in charge of the day-to-day control and Michael Weeks was responsible for store acquisition. Michael was chauffeured around the country and clocked up 100,000 miles a year in a Rolls-Royce that was changed annually. He came to see us and explained that if we didn't sell our business to them soon, in time we probably wouldn't have a business worth selling. He made us an offer, which was less than £1 million, and was confident that we would accept. What he didn't know was that another company had made an approach and indicated that they may be interested in buying our business.

Oriel Foods was owned by the large American RCA Corporation and was trying to build a European food division. They had recently acquired Discount Foods of Queensferry, an operation of similar size to us, and were keen to open further stores in the Midlands. When they first phoned to try to set up a meeting we played hard to get and said that we were really not interested in talking to them.

While all of this was up in the air, on 5 March 1977 Gill and I were married and in true discount fashion I whisked her off to the Lake District and Scotland for a full seven-day honeymoon. Dave Smith was my best man and his mother had to step in and manage the cigarette kiosk in order for him to have the day off work. Lyons Tetley, one of our key suppliers, owned the hotel we had booked in the Lake District and I therefore managed to get a sizeable discount off the room rate although I never did tell Gill. We were supposed to move on to Oban but found a hotel in Ayr with a four-poster bed, which also served meals in the room, so as it was early in the season and quite chilly outdoors we decided to stay there, having all our meals in bed and watching the TV.

On returning to work I learnt through the grocery grapevine that Tesco were planning a major price initiative to combat the

Down the aisle: St Michael's Church, Tettenhall, Wolverhampton, 5 March 1977.

The happy couple.

ever-growing threat of the discount stores. At the time, instead of offering everyday low prices Tesco gave Green Shield stamps to their customers as a loyalty reward and had been doing so since 1963.

Trading stamps had first become popular in the USA, where Sperry & Hutchinson began offering them to retailers as long ago as 1896. The retailers bought them and offered them to customers at a rate tied to the amount of the purchase. The main users were petrol stations, corner shops and supermarkets. The customer collected the stamps and was able to buy products from an S&H catalogue or shop. A British entrepreneur, Richard Tompkins, noted their success and brought the idea to the UK, setting up The Green Shield Trading Stamp Company in 1958. His biggest customer was Tesco, whose founder Jack Cohen was a great advocate of stamps.

However, offering Green Shield stamps was now costing Tesco £20 million per annum, so they decided to abandon the practice and put the money into prices rather than stamps. They launched the initiative in July 1977 and called it Operation Check-Out. It was backed with a very expensive advertising campaign and was an immediate success. Our sales suffered and we now had another competitor in addition to Kwik Save.

We quickly realised that retailing was going to become more and more competitive and in reality we were not big enough to stand up to the big boys. So when Oriel Foods phoned for a second time our skirt was now just above the knee, rather than just below!

John Page was chief executive of the company and came to visit our company with his management team. We gave them a tour around the stores and our distribution and they seemed to like what they saw. It was then up to Ralph and John to try to agree a deal. Ralph was a brilliant negotiator and arranged to meet John at his beautiful home in Solihull. We had all agreed that we would not do a deal under £1 million but as Ralph was the majority shareholder, it was really up to him to make the final decision.

We waited in the boardroom for the phone to ring and put him on the loudspeaker. I guess Ray, Derek and I were hoping the figure would be something approaching £1.5 million but when he announced that he had reluctantly agreed a figure of £1.6 million, we were blown away. In today's money the deal was worth just over £8.4 million and as I had 17 per cent of the company, my share was worth just over £1.4 million.

Deals rarely go smoothly, however, and in between agreeing the sale price and completing the deal we had another three months' trading to get through. After the Tesco initiative, sales got worse and we realised that our financial targets were not going to be achieved. We called a board meeting in which we agonised over when we should tell Oriel the bad news and worried that they might well pull out of the deal once they saw the figures. It was left up to our finance director, Derek, to call John Page, the Oriel Foods chief executive, and give him the bad news. When he came back into the room, he just shrugged his shoulders and said that John didn't seem to care; we were mightily relieved.

Our solicitors were Edge and Ellison, a well-known firm in Birmingham. The senior partner was a wonderful gentleman called John Wardle, who always insisted on breaking open the sherry bottle at exactly noon except when a deal was being done, in which case it was champagne. The sale and purchase agreement was drawn up and 25 October was chosen as the date to complete the deal and exchange contracts.

John Page arrived at the meeting waving a cheque for the full consideration but said that because Oriel Foods was owned by an American company we would have to wait for the Bank of England's approval before the deal could go through.

We had all noticed in previous meetings that John had an unusual habit of tearing off a sheet of paper from an A4 pad and slowly eating his way through it. As the clock ticked by and no confirmation came through from the Bank of England, John started to eat the cheque!

We watched in horror as he slowly nibbled his way through the cheque until it was all gone. In the event it was all a bit of an anticlimax and we had to wait until the following day for the formalities to go through.

By the time the Lo-Cost deal went through, our T&S Tobacco business had acquired another five kiosks and we had started to look further afield for expansion. I had agreed to stay on at Lo-Cost and had been offered a generous salary but as I drove home from the solicitors in my second-hand Porsche 911, wealthier than I had ever believed possible, my thoughts started to drift towards how we could build up the tobacco business.

In my heart of hearts I knew that I would not be staying with Oriel for long and so it was. The following May I left to join my pal Dave in our cigarette business.

Although I was relieved and delighted to receive the money when we sold Lo-Cost, I had mixed feelings about leaving. It had been a fantastic six years and I had learnt a great deal from my partners, Ralph, Ray and Derek. Although considerably older and wiser than myself, they had never made me feel like the junior board member. We had some great times together because throughout the 1970s there was a lot of corporate entertaining and we were invited, together with our partners, to a lot of lavish brand launches involving overnight stays and dinners in five-star hotels. Gill and I were also lucky enough to visit America, Corfu and Madeira as guests of suppliers. It was also possible to eat out every day if you wanted to spend time with the key account executives. However, I did not become too involved with the lunchtime fraternity, preferring instead to grab a quick sandwich.

Each year we held a board meeting in Jersey for a few days and took some friends along to make up the numbers. We had some incredible fun, played cards into the early hours of the morning and ate some great food as well as doing a little bit of work. Ralph had an amazing sense of humour and we spent most of the time in stitches listening to his jokes or stories. They were some of the best days of my life.

At the tender age of 29, I had worked on a market stall, run discos, bought and sold caravans, delivered pet food door to door, bought a wholesale company and finally helped to build a successful chain

Established Lo-Cost fascia for all stores.

of discount stores. I had also learnt about preparing business plans, buying and marketing, profit margins and cost control, and I could also understand a set of accounts and read a balance sheet.

I now needed to see whether I could put all that experience to work on the next venture. I had no idea that I had moved from one rollercoaster ride to a much bigger and faster one.

– CHAPTER 6 –

Chain Smoking

By the time I joined T&S in the spring of 1978, we had taken on a full-time accountant. Stephe Boddice had worked for Farmiloes, a well-known accountancy practice in Birmingham, as part of the team auditing the Lo-Cost accounts. He had become bored with his job and asked our accounts manager, Sean Traves, if he knew of any young company looking for an accountant to join them. Sean mentioned that I was leaving to work full-time at T&S Tobacco and might be interested in talking to him.

Dave and I arranged to meet Stephe at my flat one evening and he was impressed with our plans to expand the business and said that he would like to be part of the team. The problem was that we could not match the figure he was earning, so instead he took a reduced salary and we gave him 10 per cent of the business.

I had originally planned to work just a couple of days a week helping to assemble and deliver the goods to our kiosks. By the time Friday came around, I realised I had worked the whole week and continued to be full-time from then on.

The orders were delivered in a trailer attached to the back of Dave's second-hand BMW. This meant that we didn't have to go to the expense of a company car as well as a delivery van. By now we were selling a sufficient volume of tobacco products to be able to order directly from the manufacturer. There were only four main suppliers: Imperial Tobacco, Gallahers, Carrera Rothmans and British American Tobacco.

Imperial Tobacco is a British multinational tobacco company with headquarters in Bristol. It produces over 320 billion cigarettes a year and has 51 factories throughout the world. Its brands include Davidoff, West, Gauloises Blondes, Montecristo, Golden Virginia, Drum and Rizla. It is the world's fourth-largest tobacco company and the world's largest producer of cigars, fine-cut tobacco and tobacco papers.

British American Tobacco, also known as BAT, is the world's second-largest tobacco company after Altria Group, formerly Philip Morris International. BAT's largest brands are Dunhill, Lucky Strike, Kent and Pall Mall as well as Kool, Benson & Hedges and Rothmans.

In 1978 tobacco taxation was harmonised with the EU and cigarettes were taxed by retail price, rather than by weight of tobacco. This changed the cigarette market overnight. Before this change, small cigarettes were cheap and larger ones were expensive. So king size cigarettes were a luxury and small ones were more popular. After the tax change there was hardly any price difference between the two, and king size brands such as Benson & Hedges became far more popular than small cigarettes like Players No. 6.

The rationale behind the expansion was that in the late 1970s the cigarette market in the United Kingdom was huge, with nearly 20 million adult smokers buying around 120 billion cigarettes, cigars and tobacco products per annum.

We acquired a shop in the Fordhouses suburb of Wolverhampton where I had grown up and that became our first head office and warehouse. We partitioned the front of the shop for retail and the rear doubled up as an office and warehouse. However, our ambitious expansion plans were now constrained by the fact that it was becoming more and more difficult to find suitable kiosk sites.

We realised that if we were going to grow, we had to expand the range of products beyond cigarettes, tobacco and cigars. We decided to buy a newsagent business and learn more about the industry.

I had heard that a very busy newsagent in the heart of the Black Country might be for sale. The shop was situated on the High Street of Cradley Heath and had been owned by the same family for over 50 years. It had a very loyal customer base and sold an extensive range of traditional newsagent products. It was the ideal location to learn about the trade and we eventually agreed a deal with the vendor.

We then had to find someone who would run it and help build up the business. Fred Durnall was the best Lo-Cost store manager we had ever employed and I rated him very highly. He had recently been promoted as supervisor over a number of stores but had become bored with the job. I asked him if he would meet me for a chat, knowing that I could only talk him into the job by meeting him face to face. Fortunately he was ready for a change and agreed to take the job. It was one of the best moves we ever made because Fred was brilliant and became an integral part of our future success.

We now had a team of people capable of taking the business forward. Dave was to be in charge of finding new sites, Stephe was to be the numbers and systems man, I was to be in charge of buying and selling and Fred had to refine a range of products and a marketing plan to beat the competition. We quickly found out that it was just not possible to sell newspapers and magazines without the consent of the wholesaler. Unfortunately a cartel existed whereby all newspapers and magazines were distributed by two main wholesalers, WH Smith and John Menzies. You were not allowed to have an account if the wholesaler felt that a particular area was already adequately supplied.

Most newsagents, therefore, had an intrinsic goodwill value built into their business and were expensive to purchase. However, there were no such supply problems with other product groups such as greetings cards, confectionery and snacks.

We decided that we would build traffic flow by selling tobacco products at extremely low prices and then, having lured customers into the stores, sell them the rest of the product range, which carried much higher profit margins. In effect we were taking on the traditional newsagents with a discount offer on a reduced product range, in the same way we had taken on the supermarkets at Lo-Cost.

The profit margins we worked on were too low to allow us to look for shops in prime town centre locations, so we targeted just off prime but within walking distance. We targeted shops that were near to established newsagents which, by virtue of the news cartel, had a fairly secure customer base. The idea was to be cheap enough on all the product range we had in common to be able to steal the trade. People were incredibly conscious of the price they paid for all tobacco products, first because they were so expensive and second because they were purchased on a regular basis.

We operated on a profit margin of 3p in the pound on all tobacco products and out of that we had to pay all our expenses. However, if we attracted a lot of customers into the store, there was a chance that they would buy other products as well. A lot of confectionery was bought on what was known in the trade as impulse purchase. This meant that when the customer walked into the store, they had no intention of buying anything other than their planned purchase. They then saw their favourite snack line and ended up buying it because they couldn't resist the temptation.

So the plan was to build a reputation on price and fast, friendly service. Most of the products we sold were well-known brands and therefore quality was pretty much guaranteed.

If the shop was large enough, we introduced a range of greetings cards which we sold at 10p, 20p or 30p, depending on size. Greetings cards were associated with newsagents and therefore fitted neatly with the sale of confectionery and tobacco products. We made 3p in the pound on tobacco products, 20p in the pound on confectionery items and 50p in the pound on greetings cards. The problem was that we had no idea whether the overall profit on the mix of sales would warrant the development of a chain of shops.

As luck would have it, the formula worked.

Ray Ridgley, my former partner in Lo-Cost, happened to be building a similar retail operation in the Birmingham area and had come up with a fascinating method of gauging the likely sales in a particular location.

He counted the number of people passing the potential site over a period of five minutes on a busy weekend lunchtime. There happened to be a remarkable correlation between the number of people passing and the sales one could expect from tobacco sales. For some reason 100 people would equate to £10,000 per week, 150 people £15,000 per week, 200 people £20,000 per week and so on. It was also possible to predict the potential sales of confectionery, as it tended to work out at about 15 per cent of tobacco sales. We looked for stores of between 500–1,000 square feet and then, depending on the rent and rates, we could quickly work out whether the location was viable. Site selection was absolutely critical, meaning that we turned down far more sites than we took on.

We decided that the Cradley Heath store would become our retail laboratory where we could experiment with the range and price of products. Because the store was located in a working-class area, it opened at 6.00am every morning except the weekend. In fact it was busier from 6.00am to 8.00am than at any other time of the day. It also meant that we had a captive market that had been built up over a number of years. The range of tobacco products sold was twice as large as in our other kiosks and also the prices were higher than we normally charged. This gave us a dilemma in that if we dropped the prices to be in line with our other kiosks, we would gain no extra trade in the morning from people going to work because we were the only shop that was open. We decided that it was crazy to give away profit margin and we continued to work on a different price list from the other kiosks.

However, we decided that we could not carry an extended range of products just for one shop and discontinued a lot of marginal sellers. This initially upset a lot of customers but over time most switched to other products. We decided to discount crisps heavily and sold three packets for 10p. Sales rocketed from 25 cases per week to 250 cases per week in the space of three months. We also started selling ¼lb bags of sweets for 10p, which were weighed up at store level by the counter staff when they weren't serving customers, and this meant they weren't standing around doing nothing. The bagged sweets became incredibly popular with both parents and children.

We then introduced a range of sweets for younger children with price points that the mothers were prepared to pay, and we became the destination store for school kids who were quite savvy with their pocket money. However, it was a bit of a double-edged sword as they all tended to arrive at the same time and we had to control the number allowed into the store to avoid chaos at the tills.

At head office we decided to employ a bookkeeper to help Stephe and, as he was away on holiday, I conducted the interviews. The first young lady, called Dawn Sanders, arrived bang on time and we sat down together in our small office to discuss what the job entailed. Dave owned a small terrier dog that he occasionally brought into work when we were assembling orders at the beginning of the week. Unbeknown to Dawn and me the dog had come into the office, made a terrible mess under the table and then promptly disappeared. I started to tell her that as we were a young company, she would have to muck in with the rest of us with regard to tea making and tidying up. As the interview continued, the smell got worse and worse with Dawn and me looking at each other accusingly. Eventually Dawn spotted the mess under the table and unhesitatingly cleared it up without batting an eyelid. I was so impressed I offered her the job there and then and didn't even bother interviewing the other candidates. Thirty-six years later she is still with the company!

In 1979 Dave married his fiancée, Lorraine, whom he had met through her friendship with my wife Gill. We were now very much a family business with Dave's mother, Lorraine's mother, Gill and Lorraine all working in the business.

Later that year Dawn's husband Dave Sanders, who had been warehouse manager at Lo-Cost, agreed to join us and became responsible for all warehouse functions, distribution and transport.

By 1981 we had 25 stores all trading profitably and were determined to double our size within the next two years. We had been working with Vick Cook, who had gained experience of shopfitting with Lo-Cost. He now joined us full-time with responsibility for all shopfitting, refurbishment and maintenance. I now had all the people from Lo-Cost that I wanted and knew we had exactly the right team to take us forward to another level.

The shopfitting team was incredibly important to the speed of development. As they became more adept at stripping out and refitting stores, we could expand more quickly. They followed a very simple formula of battening the walls, which were then boarded with wood veneer, giving a clean and fresh appearance to the store. The wall boarding hid a multitude of problems, allowing the fitters to create straight lines that did not always exist in older shops. They then fitted a false ceiling with spotlights, a new floor covering and in most cases a new shop front.

The counter would include a stepped display area on which we could merchandise all the confectionery treats such as chocolate bars and snack items. Again the attraction of these products was enhanced with ceiling spotlights.

Where possible, the storeroom would include an area for the staff to enjoy a break and would incorporate a microwave oven to allow them the option of hot food.

The overall visual attraction of the store, one of cleanliness and colour and looking brand new, was in direct contrast to the old-fashioned newsagents, which rarely had a facelift. The staff looked smart and wore matching tabards, which were sponsored by one of our cigarette suppliers at no cost to us.

Sometimes, working late into the night, the shopfitters could turn around a small shop in as little as two weeks; and employing our own shopfitting team saved us an enormous amount of money in comparison with what it could have cost using outside contractors.

Everything we did in the business focused on tight cost control and fast turnover. The way we bought cigarettes from our suppliers was one of the cleverest innovations we ever had. Normally goods would be purchased in a calendar month and paid for by the 10th of the following month. However, we found out that it was also possible to have an account that started in the middle of the month with payment at the end of the following month. So we set up another wholly owned company called Actado and bought only on the first two weeks of the T&S account and then only on the first two weeks of the Actado account. The overall effect of this was to increase our overall credit by two weeks and, as our weekly turnover was now £250,000, it meant that overnight we had improved our cash flow by an astonishing £500,000.

Our bank manager, a wonderful man called Geoff Gallagher, had been in banking all his life firstly with Martins and then with Barclays, and had come down from Everton to run the main Wolverhampton branch in the town centre. He was an old-fashioned bank manager in the sense that you could talk to him and he also took an interest in our business to the extent that he visited our stores and understood our business model. He loved the fact that we always had money on deposit rather than having an overdraft but he also realised that when prices increased we bought more stock, and the more stock we bought the more money we could make.

However, the chancellor's annual budget was the golden opportunity to make money from cigarettes. It was politically acceptable for the chancellor to try to discourage cigarette smoking on the basis of health risk, so every year he increased the duty and we took advantage by buying as much stock as we could afford. This always led to a difficult meeting with our bank manager, Geoff, as we tried to borrow as much money as we could while he tried to juggle our requirements with his own lending rules.

He was brilliant and always bent the rules in our favour rather than the bank's, allowing us a larger overdraft than we could have got elsewhere. Obviously he charged us an arrangement fee, so it was good business for both parties. The repayment of the overdraft was never in any doubt as we sold the stock through in a matter of weeks, and there was little risk in buying the stock in the first place as cigarette duty has never been reduced in any chancellor's budget.

With cash in the bank and with a business formula that was working, we had to locate an estates company that could find stores for us quickly. As luck would have it, Robin Johnson of Picton Jones, a commercial estate agent based in Birmingham, was looking to start up his own practice and needed a substantial client such as us.

We promised him that if he could find us 30 stores in two years we would pay him a bonus of £10,000 on top of his normal commission. It was a big enough incentive for Robin to start his own business and we became his first and largest client. My partner Dave decided to concentrate solely on site development and we started to acquire stores outside the Midlands. We focused on working-class areas that had a much higher percentage of smokers and we were soon opening stores in the Manchester and Liverpool conurbations.

By 1984 we were operating 49 stores of which two thirds were selling our full range of tobacco products, confectionery and greetings cards. Three of the stores also incorporated sub-post offices, which gave us another source of income. Peter Gallagher, the son of our bank manager, had joined us with specific responsibility for confectionery buying, though he also assisted me in the buying of tobacco products. We had further strengthened the team with the addition of Brian Tennant, who became responsible for developing our greetings card sections and improving the internal control of stock levels and seasonal buying patterns.

– CHAPTER 7 –

90p Pete and the Stock Exchange

At this point it is worth looking back in time a few years, in order to examine the economic background to the growth of our business.

Yet another recession had hit British industry in 1980. A dramatic change had arrived on the political scene in May 1979 when the electorate, tired of a decade of the collective approach, voted in Margaret Thatcher, a woman who promised a new start. It had been a miserable decade for a once-proud nation. After further sharp slippage down the world's economic league, the country had reached a stage by early 1979 when the prospect was not of decline *relative* to our main competitors, but of *absolute* decline.

The country had had enough, and the Labour prime minister James Callaghan, so recently berated by the *Sun* newspaper for saying 'Crisis, what crisis?' when he arrived back from a conference of world leaders in the Caribbean in the middle of yet another winter of industrial disputes (in fact, Callaghan never said those words, but that was the *Sun's* headline and everybody believed it), realised that the country wanted a change.

The Tory party ousted its leader, Edward Heath, who had put in place many of the doctrines of his opponents, the Labour party –

restrictions on wages, prices and dividends. In his place the party elected a woman who, under the tutelage of Sir Keith Joseph, had grasped certain essentials of the remedy required to restore economic sanity to the country.

Joseph had ruled himself out as a possible leader by a speech in Birmingham in early 1975 which stated that people at the bottom of the social scale were having too many children and were ill-equipped to bring them up. Whether it was true or not, it smacked of racialism and elitism, and when he withdrew his challenge to Heath's leadership Margaret Thatcher was able to take it up.

From February 1975 until she came into power in May 1979, Thatcher and her supporters prepared the ground for a revolution in Britain's economic attitudes. She brought to that post no great technical expertise, but a handful of unshakeable principles.

They were not particularly original purposes. But they were commitments made with the fire of the zealot who could not imagine she would ever become a bore. Tax cutting was one of them. In four years as opposition leader, she had hardly made a single economic speech without alluding to the government's punitive rates of tax. Usually this was in reference to upper rates. 'A country's top tax rate is a symbol,' she said in February 1978. 'Very little revenue is collected from people in this country who pay tax at the highest rates. A top rate of 83 per cent is not much of a revenue raiser. It is a symbol of British socialism – the symbol of envy.' Restoring the morale of management, she said around the same time, was the prime requirement. 'No group is more important, and yet none has been so put through the mangle and flattened between the rollers of progressively penal taxation and discriminatory incomes policy.' So tax cuts were the first objective. They were the traditional Tory nostrum, to which the leader brought her special zeal. The second was good housekeeping.

The third fundamental therefore defined itself; the control of public spending. And again a kind of pietistic morality went hand in hand with a supposed economic law.

This was music to the ears of businessmen, but to a certain extent – even if not spelt out with quite the same rigour – they had heard it before. Heath had come to power in 1970 making not dissimilar noises, only to buckle under to corporatist solutions as soon as the going became rough. Would this woman be different?

We know now, not least from the memoirs that have been published by several of her colleagues, that Margaret Thatcher did not have the full-blooded backing of the whole of the Cabinet, or indeed of many businessmen, for some of her stronger measures.

The general financial climate from 1980 to 1982 had been the worst since the war, certainly in terms of corporate failures and rising unemployment. The result of tight monetary policies allied to another sharp hike in the price of oil following the overthrow of the Shah in Iran, which in turn brought a sharp rise in the value of the pound (viewed by this time as a petro-currency thanks to Britain's near self-sufficiency in oil from the North Sea), was to create the most difficult trading conditions that British companies had experienced since the 1930s. ICI, generally viewed as the bellwether of British manufacturing industry, cut its dividend and Sir Terence Beckett, the director-general for the CBI, promised the government a 'bare knuckle fight', saying at the CBI conference: 'We have got to have a lower pound – we've got to have lower interest rates.'

The prime minister remained firm, and declared on the day that unemployment passed the 2 million mark (Heath had lost his nerve when it passed 1 million): 'I've been trying to say to people for a long time: if you pay yourself more for producing less, you'll be in trouble.'

Heavy wage inflation, allied to the near-doubling of VAT in the first budget of the new administration (introduced within weeks of their winning power), meant that inflation soared again to an average of 13.3 per cent in 1979, 18.1 per cent in 1980 and 11.9 per cent in 1981.

The result of all this, allied to a very tough attitude towards unions and strikes (epitomised by the government's approach to a national strike in the steel industry, a battle they were determined to win whatever the cost), meant that the government's and Thatcher's popularity fell to new depths by the end of 1981. But Thatcher pressed on regardless, and although she had invited people from the whole spectrum of the party into her Cabinet, she took little notice of what many of them said. Indeed, she made it quite clear that:

> If you're going to do the things you want to do – and I'm only in politics to do things – you've got to have togetherness and a unity in your cabinet. There are two ways of making a cabinet. One way is to have in it people who represent all the different viewpoints within the party, within the broad philosophy. The other way is to have in it only people who want to go in the direction in which every instinct tells me we have to go. Clearly, steadily, firmly, with resolution. We've got to go in an agreed and clear direction.

She wasn't going to 'waste time having any internal arguments'.

Thus, at the depths of the recession and with unemployment still climbing sharply, she strongly supported Sir Geoffrey Howe's budget in the spring of 1981 which further intensified the squeeze on both companies and the consumer. Initially Howe had been against any such budget, and even the Treasury felt that some relaxation of monetary policy was possible. However, Thatcher had now taken on two extra-parliamentary advisers: Sir John Hoskyns, a former army officer who had built up his own very successful computer software business, and Alan Walters, a former professor at Birmingham University and the London School of Economics, who had established his monetarist principles long before the phrase was heard in political circles. (Indeed, he had predicted the inflation of 1974 as early as 1972, analysing the explosion of credit in that year of the 'Barber boom'.)

Hoskyns and Walters stiffened Thatcher's resolve in the early months of 1981. To them it was a matter of credibility. The government had to show everyone once and for all that it was not going to move forward 'with enormous and insupportable borrowings'. It had to convince the financial markets that it would get inflation down. And it worked. The markets saw that here was a prime minister who stuck to her guns, and they applauded her toughness and resolution. As many predicted the U-turn that tough-talking governments of both parties had indulged in since the war, Thatcher went to the party conference and told them: 'You may turn if you want to; this lady's not for turning.'

Not that Thatcher and her Conservative government worked instant miracles. Indeed, the country was immediately plunged into another inflationary crisis as more trouble in the Middle East, including the deposing of the Shah of Iran, led to another sharp rise in the price of oil. This was exacerbated by Thatcher agreeing to implement in full the awards recommended by the Clegg Commission, set up in the so-called 'winter of discontent' to grant a whole new raft of inflationary wage settlements. The belief of the new administration in increasing indirect tax (raising VAT from 8 to 15 percent) and reducing direct taxation did not help in the short term either.

By 1984 our turnover was in excess of £25 million (£150 million in today's money) per annum, we had 49 stores and as a business we were almost ten years old. At a bankers' dinner I was introduced to a gentleman called Peter Carter, who worked for Barclays Merchant Bank. He suggested that while our company was not large enough to be listed on the main London Stock Exchange, we were large enough to join the recently created junior market known as the Unlisted Securities Market (USM).

The Unlisted Securities Market, which ran from 1980 until 1996, was a stock exchange set up by the London Stock Exchange for companies that were too small to be listed on the main exchange. For example, the company might not have the full three-year trading history which was required by the main exchange. Or it might only want to float less than 25 per cent of their share capital. The USM allowed as little as 10 per cent to be floated.

In June 1995, the Alternative Investment Market (AIM) was set up when the USM no longer accepted new introductions. Companies already quoted on the USM then had to decide whether to move their quotation to the AIM or delist.

This would give us an opportunity to cash in on some of our success by selling a percentage of the company to outside shareholders. As my partner Dave and I were both approaching the age of 40, with young families, it seemed a good idea to enjoy some of the fruits of our labour while we were young enough to appreciate it.

It would also provide flexibility in financing future growth and encourage employees to participate in the future of the group through the purchase of shares in the company and through options granted under the share option scheme.

We decided that our store name of Cut Price Cigarettes didn't really do much for our image and we thought long and hard for an alternative. I eventually came up with the name Supercigs which, although not brilliant, was certainly better. Superdrug and Supersave were already well-known names on the high street so Supercigs seemed to fit quite well. We also changed the name of the company from T&S Tobacco to T&S Stores plc.

Before the listing was agreed, we had to go down to London to

High street fascia with familiar advertising.

meet the senior members of Barclays Merchant Bank who had been given a brief resumé of our careers. Over lunch one of the directors engaged me in conversation and started to congratulate me on the success of the company. For some reason, he had got very confused about the caravan business Dave and I had owned and instead thought that I had been brought up in a caravan and that my father drove a Transit van. He said, 'It's amazing that you have come so far when you obviously didn't have a proper education. Did you come from a long line of Gypsies?'

To play along I told him that it had been very difficult and that my mother had taught me how to read and write but I was really good with money! I made no secret of the fact that we also wanted to become millionaires by the age of 40. He left the lunch muttering something about never having met a millionaire gypsy before. Fortunately the rest of the group thought it was a good business story and we got the go-ahead. In the event we didn't quite make the millionaire status because having sold 29 per cent of the company we received £936,000 each (£5.6 million in today's money), but it was near enough.

The shares were priced at 90p and the company was valued at £7.2 million (£43 million in today's money). As we had 55 shops at the time of the flotation, this effectively valued each store at roughly £130,000, which was fantastic, considering we had bought them for very little.

Stephe, Dave and I went down to the stock market on 24 October, which was the date set for the listing. As we still owned over two thirds of the company between us, we were anxious to see what the share price would be at the end of the day. We were delighted to see the price open at £1 and eventually settle at 98p. Everything had gone according to plan and, from that day forward, Peter Carter, who had orchestrated everything from beginning to end, was always known as 90p Pete!

We were now on a treadmill of a different kind because our company was part owned by outside shareholders and we were responsible to them. We did not realise at that point how much pressure that would bring to bear, both good and bad, on the management of the company. Once outside shareholders owned a part of you, their interests almost had to come before your own.

As we started our first full year as a public company, the shape of the business really had changed a great deal. We had moved to a new 18,000-square-foot warehouse in Brownhills near Cannock and, apart from greetings cards, delivery of all other products was controlled centrally.

It was the early days of computers but fortunately our finance director, Stephe, had become closely involved in the development of computerised financial and management reporting systems specifically tailored for our needs. Working closely with a software company, our systems became very sophisticated and allowed replenishment of tobacco products to be controlled by the computer. The store manager only had to report closing stocks and the computer worked out the replenishment figure. This was extremely useful because we could set the computer to different algorithms to take account of seasonal factors such as Christmas and Easter. We could also change the replenishment algorithm if we were promoting a particular product.

The computerised control of tobacco products was very much part of our success as we were rarely sold out of individual lines and, with regular weekly deliveries arriving on a just-in-time basis, we never carried excessive buffer stock, thereby maximising cash flow. As far as we know, we were the first company in the UK to introduce a fully automated replenishment system and it certainly gave us an edge over our competitors.

Everyone was now incredibly busy. Fred had been promoted to the board and now had the title of retail operations director. He was in charge of the day-to-day running of all branch retail operations including staffing, merchandising, stock control and presentation. He had a team of five supervisors reporting to him, each with responsibility for approximately ten stores, and two training officers. Dave was spending two days a week with Robin driving round the country, trying to find suitable sites, Stephe seemed to have his head permanently stuck in the computer, Peter and I were buying ever-increasing amounts of goods and Dawn, who now had six girls working for her, was in charge of all office functions, bookkeeping and branch information systems.

Most of our expansion throughout 1985 was concentrated in the north-west, where our formula, if anything, worked better than in the Midlands. However, we did have major problems with robberies. Wallasey was our first store to open in the Liverpool area and in the second week, it was broken into and all the tobacco stock was stolen. In typical Scouse humour, someone had sprayed on the walls:

Welcome to Liverpool, please tell us where your next shop is opening.

Break-ins were becoming more and more of a problem to us as the price of cigarettes continued to rise, and it was getting to the point where we were experiencing a break-in or an attempted break-in somewhere every weekend. We had sophisticated alarm systems that were connected to the local police stations and steel shutters and doors to protect the perimeters. Unfortunately, this did not stop the hit-and-run thieves, who would drive a car through the shop front, grab as much stock as they could before the police could get there, and then scarper.

We had to improve our protection and our shopfitter Vick came up with a brilliant idea. We created a cage in each store by welding metal bars together to create a 6ft by 6ft strong room in which we placed the entire tobacco stock after close of business every night. In addition to this we placed a 95-decibel siren inside the cage which, when activated, made the most horrendous sound. There was now not enough time for anyone to break in and attempt to open the strong room before the police arrived.

One of our managers showed great initiative when her store alarm broke down just before Christmas. It couldn't be repaired until after the holiday and she was so concerned about her cigarette stock that she put her son's pet python in the cage over the whole Christmas period just in case anyone broke in!

We did get into trouble with a lot of the neighbours of our shops because it was impossible for anyone to go back to sleep until the manager had arrived to turn off the alarm. At a considerable cost we fitted the cages to all the stores and, fortunately, the level of break-ins dropped dramatically.

Store visits were normally on Tuesdays and we would try to fit half a dozen stores into a day's work. Fred, the stores controller, my partner Dave and I would normally do the visits together and it was great to get among our customers and talk about how we could improve. Regardless of competition our cigarette prices were always the cheapest and we operated five different price lists, each one being 1p cheaper than the previous one. It was a good job that we were computerised, because to manage that level of complexity on a manual system would have been a nightmare.

Our store visits were always unannounced so that we got a feel for reality, rather than having the 'Royal' visit when everything would look immaculate. Sometimes the stores would look terrible but by and large our standards were very good and well controlled. One day we were visiting the Liverpool area and we walked into our Birkenhead store, which had a very feisty manageress who stood no nonsense from anyone. One of my regular duties on a store visit was to put the pick and mix sweets back in the right containers, as more often than not the toffees would get mixed up with the humbugs, the chocolate éclairs with the mints, etc.

The manageress spotted me and, not knowing me from Adam, shouted down the aisle in a broad Liverpool accent, 'Oi you, get yer 'ands out me pick and mix.'

I was so embarrassed; I replied that I was the chairman of the company and just trying to help. To which she replied, 'I don't care if you are the frigging Pope, get yer 'ands out me pick and mix.'

Needless to say the story passed into company folklore and I was forever teased about it.

By 1986 I had been playing golf for five years and because the cigarette manufacturers sponsored a number of top golf tournaments, I was fortunate to be invited to most of them and play in the Pro-Am the day before the main event started. I was absolutely thrilled to be paired up with Greg Norman at the Suntory World Match Play Tournament at Wentworth. He won the competition and soon after became the world number one golfer. To this day I still marvel at the wonderful talent that he possessed, because he hit the ball so far but also had a lovely touch around the greens.

Unfortunately it was straight back to work as we had more shops to open! As we continued to expand into the East Midlands as well as the north-west, the competition just stood still and let us steal their trade. It was remarkable that established newsagent chains such as Dillons, RSM McColl, Martins and Stars did nothing to protect their own sales. It was quite ironic that Preedy had allowed us to start up in business in the first place, by offering us a week's credit when we opened our first kiosk. We were now targeting all their shops as they seemed incapable of competing with us.

During the year we had come across a novel way of merchandising loose sweets that was to increase substantially our confectionery sales. Instead of having separate displays of bagged sweets and pick and mix, we incorporated them both together in a brand new way. Over 100 different types of loose sweets were displayed from Perspex self-

Playing golf with the 'Great White Shark', Wentworth.

service hoppers to create a dramatic visual effect. Air conditioning, colour co-ordinated design with spot and neon lighting were combined to give this new range of high-margin merchandise a novel and futuristic appeal.

The new format proved to be an instant success and added a further dimension to our tried and tested retail formula.

By now our shopfitting standards were second to none. Our own teams of fitters were employed under the direction of the store development manager. The store layouts were meticulously planned by our estates department in order that the correct balance of sales to storage area was achieved.

As we approached the magic figure of 100 stores, we had started to become more than an irritation to some of the newsagent chains.

Gallaher, who controlled around a third of the cigarette market and had the brand leader in Benson & Hedges, also owned one of the largest chains of newsagents in the UK, called Forbuoys. In order to compete with us they had formed a discount operation similar to our own called Red Shops and approached us with a view to buying our company. A deal was eventually agreed in principle, valuing the company at a £5 million premium to its value on the stock market.

We went down to London to complete the deal with Gallahers, taking with us John Wardle, senior partner of our Birmingham legal advisers, Edge and Ellison. John was highly regarded in the business world as well as the legal profession and had sat on the board of a number of public companies. He was also a man not to be messed with!

As we discussed the deal, Gallaher's lawyers dropped a bombshell by insisting that the directors of T&S give guarantees as to the financial standing of the company. For private companies this was a fairly routine and acceptable request but, because numerous individuals as well as pension funds held the shares of a public company, it was a very unreasonable and unacceptable request.

A massive row ensued between the lawyers and as the buffet lunch was wheeled in with the celebration bottle of champagne, John jumped to his feet shouting, 'You can throw that rubbish into the bin, we're off to Wheelers for a bit of decent fish and we'll take the bottle of champagne as part payment for wasting our time.'

I wasn't even consulted on whether we were prepared to give guarantees. John had made his mind up that we were not selling the company and that was that. I was actually quite glad because I thought we were selling too soon in our development and looking back it was one of the best decisions we ever made. We did indeed have a wonderful meal in Wheelers and it must have been the only bottle of champagne ever drunk in celebration of a deal not being done. Instead of retiring for a second time, it was back to the coalface once again, but in my heart of hearts I knew we had done the right thing.

On 6 December 1986 we opened our hundredth store in Stockport and just before Christmas we held a big party at the National Exhibition Centre in Birmingham to celebrate the occasion. Hosted by Bob Monkhouse, it proved to be an emotional occasion as most of our employees took the trouble to attend. We had representatives from every single store, which represented not only loyalty but also a sense of pride in their company. Furthermore, as we entered 1987 the pace was once again set to increase.

It had taken eleven years to grow from one small kiosk in Wolverhampton, adding one store at a time, to achieve our goal of 100 stores. What was about to happen would mean that, in just one more year, we would double in size to 200 stores.

We had made sufficient progress since joining the junior USM market that in May 1987 we joined the main stock market, giving us greater financial flexibility and also wider shareholder coverage. I had also kept in regular contact with one of my former partners at Lo-Cost. Both Ray Ridgley and I had seen the potential of taking on the sleepy newsagents with an aggressive discounting policy and so it was no great surprise that, after selling Lo-Cost, we both pursued an almost identical business strategy.

While T&S had expanded from the Midlands into Yorkshire and the north-west, Ray had expanded Buy-Wise southwards along the M5 corridor as far as Bristol and south Wales. Because we had expanded in different directions there was very little overlap of store locations and the businesses were almost identical. The acquisition of 89 Buy-Wise stores, therefore, would offer the immediate benefit of a substantially increased geographical coverage and a near doubling of store numbers.

The T&S board celebrating the opening of our 100th store.

The other huge benefit was that all the stores in the enlarged group could be serviced from our existing central warehouse in Brownhills, giving rise to a dilution of central overheads. Ray could see the logic and, as he was approaching his 60th birthday, it represented a great opportunity for both parties. We completed the deal in August with Ray receiving just under £4 million and, after he agreed to join as a consultant, it meant that once again we would be working together.

The only downside of 1987 was that tobacco duty was not increased in the chancellor's budget for the first time in many years. As usual we had bought about twelve weeks' stock ahead of the anticipated increase and now had to sell them through at existing

prices. Fortunately, with the acquisition of Buy-Wise, we were able
to keep profits moving forward and the introduction of the Fantasia
pick and mix confectionery range added an exciting new dynamic to
the appeal of the stores.

Following the takeover of Buy-Wise we decided to review as many
operations of the company as we could and employed specialists
in the fields of warehousing and distribution. The results of the
survey were both encouraging and constructive and led to the
implementation of a sophisticated system.

The way this worked was fascinating, with a gravity conveyor
constructed to take pallets direct from the goods inwards into the
warehouse. We also introduced a two-level tobacco product picking
system for compiling shop orders. This system, known as 'carton
flow racking', delivered each product to the picking operatives at
a given picking station. As each container was emptied another
automatically slid through the gantry to take its place. The orders
were then packed into sealed boxes and taken by conveyors to the
collation area for the completed orders to be palletised ready for
dispatch. The efficiencies gained resulted in fewer staff and greater
productivity than ever before.

Within distribution, the van fleet was altered to vehicles
with higher weight capacities, ensuring that deliveries could
be completed within a shorter timescale. We also acquired a
transportation scheduling model, which was used to schedule all
store deliveries in the most economical way, taking account of
cost, time, vehicle capacity and local restrictions. By the end of
the implementation we had been able to reduce the fleet size from
fourteen trucks down to ten.

Tim Gordon had joined us in July at the height of our
modernisation programme and was appointed warehouse and
distribution director to strengthen the board.

The integration of Buy-Wise gave us a unique opportunity to make efficiencies within the business and we were ruthless in our pursuit of cost savings. By the end of 1988, from the 89 stores acquired, 33 had been sold or closed and the remaining 56 had been converted to the standard Supercigs format. Fantasia sales continued to grow and the concept was rolled out to all stores that could accommodate the range. We were now selling hundreds of tons of loose confectionery a year and our confectionery margin had improved by 20 per cent. On the tobacco side of the business we also introduced two own-label cigarettes, one manufactured in Greece and the other in Germany. After promoting them as our cheapest cigarettes, within months they were both in our top ten sellers list and as they were unique to us could not be bought elsewhere.

We even stopped selling recognised products such as England's Glory matches and instead introduced an own-label range of smokers' sundries including matches, lighter fluid and pipe cleaners. We calculated that the change to own label on smokers' sundries, alone, increased our profit by over £100,000 in a single year. Now that is attention to detail!

As we celebrated another record year my Christmas was tinged with real sadness when Fred Durnall, our retail operations director, had to retire. For years he had suffered with a degenerative back problem that could no longer be ignored. I had worked with Fred for many years and had presented him with the Lo-Cost Manager of the Year award on two occasions. He had then been hugely instrumental in developing the retail standards we were all so proud of and I was desperately sorry to see him go.

I was also concerned about how we were going to keep up the pace of progress from this point forward. We were reaching saturation point in terms of the number of sites we could open. While Supercigs was a great retail concept for working-class areas, the formula did not work in the south of the country. This was because shop rents were a lot more expensive the nearer you got to London and also fewer people smoked in more affluent areas. We had opened a few stores in the Luton area and they were just not viable. Our stores worked on such slim margins that the reduction in turnover coupled with the increased cost of higher rent and rates resulted in losses rather than profits.

As I had tucked into my Christmas dinner in 1986, proud of finally achieving our hundredth store opening, I had no idea that when I sat down for the same meal the following year we would have doubled in size. Now, in exactly the same way, as I sat down for my Christmas dinner in 1988 with roughly 200 stores, I knew there was absolutely

A bit of R&R with the boys, Jersey 1988.

no way we would double in size the following year. I was absolutely right. We were not about to double in size to 400 stores; we were about to triple in size to 600 stores!

– CHAPTER 8 –

What Next?

1989 did not start well. Fred Durnall had retired through ill health and my partner Dave was becoming restless. In addition to this, for only the second time in fifteen years there was no increase in tobacco duty, costing us £250,000 in interest payments as we liquidated the excess stock we had purchased. While the Buy-Wise acquisition had gone well, we were starting to run out of geographical locations that fitted the Supercigs formula and to keep the business growing we needed a change of direction.

Next had moved into the newsagent business with the acquisition first of 250 Dillons stores in July 1987, followed by the acquisition of 175 Preedy stores in April 1988. Dillons was Birmingham-based and had been previously owned by the newspaper publisher of the *Birmingham Post & Mail*. Preedy, another Midlands company, had been founded in 1869 as a tobacco, cigar and cigarette merchant and obtained a stock market listing in 1963.

It was not obvious to anyone why a fashion retailer such as Next would have any interest in owning two newsagent businesses. The rationale given at the time by the boss of Next, George Davies, was that the acquisition created an opportunity to have collection and delivery points for his mail order business. Nowadays 'click and collect' is a way of life, and George Davies may well have been ahead of his time, but back in the 1980s it seemed a daft idea and never got off the ground. After his dramatic sacking by the board of Next, David Jones, his successor, was looking to offload the business.

Preedy and Dillons, with 400 stores, represented the fifth largest CTN (confectionery, tobacco and news) group in the UK. While more than double the size of our own business, it represented a great opportunity for us to expand and had the added advantage of being Midlands-based. The enlarged group, with just under 600 stores and a turnover of approximately £250 million (£1.5 billion in today's money), would become the third largest CTN operator in the country.

However, there were two major problems. First, we were going to have to raise about £50 million to buy the business and second, my partner and best friend Dave wanted to retire and would not be part of the future management team.

Stephe and I agonised over the next few days whether we should go ahead and make an offer. Over a drink in the pub, we decided that it was just too good an opportunity to miss and I phoned David Jones to make an appointment.

The Next head office, situated in Enderby, just outside Leicester, was impressive to say the least. There were mock-up stores with futuristic displays and seemingly endless office space, the like of which Stephe and I had never seen before. We were shown into a very expensive-looking boardroom and in walked David Jones and his finance director, Peter Lomas.

'North of 50, Kevin' were his opening words to me, and to start with I thought he was talking about motorway directions.

'North of 50 what?' I replied.

In a very calm and confident manner he continued, 'If you want to buy the business it is going to cost you over £50 million. If you do not think it is worth that, or you cannot raise the money, we are wasting each other's time.'

Stephe and I had done our homework and had guessed that they would be looking for an offer in that region, but had been told by our merchant bankers that a price tag above £50 million would be difficult to justify to our shareholders and as we were going to have to raise the money from them it was just a bit important that we did not overpay.

I explained all of this to David Jones, who put a marker in the ground by saying that he wouldn't take a penny less than £55 million. We had both played the game before and knew that the price was therefore in the £50–55 million parish. After talking pleasantries for another twenty minutes or so we left, saying that we would talk to our bank and come back to them shortly.

Driving home Stephe and I were fairly confident a deal could be done as Next was in a financial mess and was desperate for the cash. Against this David Jones also knew that we in turn were desperate to do a deal as the business was Midlands-based and fitted in perfectly with our own expansion plans. In the end I played the old tried and tested formula of splitting the difference. He wanted £55 million, we could only afford £50 million but to secure the deal we would go to £52.5 million.

Still he wouldn't budge!

In the end both parties agreed to meet in London to try to hammer out a deal. I sat with Stephe and our advisers on one side of the table and David Jones, Peter Lomas and the Next advisers sat on the other side. However, after two hours we still could not reach an agreement on price. In the end David Jones suggested he and I go for a walk. It was a beautiful spring morning and after a couple of minutes David turned to me and said, 'I'll tell you what I'm prepared to do.'

At that precise moment a little old lady came up to us and asked for directions to some museum I had never heard of. Cool as a cucumber, David took her into a shop, then another, then yet another to find out the whereabouts of this museum. Here I was, about to do the deal of my life and David Jones was helping an old lady with directions! Eventually he turned to me and said, 'Sorry about that, now where were we? As you can't afford the extra £2.5 million to make it up to £55 million, we will lend you the difference and you can pay it back to us over the next two years.'

To start with I thought he was joking but soon realised he was deadly serious. I was not prepared to accept his offer because it effectively meant that we weren't getting a deal at all. We walked another two blocks and eventually I got him down £1 million to £54 million and we agreed to do the deal at that price. As we walked back to tell our advisers he turned to me and said, 'You're not happy are you?'

I told him that I felt that he had a great deal and we didn't but nevertheless I would go ahead. He then said, 'I can't have that, seeing as you are a nice chap and it's a beautiful day I'll take another £100,000 off the price and make you a happy bunny.'

I smiled, we shook hands on £53.9 million and the deal was done.

It's always a lot easier to agree a deal than it is to finance the method of payment. Because the acquisition was effectively two and a half times the size of our own company, we had to try to convince our existing shareholders to buy a further two and a half times the number of shares they already held. The main benefit of being a publicly quoted company was that you could approach your existing shareholders to raise the money rather than going to the bank. There is no way we could have borrowed £50 million from the bank to finance the deal as it would have been simply too big a risk for them.

As the majority of our shareholders were large pension funds,

Stephe and I had to spend three days in London and two days in Scotland trying to convince our shareholders of the merits of the deal. In fairness the commercial logic was very sound and the new shares were taken up by most of the fund managers. In the event, as is normal with banks, they earned a nice fat fee for underwriting the deal but Stephe and I did all the hard work in selling the idea in the first place.

The deal was completed on 27 June 1989 and it was quite ironic that we now owned the company that had allowed us to commence trading by granting us a week's credit for the payment of goods when we opened our first kiosk in 1975. As a company Preedy, now down to 134 stores, had lost its way and was in desperate need of attention. On the other hand Dillons, with 264 stores, had an excellent management team that was a pleasure to work with.

I felt very sad that my partner Dave was retiring. He was my best friend and we had started the business together with equal shareholdings and trusted each other implicitly. I would never have started the business without him and it was a stroke of luck that he happened to return from Marbella at just the time our first kiosk in Wolverhampton came up for sale. Our wives were also best friends and we even lived next door to each other so, needless to say, our families were very close. Because we had different jobs within the company we were able to go away on holiday together and enjoyed some great trips in spite of being very busy.

Most business partners rarely see each other socially but Dave and I played football, golf and tennis together and even drank in the same pub. We mixed in the same social circle so were able to talk about other things that were happening rather than business. For almost fifteen years we had lived in each other's pockets but we still managed to remain friends even after he had left the business. My other partner and friend, Ray Ridgley, also decided to call it a day and left the business as consultant to pursue property interests. With so many people deserting the ship, I was beginning to consider changing my deodorant!

Next newsagency business sold to T&S for £53.9m

By Derek Harris
Industrial Editor

Next, the high street retail and mail order group, has sold its Dillons and Alfred Preedy chain, comprising mainly confectionery, tobacco and newspaper (CTN) outlets, for £53.9 million.

The chain of nearly 400 stores, the fifth largest CTN operation in Britain, is going to T&S Stores, the expanding CTN business based in Walsall, West Midlands. The deal takes it into the top five in a sector which has experienced a steady erosion in the number of smaller operations, typically the corner shops.

There are still more than 45,000 CTNs with a total turnover of about £8.5 billion, but closures of the usually family-run outlets have been occurring at 10 a week or more for some time.

It is the second sale of what Next regards as a non-core business since Mr George Davies left as chairman last year. WH Smith bought some larger Preedy stores for £7.9 million this year.

Next still hopes to sell its Mercado carpet retailing chain, which might raise as much as £20 million.

Before Mr Davies left, Next had reviewed the scope of its businesses and decided to reduce them, which led to the sale of the Zales jewellery business and the Salisbury handbag stores.

At one time there were plans for the CTN chain to be used as part of a distribution system for mail order and particularly for the Next Directory. But Next says it has decided this job can be best tackled in other ways, with its Yorkshire Grattan mail order subsidiary soon to start using a £48 million state-of-the-art computerized warehouse system based at Bradford and Next Directory using its own delivery system.

Taking account of the Preedy stores sale to WH Smith, net investment in Dillons and Preedy stood at only £33.4 million, said Next. The deal with T&S consists of £52.5 million cash and the rest in loan notes.

Added to the T&S chain of 175 stores, the enlarged group will be the third largest CTN retailer after Forbouys NSS, part of Gallaher, and the Martin Retail Group. It will probably be fourth largest by turnover — WH Smith and John Menzies each has fewer out-

Building on CTNs: Kevin Threlfall (left) and Stephen Boddice, finance director, yesterday

lets but these are larger, thus producing more turnover.

Mr Kevin Threlfall, chairman of T&S, says he will build on a group of 42 convenience stores which comes with Dillons.

"The expansion it will give to our CTNs — with a wider geographical spread, especially into the South-east — will probably give us enough of these outlets but convenience stores are a natural progression from the CTN," he said.

"Some people have tried in concept terms to gear down from the supermarket into convenience stores but I believe it is best done the other way around from a strong CTN base," he added.

Convenience stores can add on to the usual CTN mix of basic food and other household lines with liquor and a video library.

Until now T&S had only 27 outlets which were also newsagents but now it will be a key player in this sector although the Preedy outlets will take the "Super Cigs" branding. The Dillons name will remain.

T&S is financing the deal through a rights issue to raise £50 million. It is forecasting a total dividend of 4p (2.625p) net for the year to December.

Announcement of the Preedy/Dillons purchase from Next in May 1989.

Now that Dave, Fred and Ray had all left the business, our management team was looking rather thin. Fortunately, the new team at DPG (Dillons/Preedy Group) rebalanced the skill shortage. Jim McCarthy, aged 33, had joined Dillons as a trainee at the age of seventeen and had even been a paper boy for many years prior to joining. He had worked his way through the business to become managing director of the group and therefore had extensive operational experience of all aspects of CTN retailing. He immediately joined the board as group retail director. John Hayward, aged 59, became my deputy chairman, having been deputy chairman of DPG for a number of years. A chartered accountant, he joined Dillons in 1969 and became managing director a year later. John now took on special responsibility for all property matters including site selection and acquisition. Tim Gordon, our group warehouse and distribution director, had joined the board in December 1988. Together with me as chairman and chief executive and Stephe as group finance director, we now had a really strong team that was capable of taking the business forward.

We had a lot to sort out, with three warehouses, two head offices and 573 stores trading under three different names, all to be consolidated into a logical and workable business. With a combined turnover in excess of £250 million we now had considerable financial muscle, and would be able to benefit significantly from increased purchasing power and savings in overheads once we had rationalised the business.

The first move was to commission a new office block and further warehousing to be built at our existing head office. By September we were able to centralise all office functions into Brownhills and the DPG office complex was closed down and the lease sold. Unfortunately delays in land acquisition and site preparation delayed the completion of our new warehouse by a year and although we were able to close down the Preedy distribution depot, the Dillons warehouse had to remain open. To facilitate the integration of the individual companies within the group, we created an executive committee with each main board directorate represented by one or more committee member.

Without doubt, one of the cornerstones of our success had been the computerisation and streamlining of all our administrative functions. Stephe was a wizard when it came to designing systems and was never happier than when he was in the computer room, which in the early days of computing had to be quite large and also air-conditioned. The existing T&S software was applied to the Dillons functions within six months of the acquisition and the integration was achieved with little disruption to the business.

On the retailing front, Supercigs remained the high street discount operation selling tobacco products, confectionery and greetings cards. Some of the Preedy shops were converted to the Supercigs format and Lorna Kirby was promoted to head up the division, reporting directly to Jim McCarthy. Lorna was one of our first employees when appointed manageress of our second kiosk in Cannock back in 1976. She had worked for us for nearly fifteen years and I was delighted for her when her dedication and loyalty was finally rewarded.

While we were extremely successful with tobacco products and confectionery, the sale of greetings cards very much depended on location. Some stores did really well but others struggled where competition was nearby. The purchase of greetings cards is by and large a planned activity and is very female-biased. Women are generally happy to browse through card racks, ensuring the card suits the occasion, whereas men always seem to be in a hurry and spend far less time on selection. Price is important when purchasing large numbers of cards, say at Christmas, but the design is more important than the price when buying on a more personal level. Apparently the biggest spend is on birthday cards to sisters, where women are prepared to push the boat out on the price they will pay.

Another problem with the sale of greetings cards is the number of occasions that have to be catered for. Valentine's Day, Mother's Day, Father's Day, Easter and Christmas all compete for space with the traditional range but, nevertheless, the displays have to be fitted in somewhere. Because Supercigs shops were very busy, browsing and fast didn't really go together and therefore we had to sell cards on a price platform rather than on a range and selection basis.

With the experience gained from Dillons, news and magazines were a better sales proposition and within twelve months we had substituted cards with news and magazines in over a third of the estate. The highly successful Fantasia range of pick and mix sweets was enhanced by the introduction of mini bars, which were branded bite-sized chocolate bars selling at premium prices. The addition neatly fitted at the end of the gondola and further enhanced the attraction of the section. The number of Supercigs stores continued to grow as we opened another sixteen stores in the north-east following the acquisition of a local chain of shops called DTC.

Over a period of twelve months we phased out the Preedy stores by either converting them to Supercigs or Dillons, and it was rather sad to see a name that had been around since 1869 finally disappear from the high street. It was quite ironic that I was the person responsible for closing down the business that had allowed T&S to start up fifteen years earlier.

Over the years the traditional newsagents had changed very little. Railway stations and town centres were monopolised by two names, WH Smith and J. Menzies, and most local newsagents were family-run businesses with husband and wife working as a team, in most cases living over the shop. Long hours were the norm, with news deliveries arriving from the wholesaler before six in the morning. The daily rounds had to be assembled for the paper boys to deliver door-to-door. Come rain or shine this seemingly archaic activity still exists, although on nothing like the scale of days gone by. In most working-class areas, newsagents would tend to be on bus routes or near factories and most men would pick up a pack of cigarettes or tobacco on their way into work.

Nearly all newsagents had done a day's work by the time other shops opened at 9.00am. At our shop in Cradley Heath we took more money between 6.00am and 9.00am on weekdays than the rest of the day put together. The workload was no easier at the weekends when newspaper rounds tended to be more extensive than on weekdays. So long trading hours and seven days a week was the norm for the majority of our Dillons stores. Over the years we had employed some very loyal husband-and-wife teams and I always felt very humble when visiting stores and regularly finding couples who had been with us over 20 and sometimes 30 years. The distribution of news and magazines was still very strictly controlled by a handful of wholesalers, WH Smith and J. Menzies being easily the largest. It was entirely in their gift whether they supplied you or not and there was no right of reply if they turned down your application for delivery. This stranglehold on distribution was a running sore within the industry and to a large extent stifled competition and innovation. Pre-war films occasionally showed a newsagent, typically with the owner's cat fast asleep on a bundle of newspapers. Ninety years later nothing much had changed, but the weight of social demand for better standards in a changing world was about to blow apart retailing as we knew it and trumpet in a new golden era called convenience.

Until the arrival of supermarkets in the 1960s the divisions of retailing had remained fairly fixed. By that I mean that greengrocers did not sell bread and bakers did not sell bananas. The early supermarkets revolutionised retailing with the introduction of self-service, but initially mainly sold canned and packaged goods. As Tesco and similar supermarkets slowly but surely improved their offer, they stole trade from the established retailers. First to suffer were the butchers, then the fishmongers, then the greengrocers and the bakers and finally the off-licences.

By the 1970s families were able to buy most of their weekly needs in one visit rather than on a daily basis. The growing use of the car and extended shopping hours made life easier still. The supermarkets got bigger and better, and even the daily milkman was becoming a thing of the past. By the 1990s supermarkets seemed to sell everything including newspapers and magazines, and the larger

Meeting Princess Anne at the NEC in Birmingham.

stores sometimes even incorporated a pharmacy. As people became wealthier, price differentiation between supermarkets and the discount stores had narrowed significantly enough for most shoppers to lose interest in the discounters and stores such as Kwik Save and my former company Lo-Cost were soon to disappear from the high street for good. But just when it seemed that bigger was better and massive was better still, with Tesco opening stores of up to 100,000 square feet, with a product range in the tens of thousands, gradually things started to change. And the change had been brought about by people's lifestyles. No longer did Mum stay at home and bring up the kids, she now went out to work – and slowly but surely people were becoming money-rich and time-poor.

– CHAPTER 9 –

Marriage of Convenience

The early 1990s brought plenty of problems. Following the boom years of the mid-1980s, by the time of the general election in April 1992, Britain had suffered a recession which, if not as severe as that of the early 1980s, nevertheless caused a great deal of pain in manufacturing industry and elsewhere in the economy. The stock market crash of 1987 had been telling the world something, but for a time it was not clear what. Investors were feeling very pleased with themselves by the summer of 1987, and by October the City was wallowing in an orgy of self-love. The Tories were in for another five years (Margaret Thatcher had been comfortably re-elected in June 1987), money – serious money – was there for the taking, the markets were going up after the usual summer hiccup, then BANG! It all stopped. First New York, then Tokyo and Hong Kong, then London, then New York again, then Hong Kong, Tokyo and Sydney, then London, Paris and Frankfurt all turned into screaming, yelling pits of hysteria as the markets lost a year's gain in 24 hours. To exacerbate the situation, the hurricane in Britain three days earlier prevented many dealers from reaching their screens.

It was only twelve years or 3,000 trading days since the FT30 index had stood at 147. Now it lost 183.7 in a single day. If anyone thought that was difficult to cope with, the Dow Jones fell by over 500 points, and it was only five years or 1,250 trading days since that index had been around 600. But that of course was part of the reason. The indexes had risen a long way, and once punters wanted to cash in some of their profits there could only be one result. Black Monday, 19 October 1987, was so called after Black Monday in October 1929 – which had itself been named after Black Friday 1869, when a group of punters tried to corner the gold market, causing a panic that led to a crash and a depression.

So many records were broken on this Black Monday – biggest one-day fall, biggest volume, more deals on the New York Stock Exchange that day than in the whole of 1950, etc. – that everyone ran out of superlatives, except that no one thought it was particularly superlative. As this was the nuclear age, John Phelan, chairman of the New York Stock Exchange, described it as 'the closest to meltdown I'd ever want to get'. In the same way that almost everyone over the age of 55 can remember exactly what they were doing when they heard that President Kennedy had been shot, every investor will remember what they were doing on 19 October 1987. It was serious. By the middle of Tuesday, as the Dow was plunging again – by then it had lost 800 points in less than five days' trading – the New York Stock Exchange was in touch with the White House and considering the suspension of trading. At that moment the market rallied and, although it might only be a dead cat bounce, it was at least a bounce and it removed the pressure for a moment. If New York had suspended trading, the effect on prices in London would have been catastrophic, as that would have been the only escape hatch. The Hong Kong Exchange did suspend trading, and that exerted extra pressure elsewhere, especially in Sydney. Why were the falls so massive? Prices could not keep going up forever. 'Why not?' asked

Sid, who had been persuaded to buy British Gas and other privatised stocks. Good question. No one knew the answer, but they never had before. This did not explain the precipitous plunge. Programme trading by computer and portfolio insurance went a long way to explaining it.

Portfolio insurance had grown dramatically in popularity in the twelve months before the crash – the pension fund assets in the USA that were managed in this way had grown from $8.5 billion to $60 billion. In simple terms, it meant that by trading in the futures market on the indexes, a portfolio could be insured against a fall. Thus you could buy with impunity, which helped to drive the market up, and if it turned you were covered in the futures market, which would just as certainly drive the market down. In theory this is great, but the concept has, in retrospect, a rather obvious flaw: if the market is falling, not everyone can be a winner or emerge unscathed. Someone has to buy what everyone else wants to sell. In the week before Black Monday, the portfolio insurers had not been able to sell the stock they wanted to, so by the Monday the pressure was immense. On Black Monday itself, as the insurers sold the futures below the prices in the market, no one would buy the actual stocks when the futures showed they could fall much further, and no one wanted the futures while the portfolio insurers were the obvious sellers. The result – a free fall.

There were moments of wry humour. In the US, Alan Greenspan, chairman of the Federal Reserve Board, was flying to Dallas to make a speech. The markets were falling as he boarded the plane, so he was greatly relieved when he arrived at Dallas to be told that the Dow Jones was down 'Five Oh Eight' – until he realised that the 'Oh' was not a decimal point.

On Tuesday in New York, in spite of another huge fall in London in response to Wall Street's 500-point drop the previous night,

we witnessed the classic dead cat bounce, and the Dow gained
200 points in the first hour. Then the insurers moved in again
on the futures and down went the market again, 225 points in
two hours. There was real panic now – any further falls (and the
futures market was signalling another 300 points) would send many
dealers to the wall. The futures market in Chicago stopped trading,
apparently believing that the decision to close New York had already
been taken. As everyone waited, the first sign of a turn came for the
little-used Major Market Index in Chicago, where there was a rally.
New York 'touched it out'; some corporations helped by announcing
that they were buying their own stock; and the day finished with
a 100-point gain – the largest ever. The immediate crisis was over.
The post-mortem began.

The consumer boom that had built up around the world in the
1980s did not lose its momentum overnight, and most of 1988 was
another good year, especially in Britain. Chancellor of the Exchequer
Nigel (now Lord) Lawson had read his economic history books and
knew that what turned the Wall Street crash of 1929 into the world
depression of the 1930s was the tightening of credit everywhere
and the mistaken attempt to balance budgets. He and others were
determined that that should not happen this time, and he lowered
interest rates to maintain liquidity in the financial system.

Unfortunately, he overdid it. Most British consumers are not
directly affected by the stock market (though many of them are
through their pension funds) and, though the crash made dramatic
headlines and hurt a few large private investors, the mass of people
went on spending, confident that their main asset – the house they
lived in – was still worth far more than they had paid for it.

The house price spiral was given a final upward twist when
Lawson announced the end of double tax relief on mortgages for
unmarried couples living together.

However, the new law would not apply until August, and the early summer of 1988 witnessed the final frenzy of house purchase at what, in retrospect, came to be seen as silly prices. What those who were buying failed to notice was that the interest rate cycle had turned. After reducing interest rates at the end of 1987 and in the early part of 1988, Lawson realised that the British economy was overheating badly. The mature British economy could grow only at about 3 per cent before it hit capacity restraints and ran into inflation and balance of payments problems. Lawson took a long time to realise that the economy was growing much faster than this. However, by early summer 1988 the overheating was obvious as the inflation rate turned upwards and the balance of payments deficit ballooned alarmingly. Lawson should probably have raised taxes in his 1988 budget instead of reducing them, but the real problem was the amount of liquidity in the economy. He tackled this by raising interest rates.

The only problem was that a national economy is a big ship, and big ships take a long time to stop and turn around. People did not realise the implications – and nor, in all fairness, did most businessmen, financial commentators or politicians. The balance of payments got worse, and interest rates went up again until they eventually reached 15 per cent. This meant that most people were paying 18–20 per cent on their overdrafts, loans and mortgages. It may have taken some time to stop the ship, but stop it certainly did, and with some very nasty related and self-feeding consequences.

Not only had house prices risen very sharply in the 1980s, but the financing of them had become very easy – 90, 95 and even 100 per cent loans had become available. On a £100,000 mortgage, 10 per cent was £833 a month – quite a lot of money, but manageable if both partners were earning £1,500 a month. The sums looked different by the end of 1989, when repayments had moved up to £1,600 a month and one of the jobs looked a little shaky. If the worst happened and one of the partners lost his or her job (and high interest rates also bring recessions), the couple would have to sell the house and move to something cheaper. And it was only then that the real calamity of the house price spiral hit home. The house that had been bought for £110,000 with a £100,000 mortgage could not be sold, certainly not at £110,000, or at £100,000, or even at £90,000 or £80,000. It could perhaps be 'given away' at £70,000. The couple faced disaster. They could not keep up the mortgage payments, but if they sold the house they owed the mortgage company £30,000. John Major, who took over from Nigel Lawson as chancellor when Thatcher determined that Lawson should take the blame for this fiasco, said: 'If it isn't hurting, it isn't working.'

We were operating in this wild economy and wondering in what direction to take the business, and had turned our attention to convenience retailing. The convenience market is huge, with millions of small stores around the globe. The developing world is dominated by small family-owned businesses selling all manner of goods. International groups such as 7-Eleven and Circle K are two of the largest and most recognised names of chain stores. Both companies originate from Texas. 7-Eleven was formed in 1927 and trades as a franchise operation with almost 50,000 outlets in twenty different countries. Circle K came from El Paso, started trading in 1951 and after a very chequered history, which included going bankrupt in 1990, now trades from approximately 10,000 stores worldwide. Japan has by far the most convenience stores of any developed country, with over 40,000 units trading at the last count. Supermarket size is restricted by Japanese law and the resulting shortage of retail space has created the proliferation of so many small stores.

Back in England in the 1990s, as the smaller supermarkets and discount stores disappeared, a gap started to open up in the market for the local top-up shop. For years the corner shops had been the place to go for odds and ends, and the symbol groups such as Spar, VG, Mace and the Co-op all still existed but were hanging on by their fingernails. Small grocery stores were closing in the hundreds but a lot were snapped up in the 1970s and 1980s by the Asian community. They tended to open longer hours than their predecessors and also traded on Sundays but standards, by and large, were low and prices expensive. Many stores applied for and obtained a licence to sell alcohol which at a stroke improved their appeal and product offer. However, most of the corner shops were far too small to carry a credible range and trying to shoehorn in more and more products actually made matters far worse in every way. Both 7-Eleven and Circle K tried to break into the British market but with very limited success. 7-Eleven could not understand why they were not selling large packs of ice cubes in the middle of December! Convenience retailing in Britain, as we know it today, evolved in many different ways.

As customers became more and more mobile, garage forecourt retailing became a growth area but again was only a bits-and-pieces solution because these sites also tended to be restricted by size and therefore were too small to offer a reasonable range of products. In addition, of course, they were not allowed to sell alcohol. The ideal size, to accommodate the necessary range of products, was a store somewhere between 1,500 square feet and 3,000 square feet with adequate parking allowed nearby.

The second type of convenience store (or C-store) to emerge was from a reduced range of grocery products that then allowed space for the addition of newspapers and magazines and an off-licence section. Instead of having two different sizes of, say, Kellogg's cornflakes and Nescafé coffee, only one size was stocked and the trick was to offer a range of products in a particular category that was just sufficient to cover the basic distress purchase but that in no way purported to be a full supermarket offer.

The third type of C-store grew from an enlarged traditional newsagent with grocery and off-licence added to the mix of products sold. The problem was that the C-store companies that evolved from a grocery background were not very successful retailers of news and confectionery. But, in the same way, the C-store operators that had developed from a newsagent background knew very little about grocery retailing.

However, the biggest challenge to us all was to find a way of successfully retailing chilled and fresh goods. These product groups, by nature, have a very short shelf life and need to be refreshed, ideally on a daily basis. This gave us what came to be called the 'chicken and egg' problem. We needed good fresh displays in order to build up a reputation and therefore sales, but the waste involved was so large and costly that we could never afford to keep going long enough to build up the sales in the first place!

This was an issue that would take years to resolve and became a logistical nightmare for the early C-store operators.

I had absolutely no idea when we bought the Dillons/Preedy Group that the small 38 C-store division was to be the seed from which most of our future growth would come. I had not been impressed by any C-store operation that existed and in fact had famously said that I didn't see much of a future for convenience retailing.

How wrong could I have been?

I much preferred the Dillons type of convenience store which had grown from a newsagent legacy rather than the downsized grocery approach. The more Jim and I visited the stores, the more excited I became about the concept. All the Dillons C-stores traded from 6.00am until 10.00pm seven days a week, with most of the stores offering video rental as well as the core product ranges. Another little 'jewel in the crown' of our retail operation was that, in addition to the three retail formats, we also operated 74 in-store Post Offices. As well as forming a highly profitable division in their own right, the Post Offices were also valuable traffic builders for the stores.

We started to concentrate more and more on the development of our C-store format and introduced the Fantasia range of pick and mix into all the stores. It was an instant success and added yet another point of differentiation between us and the competition. I have always believed it is virtually impossible to copy someone else's formula because so many small and intricate nuances are added along the way that an individual company ends up with a unique identity not only in its face to the public but also in the ethos and culture at its core. Supercigs took a simple no-nonsense, fast-track approach to discount retailing and many companies tried to ape what we were doing, but very few, if any, succeeded.

In 1991 we strengthened the board with the appointment of David Turner as group property director. Aged 38, he had worked under John Hayward for five years and his appointment turned out to be a master stroke as he was hugely influential in engineering most of our future growth. We were a young team with the average age of the executive board under 40. John Hayward retired from full-time duties and became non-executive deputy chairman working alongside our other non-executive, Ian Vickerey, who had joined the board the year before. Ian had been part of the team at De Zoete and Bevan bank that had brought us to the Unlisted Securities Market back in 1984.

The acquisition of the Bristol-based 22 JCR convenience stores was complemented by purchases of other C-stores as far apart as Barrow-in-Furness, Llanelli, Cambridge and Plymouth. In total 39 C-stores were opened, which doubled the size of our C-store estate. Sales in C-stores continued to forge ahead by 63 per cent year on year

The famous Fantasia range of pick and mix confectionery.

with like-for-like sales ahead by 12 per cent. As a group we were now selling over five tons of pick and mix confectionery every single day of the year and had become the number two retailer of pick and mix in the UK.

By the spring of 1992 we had centralised all warehouse, distribution and office functions and a complete review of staffing levels and management structure was undertaken. The country was in the grip of a recession and we needed to cut overheads and reduce costs to combat a more austere retail environment. We announced 52 head office redundancies and the closure of all four divisional offices. While making people redundant is inevitably a painful experience, it is necessary for any company to prune the management tree from time to time, as it tends to grow like Topsy if left unchecked. It is essential that better and more efficient systems of working are continually developed. I think the time and motion boffins call it business process re-engineering, but I believe pruning is a much better definition.

In the warehouse we had moved to a paperless system of picking orders. The system replaced printed picking lists with hand-held terminals (HHTs) connected to the central computer systems by radio link. Bar code scanning and quantity input at the point of order assembly greatly reduced the risk of human error.

One of the problems with an ever-expanding business is that management infrastructure has to grow to control the beast you are creating. T&S was no different and our management tree had grown so many branches we could hardly see the sky. In the early days we boasted about the fact that our delivery van cost no more than the company car because it was just a trailer that fitted onto the back of the car. Twenty years later we operated a fleet of lorries that delivered to the stores from Newcastle in the north-east to Plymouth in the south-west. On the retail side, as well as the staff in the stores, we now employed 60 area managers, ten regional managers and three operations managers.

At head office, in addition to a large group of general office people, we also had the following departments: information technology, computer, personnel, training, shopfitting, estates, Post Office and buying. At one time we even had someone going around asking if anyone required stationery; but I soon put a stop to that by refusing to buy any more pencils and pens, issuing pencil sharpeners instead. I think the staff had forgotten that you can actually sharpen a pencil and then it really does last a long time. As departments grow, so they need secretarial support and suddenly everyone seemed to have a secretary, so we halved the number we had and made departments share secretarial support. Once the moaning had settled down and people got used to the idea we halved the number again until the pips really did start to squeak.

As over 100 people enjoyed the benefit of a company-expensed car, it effectively meant that every six stores had to support the running costs of at least one vehicle. We monitored petrol costs very carefully and introduced a monthly prize for the person who paid the lowest price for a litre. Furthermore, daring to fill up the car at a motorway service station was almost a hanging offence.

Our vehicle insurance costs seemed to escalate every year as more and more of our staff had accidents so our transport manager, Clive Smout, made everyone, including myself, go on a half-day drivers' awareness course with a company that employed retired police drivers. The results were astonishing and the costs of the course were more than covered when the number of accidents fell dramatically and our insurance premiums started to go down. I was also staggered by how many trivial expense claims were made each month by various people and I was furious when I discovered an area manager had claimed 20p for a car parking expense. I phoned him up to explain that it cost us far more than 20p to process the claim and from that point on we did not allow expenses under £2 to be submitted. We paid our people well and I thought it was an abuse of the company that every single expense should have to be borne, let alone the expense of processing it.

Break-ins, robbery and theft were problems we had to cope with every day of the year because we stocked and sold so many cigarettes. We could no longer insure against theft in the shops, as our annual premiums never covered the losses from the numerous break-ins and the insurance companies quickly lost patience with our claims record and refused to insure us. However, we did insure cigarette stocks at the warehouse and had to install highly sophisticated alarm systems as well as night watchmen to satisfy all the insurance requirements. Obviously patrolling a warehouse at night is a boring job, but we had to sack a particular employee who ran up a bill of £1,500 in one month alone talking to girls on expensive chat line numbers!

We also insured for goods in transit as the value of a van load of cigarettes ran into the tens of thousands of pounds. We always sent a driver and a mate to ensure that when deliveries were made to stores, the goods were never left unattended. However, we were not prepared for what happened one December morning as one of our vehicles was on the A38 making its way to deliver to shops in the Derby/Nottingham area. A police car overtook the lorry and indicated to the driver to pull over into the lay-by just ahead. Keith Aston, the driver, duly obliged and the two policemen got out of the car and approached the vehicle very slowly. Suddenly two sawn-off shotguns were produced and Keith and his mate were ordered to get out of the lorry and marched into a field at gunpoint. They were then handcuffed together and tied to a tree as the two robbers made good their escape, one driving the police car and one driving the van. Incredibly they left the keys to the handcuffs in Keith's shirt pocket, telling him that whoever found them would be able to release them immediately.

It really was not the robbers' day because, unbeknown to them, Keith was double-jointed and within minutes had managed to get the keys out of his shirt pocket and unlock the handcuffs. He immediately flagged down a car, told the driver what had happened and the alarm was raised. Fortunately all our vans had identification numbers on the roof and the police helicopter spotted the van speeding down the M1, followed by the bogus police car. After a twenty-mile chase the real police had the men in custody and all our stock was recovered. Keith and his mate, while obviously shocked, were unhurt. Their quick thinking had saved the day and also saved the insurance company a lot of money.

The robbery had obviously taken a great deal of planning and it turned out that one of the culprits had been informed of the timing and route of the lorry by one of our female area managers with whom he lived. The courts were never able to prove her collusion in the robbery but the two bogus policemen received long prison sentences due to the severity of the crime. They were charged with the separate crimes of impersonating police officers, armed robbery and kidnapping, which taken together was a very serious offence.

As if all of this was not enough excitement, in the following month, January 1994, we completed the £6.7 million acquisition of Gibbs News Ltd. Located within the southern counties, the 74 stores traded as traditional newsagents with a strong news base, underpinned by a significant element of home delivery. The acquisition added £25 million to group turnover and took the number of CTN stores within the company to 340 and deliveries of news to some 120,000 homes. Securing the business allowed us to look for C-store opportunities in the vicinity of the shops and greatly enhance the value of the business we had bought.

On 28 March the same year we announced the purchase of a further 27 C-stores, trading as Mac's, from the Rowlandson Organisation for £5.95 million. The main attraction of this acquisition was that the stores, which averaged 2,500 square feet in size, were all situated on modern housing estates located in the Midlands and Home Counties. The increasing value of C-stores was reflected in the fact that we had paid just under £100,000 for each Gibbs newsagent but had paid nearly £250,000 for each Mac's convenience store.

In August the Sunday trading laws changed, allowing supermarkets

T&S takes 27 Macs as profits rise to £12.6m

CTN and convenience store multiple T&S Stores this week added another 27 shops to its trading base while announcing a rise in profits.

T&S took over the 27-strong Macs Stores convenience chain in a deal worth just under £6m. T&S runs Dillons, Gibbs and Supercigs in the CTN sector, and is a growing force in the convenience store market.

The Midlands-based company this week announced pre-tax profits for last year of £12.6m, up £100,000 on 1992. Turnover grew £7m to £345m.

Commenting on the results, T&S chairman Kevin Threlfall said the company plans to add 130 further stores this year. He made clear how much T&S is counting on the National Lottery, due to launch within the next year, to provide an extra boost to revenue.

"We are particularly excited by the opportunities which will arise from the sale of National Lottery tickets – a

Kevin Threlfall: despite the depressed economic climate news and convenience stores have turned in a "solid trading performance"

market forecast to grow rapidly to between £3bn and £4bn annually," said Mr Threlfall. T&S has already begun to prepare its stores for ticket retailing equipment and meetings have been held

with National Lottery bidders.

In his statement to shareholders, the T&S chairman played down fears over the Government's shake-up of the news market. He concluded the effects of the

MMC and DTI's recommendations on newspaper supplies would be "broadly neutral", reflecting T&S's identity as both newsagent and convenience retailer.

Mr Threlfall said last year's continuing depressed economic climate was reflected in the group's sales but added that despite this newsagent and convenience stores had turned in a "solid trading performance".

Dillons newsagents turned in an average branch profit of £21,740, up by 9.4 per cent on 1992.

The newly acquired Macs Stores are mainly in the Midlands and Home Counties. T&S takes them over from retail property developers The Rowlandson Organisation as the first stage in a working relationship between the two companies.

RO will develop further neighbourhood shopping centres in England and Wales which Dillons convenience stores will occupy as 'anchor tenant'.

Acquisition of Mac's convenience stores.

to open for a maximum of six hours between 10.00am and 6.00pm. Obviously this was a huge blow to us as sales of Sunday newspapers in our CTNs and C-stores were badly affected, with supermarkets having another string to their bow. However, as one door closed another one opened with the announcement that the National Lottery was to be launched in November. With lottery terminals being located in most of our stores and 5 per cent commission on all sales, it was to prove a massive boost to our business, far outweighing the damage caused by supermarkets being allowed to trade on a Sunday.

– CHAPTER 10 –

Following a Paper Chain

1994 was a year of low inflation and two significant retailing milestones that impacted upon the sales performance of the group. There was the relaxation of Sunday trading laws and also the Mergers and Monopolies Commission investigation into newspaper distribution. The commission decided that it was against the public interest for wholesalers to refuse to supply newspapers on the grounds that an area was adequately covered. As a result this broke the long-established cartel the wholesalers had enjoyed and opened the floodgates for other entrants. Thousands of new outlets started to sell newspapers and magazines, including supermarkets and garage forecourts.

However, the introduction of the National Lottery further enhanced the attraction of our stores and apart from making money from the sale of lottery tickets it encouraged more store visits and resulted in a greater number of impulse purchases. By the end of the year we had installed 300 lottery terminals and had secured over 2 per cent of national sales.

Although I had been company chairman since the outset, my main day-to-day responsibility had always been on the trading side of the business and I had gained considerable experience in my role as buying director of Lo-Cost Discount Stores back in the 1970s. I was privileged to have a formidable team around me and, with the likes of Peter Gallagher, John Lyons, Doug Flello and Kevin McAndrew, I had assembled probably the most respected and capable buying team within the industry.

As my role increased with the size of the business we searched long and hard for my replacement and eventually appointed Geoff Purdy to the board as group buying director in June 1994. Geoff had enjoyed 30 years' experience in retail and buying, having previously been trading director of Spar Landmark Ltd. From the minute the interview started I knew instinctively he was the right man for the job, with his down-to-earth manner and cockney accent. He was to prove a tremendous asset to the company and we remain good friends to this day.

As the economy picked up again and confidence returned to the retail sector, our three trading formats benefited enormously. At Supercigs we had become less dependent on the sale of greetings cards and introduced newspapers and magazines into a further 60 stores. By the end of 1994 we were selling discounted newspapers and magazines in 140 stores out of a group total of just over 200 stores.

Our newsagents division with 324 stores had been enhanced by the purchase of Gibbs News Ltd, which widened our geographical coverage of the country and also provided us with a useful base for the further development of our C-store estate. Obviously our news sales were affected by the relaxation of supply but as over 60 per cent of our sales were from home news delivery, we were not as badly affected as we could have been.

Including the Mac's acquisition we had added a further 55 C-stores and with like-for-like sales ahead by an impressive 7 per cent, we started to realise that convenience retailing was going to be very much a growth area for the foreseeable future.

In our tenth year as a publicly quoted company we had produced record profits. It had been a period of rapid growth in which store numbers had grown from 57 to 704 and profits from £0.8 million to £13.9 million.

At the end of 1994 Stephe Boddice decided to retire from business life and I was extremely sad to see him go. We had worked closely together for almost twenty years in which time the company had grown from three kiosks to over 700 stores. He had installed all of our computer systems and written a lot of the software himself, and I was convinced that this had given us a massive advantage over our competitors. He had installed Retail Information Technology into all the stores, allowing electronic management of cash routines and all aspects of newspaper and magazine control. At an early stage in the history of electronic data development he had already laid down the foundations for a future fully integrated Electronic Point of Sale system, or EPOS as it is known.

We had become close friends as well as colleagues and his enthusiasm and talent had been hugely influential in our success. In many ways, with Dave Smith, Fred Durnall and now Stephe all having left the business, I was the only one remaining from the original board of directors and it really did seem like the end of a golden era.

David Crellin replaced Stephe as group finance director, having joined the company five years earlier as operations director for finance. David was a very safe pair of hands and, having qualified as a chartered accountant in 1962, had worked with well-known names such as Tower Houseware, Evode and Scotcade.

With Stephe having been so heavily involved in the development of our computer systems we felt it was vitally important to keep the momentum going and we made a further board appointment with Melvin Kenyon joining as group information systems director. An Oxford graduate, he had more than fifteen years' experience in retail and information systems and had previously worked for the John Lewis Partnership and Boots plc.

We knew that at some stage we would have to convert our tills and select a fully integrated EPOS and back office system for our C-stores. This was going to be a major project requiring significant investment as well as careful planning and execution, and would require the full attention of a board director.

Online lottery proved to be an instant success and was complemented in March 1995 with the introduction of the scratchcard game. While it was impossible to estimate the effect that lottery sales had made to other product groups, we knew there had been a trade-off in the busy Supercigs stores where weekend queues had discouraged shelf browsing. Because fast customer service was essential to our Supercigs operation, we quickly had to solve the problem of lottery queues. We employed extra staff and more appropriate till locations and slowly came to terms with this brand new addition to retailing.

Combined sales of lottery products reached £100 million in the first full year of introduction and our market share had grown to 2.5 per cent of the total UK market, making us one of the largest distributors in the country.

Britain enjoyed a wonderful summer and the UK ice cream market grew by a massive 20 per cent; for the first time sales topped £1 billion. We piloted a 24-hour C-store trading format but staffing problems and security issues made us realise that, with the exception of a small number of stores, it was not going to be the way forward.

In 1988 we had introduced two own-label cigarette brands named Triumph and Supreme that were unique to our stores. They were our cheapest-selling cigarettes and had proved to be an instant success because they offered such value for money and sold for just under £2 for a pack of twenty. With yet another budget increase in tobacco duty, the price for these two brands had gone through this very sensitive price barrier. We therefore introduced another own-label cigarette product unique to us called Warwick but reduced the pack size to eighteen instead of the normal twenty, in order to keep our selling price just under £2 a packet.

Because the four major manufacturers effectively controlled the UK cigarette market they were not prepared to see sales of their own brands threatened by our own-label names and refused to manufacture them for us. We therefore had them manufactured in Greece and Germany and shipped directly to our warehouse in Brownhills. By 1995 our own-label brands represented 12.5 per cent of all our tobacco sales and we were fast developing a franchise for brands that were not only good value for money but also could not be bought anywhere other than in our stores.

As if the relaxation of the Sunday trading laws, a review of newspaper distribution and the introduction of the National Lottery weren't enough retail changes to cope with, Christmas 1995 was to bring about another substantial shift in retailing.

The Net Book Agreement had come into effect on 1 January 1900 and involved retailers selling books at agreed prices. If any bookseller sold a book at less than the agreed price, the book's publisher would no longer supply them. In 1905 *The Times* newspaper even tried but failed to challenge the agreement by setting up a low-cost borrowing club. In 1962 the Net Book Agreement was examined by the Restrictive Practices Court but once again survived as it was decided that it was of benefit to the industry, since it enabled publishers to subsidise the printing of the works of important but less widely read authors using money from bestsellers.

However, there was a ridiculous loophole in that the agreement did not cover books that were damaged. So in order to sell at lower prices retailers adopted one of two strategies. Either they punched a hole in the cover of the book or used a marker pen to deface the edge of the pages. The marker pen method was the more popular as it took less effort. It was only a matter of time before common sense prevailed and in August 1994 the director general of the Office of Fair Trading decided that the Restrictive Practices Court should review the agreement. And, although it was not until March 1997 that the Net Book Agreement was finally made illegal, to all intents and purposes it collapsed in 1995.

Once again this paved the way for the supermarket industry to enter another area of retail, previously barely touched. It allowed them to take a chunk of the book business, typically offering a small number of best-selling titles at deeply discounted prices. Interestingly enough some ten years later, although 500 independent bookshops had closed since the collapse of the Net Book Agreement, the volume of books sold in the UK had increased by some 30 per cent.

Needless to say, we also took advantage of the abolition of the Net Book Agreement and at Christmas introduced into our C-stores and selected CTNs a small range of bestsellers at discounted prices. The results were so encouraging that we continued the process for Mother's Day and Father's Day, when bestselling titles were offered alongside our traditional confectionery offers.

For some time we had been trying to acquire Paperchain, which was a multiple neighbourhood retailer with 109 outlets, 79 of which traded as newsagents and 30 as C-stores. The main attraction for us was that the stores had a strong presence in their principal area of East Anglia and Essex, where we were very under-represented.

The group was slightly larger than the Gibbs acquisition but again was a great geographical fit, with minimal trading overlap with our own stores. Paperchain's portfolio of convenience stores provided a solid base for the continued development of our own C-store format. In particular, Paperchain's newsagents estate provided opportunities to develop further the convenience format as and when stores became available for conversion. It also gave us a foothold and critical mass in an affluent area of the country, which would have taken us a number of years to build up on a piecemeal basis.

In December 1995 we finally agreed a deal at just over £10 million, which represented approximately £100,000 per store. We were delighted with the acquisition as it took our total store numbers to over 800 and increased our C-store estate towards our target of 250 stores. We financed the deal by selling new shares onto the stock market and then satisfying the consideration in cash. Once again we were able to benefit from increased purchasing power and by April 1996 all distribution functions had been transferred to our centre in Brownhills. We closed their Norwich head office in the same month and saved a substantial amount of money by absorbing all their office functions into our own facility.

In many takeovers not everything goes exactly to plan and the Paperchain acquisition was no exception. Over the years the retail disciplines had declined and we identified a lot of slow-moving lines that needed to be sold. Unfortunately this included substantial stocks of giftware, glassware and toys that had accumulated over the years. In the end we decided it would take too long to sell off at store level and returned all the surplus goods to Brownhills to be categorised and sorted. The result was a nightmare of complexity and we ended up with almost 100 pallets of assorted rubbish that would have taken years to clear.

We had learnt from previous experiences that it is better to bite the bullet and address the problem by taking one big hit, rather than experiencing death by a thousand cuts. The value of all the returned goods added up to just under £250,000 and in the end the most we could obtain from a market trader was 10 per cent of the value or £25,000. Painful as it was to take the loss, it freed up a lot of space and turnover increased as the stores benefited from selling our established range, as well as from planogram disciplines and increased service standards.

Nevertheless, we did make operating profits of £2 million from the acquisition in the first full year of ownership, which represented a very healthy 20 per cent return on capital.

In 1996, after twenty years of continual growth, our Supercigs division began to suffer from a combination of fewer customers on the high street and the annual decline in the number of smokers. Annual duty increases coupled with health awareness meant that the UK tobacco market was shrinking by approximately 3 per cent per annum.

Because we operated on only a 3 per cent gross profit margin on the sale of all tobacco products, we relied very heavily on the sheer volume of product we sold in each store. We were serving 69 million customers a year, with an average transaction value of just £2.69, and we relied on the traffic flow in our shops for confectionery sales. Obviously with fewer smokers and fewer people visiting our stores, total confectionery sales started to decline. With profit margins extremely slim, sales declining and high street rents increasing, the formula that had worked so well for twenty years was now under pressure. Having said that, each store was still making an average of £15,000 per annum, and with approximately 200 stores in total Supercigs was contributing circa £3 million to group profits.

On the other hand our C-store division was going from strength to strength. We were serving nearly 2 million customers a week and with like-for-like sales increasing by 4 per cent, the division made almost exactly half of the group operating profit of £20 million in 1996. We now had 250 C-stores, each contributing an average of £40,000 per annum. Within a maturing food retailing industry, they were fast becoming a growth story largely at the expense of the traditional high street supermarkets and weaker independent symbol formats.

We were finding that convenient accessibility combined with changing social structures and behaviour patterns were providing the key driving forces behind the impressive like-for-like sales growth. Important social factors contributing to the popularity of C-stores included a greater number of working women with increasing time constraints, an ageing population, smaller single-occupancy households and more snacking. These were all factors conducive to local shopping.

The development of our C-store identity necessitated continual appraisal of the product range and services offered to our customers. New sales initiatives such as hot drinks, fast food and in-store bakery, coupled with the continuing development of chilled and fresh products, were definitely seen as strong drivers of the future. Other services such as Post Offices, online lottery, video hire and dry cleaning agency were all added where possible.

Because the early Dillons stores incorporated a number of in-store Post Offices, it was a business that we had learned to understand better than most of our competitors. The provision of an in-store Post Office creates a destination outlet for customers that anchors the retail offer and supports the total service ethos you are trying to engender. We were now operating a total of 159 offices throughout the country and stores that benefited from the service generally outperformed the average financial contribution.

With C-store development becoming the main focus of future growth we decided to accelerate our acquisition programme and added a number of experienced executives to the team. A C-store launch team was formed at the beginning of 1996 to provide dedicated focus and to free established field management from this specialised task. The effect of this was to improve and make more consistent the high-profile launch of new stores.

We continued with our policy of selling off underperforming

stores and disposed of 37 small mature neighbourhood newsagents, which obviously improved the overall estate quality while at the same time releasing cash for further investment in our C-store estate. To put this in perspective, although since the acquisition of Dillons/ Preedy in 1990 we had acquired a further 440 stores, we had also in the same period sold 202 underperforming stores. This represented extremely sound property management and allowed us to focus on those stores with a future rather than keeping mature stores that had seen better days.

As our business grew so did our infrastructure and we appointed a group head of training and also a group retail director. We made a significant investment in the personal computer network within the Apex Road facility in Brownhills. We were also very aware that the substantial EPOS investment would soon have to be made for our C-store estate and, following extensive investigation, discussion and tender process, we shortlisted three potential suppliers.

As 1996 drew to a close we were all delighted that group turnover had just managed to finish above £500 million and operating profits just above £20 million. With 804 stores, we could see that in maybe another five or six years we might achieve the magic goal of 1,000 stores.

It was to happen a lot sooner than that.

CHAPTER 11

1,000 Stores

In the early 1990s the British economy was still suffering from the hangover of the boom years of the late 1980s set up by Chancellor of the Exchequer Nigel Lawson.

The rate of inflation had risen to double figures, interest rates were at 10 per cent and unemployment was moving sharply upwards. To add to the feeling of crisis, on 16 September the pound sterling fell out of the ERM (Exchange Rate Mechanism). This is how the prime minister, John Major, described that day in his autobiography:

Black Wednesday – 16 September 1992, the day the pound toppled out of the ERM – was a political and economic calamity. It unleashed havoc in the Conservative Party and it changed the political landscape of Britain.

On the day of the crisis itself, interest rates in the UK were raised to 12 per cent. However, sterling kept falling on the foreign exchange markets and the government threatened to raise them to 15 per cent. This would have caused multiple bankruptcies and the alternative of leaving the ERM was adopted instead.

By the end of that awful day, the Bank of England had made the largest intervention in the currency markets in its history, having sold over £15 billion of its reserves (over the Tuesday and Wednesday combined). The final cost to the taxpayer was between £3 and £4 billion, equivalent to £20 for every man, woman and child in the UK.

It was a frightening experience for many people and the recession continued. The chancellor of the exchequer kept talking of the 'green shoots' of economic recovery but, in truth, the recession lasted throughout 1993 and 1994 and real recovery only began in 1995.

After the surprise victory of the Conservative Party in the 1992 general election, the party was severely damaged by Black Wednesday as one of the main reasons for its victory had been the belief of many voters that it was economically more competent than the Labour Party. Furthermore, the party suffered a series of lurid scandals. Prime Minister John Major made a speech on morality and used the phrase 'back to basics'. As each scandal of adultery, children born out of wedlock, a sex death when a kinky stunt went wrong and rumours about Major's own affairs were exposed, the press had many field days using again and again Major's phrase 'back to basics'.

In the meantime, the new leader of the Labour party, Tony Blair (Neil Kinnock had resigned after the shock Labour defeat in 1992 and his replacement, John Smith, died of a heart attack), did a brilliant job of modernising the Labour Party. In conjunction with Gordon Brown, he made Labour look like the sort of party many in the country felt would make a competent government.

The Conservative Party held on as long as it could but, in the spring of 1997, its eighteen years in power were up and it was forced to hold a general election. New Labour won 419 seats, the largest number ever for the party. Its majority in the House of Commons was also a modern record, as was the 10 per cent swing from the Conservatives.

The new chancellor of the exchequer, Gordon Brown, immediately made a surprising move by handing control over interest rates to the Bank of England. Most other countries, including the economically important USA and Germany, had long ago run monetary policy independently of politicians. Brown's decision was an excellent one and gave the exchange markets confidence in sterling.

Brown followed this up with cautious moves on the economy, generally giving the middle classes reassurance that a Labour government would not automatically raise taxes on middle-income families.

The British economy during the Labour government from 1997 to 2001 grew steadily at 2.8 per cent a year, above the post-war average, and a rate of inflation lower than for many years. Britain's gross domestic product (GDP) per head was above that of France and Germany and she enjoyed the second-lowest jobless figures in the European Union. The number of people in work increased by 2.4 million. Incomes grew, in real terms, by about a fifth. House prices rose, making the middle classes feel prosperous.

Furthermore, the increasing availability of cheap air travel, pioneered by Freddie Laker in the 1970s, gave the British people opportunities to travel to the sunny resorts of Europe. In retail outlets, evolving electronics and cheap clothing imports kept most shops busy. Internet shopping also grew apace.

With convenience retailing becoming more and more popular, it was obvious that sooner or later one of the major supermarket groups would enter the arena. A shiver went down my spine when, early in 1997, Tesco and Esso formed a business alliance that included several petrol filling stations on lease from Esso, with Tesco operating the attached stores under their Express format.

I knew that, with their expertise, it was only a matter of time before they got the formula right, and we would all be in trouble once they realised how much money there was to be made and the potential there lay in the business. We were determined to move quickly and establish a major foothold in the marketplace before competition for sites became so intense as to make acquisitions too expensive.

For a couple of years we had been stalking a publicly quoted convenience store company called M&W plc. Founded in 1848, the company operated 179 convenience stores, primarily located in the south of England, East Anglia and the East Midlands. Geographically the stores were a perfect fit with our own, as there was virtually no direct competition within the T&S and M&W store portfolios.

In addition to this, M&W operated a central warehouse based in Nursling, near Southampton. The modern 85,000-square-foot facility was an almost identical size to our own warehouse in Brownhills, West Midlands. This meant that that the Nursling warehouse would be able to supply the southern-based Dillons stores and the Brownhills warehouse would be able to supply the more northerly M&W stores. The two warehouses would provide a perfect distribution spread for the two companies.

One of the other major attractions of M&W was that it had a seven-year history with EPOS. As we were about to install our own system, the experience they had gained would help facilitate the successful implementation of the programme. The cost of installing EPOS had always frightened me to death, as I knew it would run into millions of pounds and would be extremely difficult to install. While our back office control and cigarette stock and order systems were state of the art, our point of sale information was now behind the times.

The final benefit of the acquisition lay in the economies of scale that could be derived from putting the two companies together. The additional turnover of £120 million a year would significantly enhance the enlarged group's ability to negotiate more favourable terms with suppliers, resulting in benefits to purchasing, promotion and marketing.

With our own plans to open 80 new C-stores in 1997, the acquisition would take us over the 500 C-store mark and we would become the largest company-owned and -managed convenience store estate in the country.

The only problem was that they didn't want to sell!

On three separate occasions Jim McCarthy and I had gone out to lunch with the chairman, Michael Weston, and his managing director, Basil Taylor. We always met halfway between Brownhills and Southampton at the prestigious Le Manoir in Oxfordshire and attempted to seduce them both (not literally) with great food and fine wine. Michael, who was a delightful gentleman in spite of supporting Southampton Football Club, always liked a bottle of Meursault which had never been on my price radar, but no expense was to be spared in our attempt to impress him.

We would have a lovely three-hour lunch and then right at the end, when we were having coffee, I would ask again if they had any interest in becoming part of T&S. Michael would always give the same frustrating answer that, although the logic of putting the two companies together was indisputable, they preferred their independence for the time being. Although M&W was a publicly quoted company, with its shares listed on the Stock Exchange, it was futile launching a hostile takeover bid, as shareholders tend to vote with the management and it creates ill feeling among the workforce.

We would pay the bill and agree to meet in another twelve months' time but by 1997 I was becoming frustrated by the lack of progress and, as the Godfather would say, decided to make an offer they could not refuse. For the three years prior to 1997 the pre-tax profits at M&W had hardly increased and the share price remained becalmed at £1.55. I phoned Michael and told him we were going to make an offer for the company that was incredibly generous and I wanted his assurance that it would get his backing. Again he was hesitant but when I told him we would be bidding at £2.55 per share, a full £1 premium to the quoted price, it all went very quiet. After he got back off the floor and climbed into his chair again he knew the offer had to be backed by the board.

Michael wrote to his shareholders on 23 September 1997 and recommended that our offer was fair and reasonable and should be accepted by the shareholders. I should imagine they were over the moon to receive the letter and on 14 October the deal went through. We had paid £42.8 million for 179 stores, representing an average price of just under £240,000 per store. I was delighted because although we had paid a lot of money, the quality of sites we had bought gave us a great opportunity to improve sales substantially. M&W were making half the trading margin we were achieving in the T&S C-stores and I knew that bringing the two companies together would make one and one add up to far more than two.

The deal cemented our position in the marketplace and at a stroke we had created the UK's largest chain of company-owned convenience stores. It also impressed the shareholders as our share price reacted positively after the announcement and more fund managers started to take an interest in our business. The only thing that worried me that was our company debt had risen to just under £100 million, which left us exposed to any sudden increase in interest rates. We sensibly purchased a variety of hedging products to ensure that any future interest costs would be capped at a set level.

For years T&S always had money in the bank, except just before the chancellor's annual budget when we bought several weeks' stock of tobacco products. I had been brought up believing that all retail operations should be cash positive and it always gave me a warm feeling to be lending to the bank rather than borrowing from it.

Once again we improved the quality of the board with the appointment of Graham Maguire, who took over a lot of responsibility from Jim McCarthy and became group retail director. Graham had held the same position at the Victoria Wine Company, where he had worked for the last eight years. We were also pleased to secure the services of Bob Davies as a non-executive

T&S intensifies c-store battle with bid for M&W

by Juliet Morrison

NEWSAGENT and convenience store operator T&S Stores is buying rival M&W to create what it claims will be the UK's biggest company-owned and managed convenience store group.

T&S, which owns the Dillons and Supercigs chains, said the £42m takeover would give it an opportunity to expand its convenience store network – one of its stated strategies.

M&W also fitted its business geographically and operationally, and there was virtually no competition between the two networks, T&S said.

The move came as T&S announced first half pre-tax profits up 17% to £10.3m on turnover two per cent higher at £253.8m, compared with the same period in 1996.

Walsall-based T&S has 800 outlets, including 296 convenience stores, 324 newsagents and 183 high street discount newsagents.

Last year, the company said it planned to increase its network of convenience outlets to 500 by the year 2000.

The seller and the buyer: Michael Weston, chairman of M&W (left), and T&S chairman Kevin Threlfall

M&W has 179 convenience stores, mostly in the south of England, East Anglia and the east Midlands. Its shops had an average weekly turnover of £13,610 in the year to 30 March, and for the year to September 1996 the company reported pre-tax profits of £2.8m.

T&S said the acquisition would give it 475 convenience stores, which would have had a combined turnover in excess of £160m for the last reported six months.

T&S chief executive Jim McCarthy said that it was likely that the M&W name would be dropped. "We will probably change the trading name to Dillons throughout 1998," he said.

Press announcement of our takeover of M&W plc.

director. Bob had worked for Coopers & Lybrand Management Consultancy, Waterford Wedgwood and Ferranti International, finally becoming chief executive of East Midlands Electricity plc. The final appointment was Basil Taylor, who had been chief executive of M&W for seven years. Basil had agreed to join us for a year to help with the integration of M&W and also to help with our EPOS implementation.

Following the acquisition of M&W, store numbers had increased to 980 and we were now within touching distance of the magic 1,000 target. With further store openings in the pipeline it was not long before we were celebrating the opening of our 1,000th store in Poole, Dorset on 10 December. I had met Willie Thorne, the famous snooker player, while on holiday in Marbella and we had become friends. When I told him about the event, he offered to come and cut the ribbon on the big day. As we drove down I was quiet and preoccupied as I reflected on the previous 22 years, in which the company had grown from a single kiosk in Wolverhampton market to 1,000 stores. Needless to say, it was a very special and proud moment in my life and a day that I shall never forget.

Once again we celebrated at the NEC in Birmingham and over 1,000 guests enjoyed the immense talent of Bob Monkhouse, who ensured that it was a night to remember for all of us.

The test of any management's strength is in its ability to adapt to the ever-changing needs of its customers. Supercigs as a business had peaked and with store numbers declining it was important that we managed the transition of our business very carefully. This was to be a very delicate balancing act as the purchasing power of Supercigs, with its high sales volumes, brought a lot of benefit to the group as a whole. Having decided that our future lay in convenience retailing, we had re-engineered our business and opened over 400 C-stores in five years. We now anticipated that within the next five years all investment would be focused on the C-store development while

Snooker Star Willie Thorne opens our 1,000th store in Poole.

Supercigs, together with the smaller newsagents, would, over time, slowly be managed out of the business.

In spite of the ever-growing popularity of convenience shopping, most fund managers did not really understand the marketplace, nor did they see the huge potential that lay in store for operators of this fast-evolving trend.

The transition from a sector of undifferentiated family-run stores to specialists offering premium products at premium prices was incomplete. Up to the point where we bought M&W, convenience store chains remained largely regional and for that reason were not well known. The UK market did not have well-established national brands, unlike the US and Japan where the

sector had long been established with household names such as
7-Eleven and Circle K.

There really was a perception that companies such as ours were
the unglamorous and poor relations in a grocery world dominated
by the large superstores such as Tesco, Sainsbury and Asda. Our type
of company was valued at single-figure multiples of annual profit,
whereas the well-known supermarket chains always commanded mid-
teen multiples of annual profit.

Nevertheless, in 1996 the convenience market was valued at £14.9
billion, representing 18 per cent of a total UK grocery market of
£82.4 billion. It may have still represented small beer in comparison
with the big boys but it was now growing at the rate of 20 per cent per
annum, or almost ten times the overall rate of growth of the market.

We now had to convince the institutional investors that
convenience retailing was the growth story and that our company
share price was way too low when compared with those of the
established grocers.

One of the responsibilities of being chairman of a public company
is to communicate your results twice a year and this involves a lot
of time and effort. First and foremost you announce half-yearly
or interim results and then at the end of your financial year you
announce preliminary or final results. These are communicated to
the Stock Exchange on an agreed date and are normally published
just before the stock market opens for trade on that particular
day. Obviously the results are always cloaked in secrecy before the
announcement, as prior information could lead to insider dealing.

Some of the larger companies report masses of information that
can run into hundreds of pages, while others communicate just the
headline figures combined with a basic narrative.

A more comprehensive review of activities is then contained within
the published report and accounts booklet, which is sent to individual

shareholders. At T&S we had hundreds of individual shareholders as well as some of the major well-known pension funds such as Legal & General, Scottish Widows, Standard Life and the Prudential.

Shareholdings would vary from a few hundred owned by a particular individual to a few million owned by one or more of the larger pension funds. We regularly received a list of our shareholders and it always fascinated me to know why certain individuals had picked our company to invest in and what had been the trigger. I was delighted that, in spite of the fact that we sold a lot of cigarettes, my own doctor's wife had accumulated quite a sizeable holding. She was obviously a very savvy investor because over the years she made a lot of money out of her stock market investments.

We normally made our announcements on a Monday and my chief executive, Jim McCarthy, and I would travel down to London the night before as the day always started with an 8.00am presentation to broking company analysts and the press. We normally stayed at the Hilton on Park Lane as we had negotiated a good corporate rate and it was a convenient location from which to get around.

Each broking house would have different specialists following the various sectors that existed within the business world. So they would have one specialist for the engineering sector, another for financial services, one for retail and so on. We obviously fell under the retail food sector and it was very important that we had good relationships with the analysts, as they would be writing about our results and giving out a hold, sell or buy recommendation based on the quality of our results against expectation. I stress the word expectation because we always had to steer the analysts towards a profit range that we felt comfortable with communicating. This is why share prices can go up in value even if a company reports horrendous results, and sometimes can go down if a company reports really good results. The reaction of investors, and therefore the share price movement, all depends on how the results compare with market expectations rather than the results themselves.

Jim and I would be picked up from the hotel around 7.00am, which would give us time to set up our PowerPoint presentation before everyone arrived. We would then go through the figures, giving reasons why they were better or worse than the previous year, and also try to give an overview of our plans for the coming year. Our same store sales figures, in comparison with the previous year, were probably the most important element of what we reported as this gave a strong indication of whether the business was growing or going backwards. We would normally finish the presentation with an appraisal of our prospects for the coming year and then invite questions from the analysts and journalists.

Over the years we got to know a lot of people, although the journalists moved around so much it was difficult to build any sort of meaningful relationship with any of them. On the analyst side we got to know Jeremy Hilditch of Williams De Broe very well and also Clive Black, now of Shore Capital Stockbrokers.

Jeremy has since retired but Clive is often quoted in the financial papers and is probably the most highly regarded retail food analyst in the country. I will always be grateful to Clive because, together with Darren Shirley, he wrote a number of very in-depth reports on our company and gave a lot of credence to the way we were running the business.

After the presentation, Jim and I would rush to see if there was any movement in the share price, as this would really set the scene for the rest of the day when we would be visiting our larger shareholders on an individual basis. The individual meetings would normally last an hour and Jim and I would work through our 'presenter packs', taking questions along the way. Time allowed only a couple of these in the morning so we would normally invite up to half a dozen shareholders to a lunch briefing that was normally held at our broker's head office. In the afternoon we would typically see another three investors before crashing out back at the hotel for a well-earned rest. It was always an extremely stressful day that demanded a lot of concentration although, towards the end of the day, we were almost word-perfect on the 'presenter packs' and had memorised most of the important numbers. The following day we would visit another half-dozen major shareholders before being taken to Heathrow for the evening flight to Edinburgh. There we would host a dinner for some of the Scottish institutions that maybe didn't hold shares but were interested in our story.

Our major shareholder, with over 10 per cent of the company, had their main office in the city and we would normally see them for a two-hour breakfast meeting before moving on to our other shareholders that were based in Edinburgh as well.

After lunch we would travel by train to Glasgow and spend the afternoon visiting more Scottish investors before catching the 19.45 flight back to Birmingham. In all, over the three days we would probably see up to twenty of our largest shareholders who in total held about 50 per cent of all the shares in issue.

In the early days of our City visits we were known as 'T&Who' or 'the boring boys from Birmingham' because our profit figures were almost always bang in line with the analysts' forecasts. For sure it was time-consuming to have to ply our story twice a year to the City and over three days each time but, as fund managers were investing their clients' money, they had a duty to understand the nature of our business.

One of the benefits of being a PLC (public limited company) is that it does make you focus on your future strategy because, if you are not clear about the future, you can bet your bottom dollar that your fund manager won't be either. And of course being a PLC does force the pace; there is no time to have a mid-term sabbatical or go backpacking and have a year out.

I encouraged the fund managers to come to Brownhills and have a closer look at the business. I used to say that if they wanted to know the quality of their investment don't just look at the pin-stripe suit, have a look at the colour of the vest underneath. It annoyed me that so few of them took up my offer because the only way to find out how a company works is to go and visit it, look in the bins to see how much is being thrown away and look in the storerooms.

It is the only way that you can sort out the bullshit from the truth and far too many fund managers were prepared to make commercial judgements from reading analysts' notes rather than getting right inside the fabric of the business. Having said that, over the years we developed a great relationship with our shareholders and many owned their shares for a number of years.

There was only one occasion when the proverbial hit the fan and a junior fund manager came close to losing his life one rainy morning in March 1993.

Business had been very difficult in 1992, with the country being in the grip of a recession and the increased competition from the supermarkets with the change to the Sunday trading laws. Nevertheless we had fared better than most, but it was still the first and only year in our history where profits were worse than the previous year. At the operating level they were almost identical with the year before, so it was no big disaster.

However, along with most other companies our share price had suffered and had fallen from a high of £2.50 in June 1992 down to £1.65 in March 1993 when we were visiting the City and reporting our results. Most fund managers were sanguine about the situation and didn't give us a hard time. They had seen it all before and knew that business went in cycles and that the country would in time recover from the recession.

However, one particular fund manager did not quite see it that way and asked to see us at the unearthly time of 7.30am. This felt like the headmaster summoning us to his study in order to make it really difficult. It was a long-established and well-known firm of investors that held 2.5 million shares, or 4 per cent, of our company and for this reason we had to show willing and go along for the grilling!

The offices were famous for the expensive paintings that hung in the corridors and the reception area could have graced a five-star hotel. We were shown into one of the meeting rooms and five minutes later the door flew open and in walked Mr Angryman and his junior bag carrier. Without introducing himself he dispatched the bag carrier to go and organise the coffee and started pacing round the room. Throwing his papers down on the table he turned to Stephe Boddice and me and said in no uncertain terms that he was not happy with our results. He then went on to explain that he had inherited a portfolio of investments that included our bag of s**t and under no circumstance would he ever have bought the shares if it had been his choice.

Staying calm, I suggested that if he wasn't happy, the best thing to do was sell the shares. With this he then went ballistic and started shouting and screaming that because the shares had been bought at the top of the market, he would lose almost £2 million if he sold them.

Going redder in the face, he turned on me and said that I wasn't working hard enough and that I was spending too much time on the golf course and not enough time looking after the business. What he didn't know was that I also had a temper and he had just lit the fuse. The red mist hadn't escaped from its box for a number of years but he was slowly and surely about to blow it wide open if he carried on in this manner.

He did, and in the end I had taken just about as much of this verbal tirade as I could stand. He had no idea how hard we had

worked in a difficult environment to come up with the profit figures
in the first place, and my working week certainly did not involve any
visits to the golf course.

In the end something just snapped and while he was still rabbiting
on I got up from my seat, walked round the table and lifted him by
his lapels straight out of his chair. I then proceeded to start banging
him back and forth against the wall with his feet off the floor and
told him in a very measured voice that he had precisely ten seconds
to apologise or lose his front teeth.

He turned into a gibbering idiot and, begging me not to hit him,
started to apologise profusely. He tried to explain that he was under
immense pressure to succeed and it was just unfortunate that he had
taken his frustrations out on us.

Gathering up our papers, we stormed out of the office and down
the hall to the reception but as we were walking down the corridor
the junior bag carrier appeared round the corner carrying a silver
tray with a pot of coffee, four cups and a small jug of milk. You know
what is coming next don't you?

I smashed the whole lot up in the air and the boiling hot coffee
came flying out of the pot all over one of the fine paintings hanging
on the wall. For one split second I thought we might have to pay
for the restoration of an Old Master, but to be honest I didn't care
because it just felt so wonderful to get my own back.

Later that afternoon we had a meeting with the senior partners
of the firm and they apologised profusely for what had happened.
They tried to explain that it was a young man who had joined them
recently and was trying to make a name for himself. Well, he certainly
did that.

I asked them to sell the shares because we would never be
returning to their offices and we did not want them as future
shareholders. They sold the shares at a loss of £2 million but what

T&S board photo, 1998.

pleased me the most was that if they had hung on to them, ten years later, instead of losing £2 million, they would have made £4 million.

I have to say that in over eighteen years of visiting fund managers I probably attended in the region of 500 meetings that for the most part were cordial and meaningful. I can only imagine the painting wasn't too badly damaged, as I have never received a bill for restoration.

– CHAPTER 12 –

Non-Stop then One-Stop

The acquisition of M&W really was a step change to the future of our company as suppliers and investors alike started to take us more seriously. The main focus for 1998 was to integrate M&W into our existing business and also develop the other 78 C-stores that we acquired during 1997. Store numbers actually declined as we took the opportunity to sell 40 small newsagents and 10 underperforming Supercigs stores.

We were fortunate that the small newsagents were still fetching reasonable money, and by selling 40 we were able to reduce our debt by over £1 million but at the same time take some overhead costs out of the business. There is always a difficult decision to make about keeping marginal stores, because, although they contribute towards much-needed turnover, they also cost as much to look after as better-performing stores.

Although our stores were small in comparison with the average supermarket, it was amazing how many individual products were sold in total. In 1998 we sold 3 million Crème Eggs, 20 million bags of Walkers crisps, 52 million pints of milk and 90 million sticks of Wrigley's chewing gum as well as selling 3 per cent of all cigarettes sold in the UK.

The attraction of the convenience store sector was growing every year as more and more services and product innovations were introduced to the stores. We had introduced Pay Point, a brand new method of paying utility bills electronically, into 305 stores. We had Post Office facilities in 162 outlets, online lottery in 380 locations and 97 in-store bakery facilities.

We had forged an exciting partnership with the Alliance & Leicester building society, which resulted in the installation of our first ATM. We knew that the introduction of ATMs across the C-store estate would bring considerable value to the overall retail proposition and add yet another dimension to the attraction of services available to the customer. Dillons C-stores, situated predominantly in the heart of the community, now provided a really credible local top-up shop covering long hours and in a well-lit, modern and clean trading environment.

The product ranges were now complemented by an ever-increasing variety of customer services which now included online National Lottery terminals, Pay Point electronic utility payment systems, cashback, video rental, home newspaper delivery, ATMs and a national network of Post Offices. All of this contributed to a powerful convenience offer that was gaining momentum and increasingly becoming more relevant to the ever-changing shopping habits and demands of a more mobile and busy UK consumer.

By 1998 the British population had grown to about 60 million, with a small increase forecast for the first decade of the new millennium. Food retailers, therefore, were working in an affluent but ultimately low volume growth market.

The structural composition of the food retailing industry was also showing signs of maturity, with the top ten retailers controlling 84 per cent of the market. The scope for market share gains lay in store expansion, retail excellence and/or corporate activity. The scope to open larger outlets, especially edge-of-town, had become more challenging as a result of the relatively tight British planning regime. Similarly, the regulator served to be a major 'conditioner' of industry organisation through the competition policy.

While the overall food retailing market had low growth credentials, changes to social structures and lifestyles were providing value-added opportunities that we had identified and exploited. More working women, more people commuting, more people working longer hours and more people eating at different times all added to the fact that convenience, prepared food and associated services had a growing place in people's lives.

Drilling down a little further into the characteristics of the market supports the view that convenience stores are favoured by an ageing population. These are people who do not wish to travel to superstores and have the time and inclination to do small daily shops for newspapers, treats, necessities and mainstream food. The average basket size is £5 per visit compared with £50 for the superstore visit.

For shift workers who return home at different times, the convenience store provides a useful service through access to quick meal solutions, services and impulse purchases. Within this category working women appreciate the convenience store as a means of accessible top-up for food (e.g. meal solutions and milk), services (e.g. phone card or lottery), discretionary spending (e.g. sweets, crisps and drinks), and distress purchases such as toilet rolls and cleaning materials. Interestingly, Sainsbury's even built a convenience store into the body of one of their London superstores to satisfy the demands of the convenience shopper.

The successful C-store can, therefore, be regarded as the fusion of the neighbourhood CTN with its store accessibility and regular footfall, the supermarket one-stop with a core ambient grocery range, and the partial authority of the superstore with its category strength and moves into prepared food.

Therefore we concentrated on exploiting the potential of higher-growth categories such as fresh snack food, soft drinks, bakery and alcoholic drinks while downsizing the space given to the more traditional grocery items such as canned and packaged goods, frozen foods and household products.

We were well aware of the potential extra sales that could be gained by offering a credible range of fresh and chilled food, but the reality of actually achieving it was to prove far more difficult. The disciplines in serving long-life brand-oriented confectionery and tobacco products compared with short-shelf-life chilled and fresh food are very different.

The logistical requirements for chilled food and fresh products with short shelf-life dates are extremely difficult to control at store level. The products have to comply with relatively rigorous food safety and consumer protection regulations and there is the important operational challenge of managing wastage.

Managing waste was a complete nightmare as sales patterns were impossible to predict. One day we would sell out of sandwiches well before the store closed and another day we would sell only half of what was delivered. This resulted in us either disappointing a potential customer, who may not use us again, or losing any profit we may have made by having to dispose of the sandwiches that remained unsold! It really did prove to be the most difficult part of running a C-store and to this day the biggest challenge for any operator is to achieve that balance of wastage versus availability. Too much waste and the store loses money, too little choice and you quickly lose your customers.

A fascinating fact that emerged from one of the many surveys we conducted was that typically over one quarter of sales came from customers who lived within 100 metres of the store and more than 55 per cent of revenue came from people living within a one-quarter-mile radius.

However, the growing appeal of the convenience sector had not gone unnoticed by the superstore operators. We knew it was only a matter of time before they would all join in the new retailing 'gold rush' and then life would become ever more difficult.

Tesco had already put its toe in the water with its Express format opening on a number of Esso sites. Sainsbury's also entered the market in 1997, when the first outlet opened in London's Fulham High Street. Trading as Sainsbury's Local, they had plans to open several hundred stores in the south-east of England. However, unlike Tesco, they did not do the initial detailed work on C-store retailing and, in the face of considerable challenges elsewhere in the company, the plans for Local were massively scaled down.

Beyond the 'big two' there was varied interest in the convenience market. Asda and Wm. Morrison showed little interest in smaller units, with their focus remaining upon the much larger superstores. Safeway had created a similar forecourt joint venture to Tesco, with its association with BP.

We became paranoid that the superstores would sooner or later muscle in on our turf and we began to look around at potential targets that we could acquire before it was too late.

As we approached the new millennium the British food retailing market was estimated to be worth in the region of £100 billion, of which convenience retailing represented between £18 and £20 billion. With over 56,000 C-stores in the year 2000, the C-store market was highly fragmented and split into several compartments. 63 per cent of stores were run by independents, 18 per cent by garage forecourt operators, 12 per cent by symbol group operators, 5 per cent by multiples such as us and 2 per cent by the Co-operative movement.

The independent trade, the backbone of food retailing for the previous 30 years, was in structural decline, with stores closing at the rate of twenty a week or over 1,000 per annum. The reduction down to 35,000 operators was due partly to fewer offspring wishing to follow their parents into the business, and partly to the progress of the more sophisticated competitors, such as us, in taking away market share.

Garage forecourts, with 10,000 sites, were the next largest category and while numbers were in decline, the overall offer and presentation of the remaining sites was visibly improving.

Spar, Londis and Costcutter dominated the symbol groups with roughly 7,000 stores, and this format provided for independent operators to be supplied by and trade under the banner of a trusted brand.

The specialist neighbourhood retail chains such as ours represented about 2,700 stores; the Co-op movement was the smallest with about 1,250 outlets.

While we were happy to pick off individually owner-operated stores on a one-by-one basis, we knew that to expand quickly we needed to make another acquisition, ideally of a similar size to the recently acquired M&W group. Within our trading segment, there was not exactly a massive choice within our field of interest, with the stand-out candidates being Alldays, One-Stop, Day & Nite, Bells and Jacksons. Alldays, with over 600 stores, was far and away the largest group but was sinking fast with over £200 million of debts and, in spite of sales in excess of £500 million per annum, was still losing money. After looking at it closely, we concluded that it was just too big a risk for us to take and something that might bitterly be regretted at a later date.

Our attention turned to a much smaller but better-run outfit called One-Stop. Trading from 218 stores, primarily in the south of England, One-Stop was owned by the Portsmouth & Sunderland

Newspaper Group, which itself was the subject of a takeover approach from the fast-expanding Johnston Press plc. As it happened, the chief executive of Johnston Press was a Wolverhampton man called Tim Bowdler. I had gone to school with Tim and knew the family well. Quite by coincidence his father had been a former director of Alfred Preedy & Sons before we bought it from Next plc in 1989. I phoned Tim and suggested that if they bought the whole company, we would be prepared to do a back-to-back deal and take on the convenience estate in its entirety.

In the event the sale became a little bit of a 'Dutch auction' and we weren't sure which companies were bidding against us. But the more we looked at the quality of the One-Stop estate, the more we liked what we saw. It was a pure convenience group with 218 stores, which also included 97 in-store Post Offices, 151 online lottery terminals, 10 in-store pharmacies, 53 in-store bakeries and 32 ATMs. In other words, the profile of the stores was already well developed along similar lines to our own, and the inclusion of ten pharmacies gave us an introduction into another area of local service that would be important to us in the future.

Another attraction of the proposed acquisition lay in the fact that One-Stop used a third-party contractor to supply all of its stores. However, because we had sufficient spare capacity at our warehouse in Southampton to accommodate the One-Stop distribution requirements, we realised that it would result in an overall dilution in distribution costs. In addition to this, One-Stop would benefit from our buying terms, which were far better due to our overall size.

Obviously the additional turnover would also enhance our ability to negotiate even more favourable group terms with suppliers, resulting in benefits on purchasing, promotions and marketing.

However, as mouth-watering as the deal appeared, we could only go so far on price as we were not prepared to upset our shareholders by growing at any cost. There is always a delicate balance between growing a company so as to benefit from the economies of scale and the risk of getting no further forward by overpaying in the first place. It is also important to be careful that not too much debt is taken onto the balance sheet by the desire just to become bigger and bigger.

Too many companies have gone bankrupt by taking on excessive debt and then being unable to pay the interest charges when rates have increased. We were aware that the acquisition would take our bank borrowings to around £120 million and our interest payments on that debt to £8 million per annum. In the end we considered that £300,000 per store was the maximum we were prepared to offer and we would walk away at any price above that. After heated negotiations that went on well into the night we eventually agreed to pay £67 million: only slightly above our stated maximum.

For some extraordinary reason most of the deals we ever did went on late into the night and always involved teams of lawyers and bankers shuffling between rooms to try to complete the paperwork before it got light. On three separate occasions I stayed up all night as lawyers argued about technical legal details which when finally resolved invariably led to a knock-on banking issue.

In one instance, I had to phone a senior Barclays manager at 4.45am and explain to him that we were supposed to be announcing a deal to the Stock Exchange at 7.30am and that if he didn't sort out the problem, he would not only be losing Barclays' fat fee but as of that morning he would also be losing our company as a client. Needless to say, within ten minutes a problem that had been unsolvable for three hours was suddenly sorted out and with minutes to spare, all the documentation was sent to the Stock Exchange for the 7.30am announcement.

I am convinced that lawyers and bankers try to justify their extraordinary fees by working to incredibly tight time deadlines that

I'm sure in most cases are completely unnecessary. Needless to say, having worked all the previous day and night, rushing back to the hotel for a quick shower and change of clothes wasn't exactly the greatest preparation for a series of meetings to announce to the press and the analysts the finer points and benefits of the deal.

We announced the deal on 31 April 1999 and completed the acquisition on 20 May. Investors certainly seemed to warm to the deal, as our share price jumped from just under £3.00 per share to just over £4.00 per share in the space of three months. Satisfying shareholders, however, is a precarious game at best and a frustrating game at worst. There are basically four elements that combine to make the case for investment in a company: growth prospects, increasing earnings per share, a progressive dividend policy and a strong and well-established management team.

The first element is essential for the long-term viability of a company and as people will always need to eat, we were in a sector that was not susceptible to fashion changes. The bonus for us lay in the fact that the convenience market was growing at a faster rate than the overall food market, so at least the first box was ticked.

Earnings per share are equally important as a measure of success because while a company's profit may double, if the number of shares in issue has also doubled to achieve the growth, then in reality the company has stood still. Over the previous four-year period our earnings per share had grown by over 50 per cent, so again the second box was ticked.

The third element, dividend payment, is also extremely important to fund managers as it represents the financial lifeblood of pensioners in particular, who once retired, need the liquidity of dividends to meet their day-to-day living expenses.

A lot of companies that do not pay dividends are known as growth stocks because hopefully the investors will be rewarded

with long-term capital gain rather than a drip-feed payment
in dividends. Other stocks such as utility companies fall into a
category known as income stocks because they are normally mature
conglomerates that produce a regular, if not growing, profit from
which dividends can be paid.

Because fund managers are greedy they normally like companies
that offer both growth prospects and a progressive dividend
policy. With our earnings per share and dividend payment having
increased by 50 per cent over a four-year period from 1995–99, we
fell into both categories.

Finally our management team was well established with our chief
executive, Jim McCarthy, rated as one of the leading executives in
British retailing. The result of all these favourable factors was that
the investment case for buying shares in our company was fairly
convincing, but nothing in the City ever moves in a straight line and
occasionally it takes something like a takeover to get the share price
moving. The frustrating part then sets in as the greed and fear illness
starts to take root.

It works something like this: because we had announced what
appeared to be an excellent acquisition, the share price rocketed
from £3.00 per share to £4.00 per share as fund managers pushed
up the price by piling into the shares. Then at £4.00 per share most
investors are sitting on a healthy profit, so what do they do? They
sell out before the price starts falling. So in effect, greed takes the
share price up and fear takes the share price down. Eventually the
price finds a level, usually somewhere in between the high and the
low point, and it sits there until a new piece of news sets it off again.
However, on a day-to-day basis most company share prices always tend
to move in step with the sound of the stock market drum.

We were now operating 1,200 stores of which just under 800 were
C-stores. Our pace of expansion was so fast that there was a real

danger that we would trip up along the way. It was now time to batten down the hatches, consolidate what we had, improve the operating margins and then move forward again. As we now had a national chain of C-stores, we thought it was about time to brand them all with an identity that everyone would recognise. We decided to name them One-Stop and all the newsagent stores would remain Dillons. This was really infuriating, as we had only recently finished rebranding the 179 M&W stores to the Dillons format!

We further strengthened the board with the appointment of Chas Lawrence as a non-executive director who had specific experience in logistics and supply chain management. David Crellin decided to retire and we conducted an extensive search for a new group finance director, eventually settling on Dean Moore, who had worked with Alan Lloyd at Lloyds Chemist. I knew Alan personally and phoned him to seek some advice on Dean's appointment. Alan had to pull over into a lay-by as he was in France driving a low-loader down to Le Mans, where he would be participating in the famous 24-hour race. As I wished him luck in the race, he assured me that Dean was a first-class accountant who would do a great job for us.

With record profits certain for 1999 and the acquisition of One-Stop completed, everything looked rosy in the garden for T&S as we were about to enter the new millennium. On a personal level I was very happy with life but had been suffering with stomach pains for a few months and decided to go and see the doctor. He referred me to a specialist who diagnosed irritable bowel syndrome, which he suggested had probably been brought on by the stress of work. He recommended I take it a little easier and gave me some tablets to ease the pain. Unfortunately nothing seemed to work and I asked him whether I could be suffering from a rumbling appendix. He discounted the theory because he said the pain was coming from the wrong place for potential appendicitis.

I continued to go to work and had arranged a trip up to the north-west to see some of the Supercigs stores, in particular one that had recently opened in Barrow-in-Furness. I left home at 6.00am on the Tuesday morning to ensure that I met the field team before the M6 motorway got too busy. I felt lousy but didn't want to let the side down, as it had been a few months since my last visit to the north-west and also Barrow was the only Supercigs store in the whole estate which I had not yet seen.

Barrow is a horrendous place to get to from Wolverhampton but when I eventually arrived I was in a really bad way. By mid-afternoon the pain in my side was so excruciating that I was bent over double in agony, not knowing what to do with myself. I was now convinced that this had to be an appendix problem and I started to be sick on a regular basis. I phoned my specialist and having talked through the symptoms, he said he would have to operate that evening and could I get back as quickly as possible.

I was driven back by one of our area managers with me lying on the back seat of his car clutching my side for most of the way. It was one of the most horrendous journeys of my life, with traffic jam after traffic jam delaying our progress until he eventually got me back to the hospital at about 7.30pm. I was rushed straight to the operating theatre and just couldn't wait to be put to sleep to escape from the terrible pain that I was in. The injection went into my arm and as I waited to drift away into the darkness I began to realise that something had gone horribly wrong. Although I was paralysed by the muscle relaxant that they administer, I was still wide awake as they started to insert tubes down my throat.

From a previous operation, I knew that once they have given you the muscle relaxant it is impossible to move even your little finger. As they prepared to cut me open my mind went into a blind panic at the thought of having my appendix removed without anaesthetic.

I heard the anaesthetist say to the surgeon that my pulse rate had shot up to 180 beats per minute and he couldn't understand why it was happening. For a split second I thought they might examine the equipment and realise that something was amiss. Then I tried desperately to scream as I felt the surgeon's knife cutting into me.

I must have fainted because the next thing I remember was the surgeon saying that it was not surprising that he couldn't find my appendix as it was tucked up the back of the caecum. I had never heard the word caecum before and it was one of the ways I was able to prove after the operation that I had been awake. Then I remember more agonising pain as they started to cut out my appendix. Again I must have fainted because the next thing I remember hearing was the surgeon saying how bad his golf game had become and that he was seriously thinking of packing it up. I continued to drift in and out of consciousness but it probably saved my life as I slowly came to terms with my situation and knew that eventually the operation would be over. I knew that when the muscle relaxant wore off I would get my movement back and I would be able to tell them all of my living nightmare.

Eventually I came round again to the pain of being clamped as the closing stitches went into my body and I knew that the operation was coming to an end. It was the most horrendous feeling lying there unable to breathe or move a muscle and I can only imagine that it must be like drowning without the water actually entering your lungs. Finally as the effects of the muscle relaxant started to wear off I tried to pull the tubes from out of my throat and they had to restrain me on the operating table.

I broke down in tears as I explained that I had been awake throughout the whole operation and they tried to calm me down by saying that it was a common impression for patients to have as they were coming round from anaesthetic. It was only when I related things that had been said by the surgeon during the operation that they started to take me seriously.

Eventually they found the fault that had caused the problem. The top of the cylinder that mixed the gases for the anaesthetic had not been secured after cleaning and had just been placed on top of the cylinder rather than being screwed on tightly. As the operation got under way the anaesthetist must have knocked it slightly, allowing oxygen to be drawn into the machine, which elevated me to a state of consciousness.

It was one of those million to one chances. In fairness the hospital completely owned up to its mistake and did not try to cover it up in any way. For twelve months after the experience I was treated for post-traumatic stress as I regularly woke up reliving the nightmare and being unable to move. Slowly the episodes became less frequent and now it is just a distant memory that rarely bothers me.

Since the operation they have come up with ways of isolating an arm with a tourniquet so that the muscle relaxant drug knocks out the whole body except the arm, and in the event of consciousness the patient would be able to communicate with the operating staff.

CHAPTER 13

Working Day & Nite

Having survived the operating table and with the dawn of a new millennium, I started to become a little more philosophical about life because the years seemed to be slipping by far too quickly.

Although the S in T&S had been retired for ten years, Dave and I remained good friends and so had our respective families. We had bought a villa together on a golf course in Portugal and our wives, Gill and Lorraine, had thoroughly enjoyed being involved in the design and furnishing of the property.

Golf was very much my passion and I was determined to play a little more and also spend some time with my children before they finally flew the nest and embarked upon their own lives. Having acquired my private pilot's licence, I had also bought a small single-engine aeroplane that became my pride and joy. I was incredibly fortunate that Halfpenny Green Airport was only fifteen minutes away from my home and therefore easily accessible. This was really useful because with flying being so weather-dependent, it meant that I could make a decision to go flying on the spur of the moment and twenty minutes later be airborne over the wonderful Shropshire landscape.

With golf, flying, the villa and my non-executive role at the

A corporate golf day with 'Monty' and Jimmy Tarbuck.

building society, as well as my normal duties at T&S all vying for diary space, I was incredibly reliant on my secretary, Rita Britton, to organise my affairs. Rita had been with me for fifteen years and had a wonderfully calming demeanour, which meant she got things in perspective very quickly and, regardless of how much was going on, she never seemed to get flustered. With her soft Scottish accent she could be charming yet firm and, if I needed to see people urgently, she always seemed to be able to organise other people's diaries and find me a slot.

On one occasion she stepped in at exactly the right moment of a very difficult situation. I used to try to meet at least one major supplier each week, either with the buying director Geoff Purdy, or just on my own. On this particular day I was meeting a gentleman called Andrew Brownsword, who owned an up-and-coming company that manufactured quirky, modern, humorous greetings cards. The cards sold well in the stores where we had them and I was anxious to extend the distribution to all the stores where we had sufficient space to display them.

However, Andrew was quite a feisty gentleman and was determined to run the account to suit him rather than us. He was also not prepared to improve our buying terms even though our sales had doubled over the previous year. I decided that a face-to-face meeting was the only way we were going to settle our differences and invited him along to a meeting at Brownhills to discuss the issues.

Rita went down to reception to meet him and bring him up to my office. There was immediate friction between us as I sensed that he was determined to be top dog from the outset. The atmosphere remained cordial for a few minutes as he opened up his briefcase and showed me a new range of cards that was about to go into production.

He then turned to me and, in a very arrogant manner, explained that his company worked on the principle of the 'three Ps'. First, price was not negotiable and we would have to pay the list price regardless of whether we had one shop or a thousand. Second, payment for goods had to be on time otherwise penalties would apply. Finally, proximity of other card shops he was supplying would determine whether we qualified for distribution.

I sat there with my mouth open wide and suggested that I felt very privileged to have been supplied by him in the first place. He looked me straight between the eyes and repeated that those were his terms of business and if I wasn't happy, well tough.

After a few seconds' reflection I told him that we also operated on a principle of 'three Ps' but ours were slightly different from his. First, pretend you didn't come; second, pack up all your stuff; and third, p**s off!

Rita, who had seen the drama slowly unfold, knew me well enough to intervene. She opened the door and in her soft Scottish lilt told Mr Brownsword that the meeting was now over and that she would show him the way out. It was brilliant timing and within seconds he had indeed packed up his belongings and p****d off!

Rita never called me Kevin and in all the time she worked for me it was always Mr Threlfall. When she returned to the office she just smiled and said, 'I hope you didn't mind me intervening, Mr T, but I thought it was time for him to leave.' By now my blood had stopped boiling and I just smiled back and thought how priceless she was.

In fairness to Mr Brownsword he did go on to build a very successful company that he eventually sold for a lot of money. He managed to exist quite well without us, but we also managed to exist quite well without him.

Life at T&S was becoming far more complex and we invested heavily in systems within the business as it continued to grow. In March 2000 we embarked on installing EPOS into our C-store estate and by Christmas all 800 stores were up and running with the new technology. This was a massive step forward for the business, as scanning every product at the checkout resulted in our management receiving actual sales data at the touch of a button. It allowed our buyers to understand data on sales patterns and stock availability that was not previously accessible to them.

Altogether we invested £23 million into modernising and improving sales data capture, supply chain efficiency, financial control and payroll. Indeed supply chain became so important to us that in October 2000 we appointed Stuart Ross to the main board as group supply chain director as distinct from Tim Gordon's role as group distribution director.

In just 25 years the world had changed dramatically and it didn't seem that long ago that the checkout girls at Lo-Cost had remembered the price of all the goods and replenishment was just a basic manual order system.

Over the previous three years we had added over 400 C-stores to our estate with the acquisitions of M&W and One-Stop, but there was one more store group that we had in our sights. Day & Nite was a Preston-based C-store chain with 100 stores operating in the north of the country. Its two owners, Frank Heald and Frank Dee, had built up the business over a number of years. The Dee family was well known to me, as Frank's father had built up a chain of discount stores called Dee Discount that was a very similar operation to my own Lo-Cost Discount chain.

The two Franks were very aware of how well their business would fit in with ours and were therefore very much in the driving seat as far as negotiations were concerned.

Discussions continued for a few months, with Jonathan Grassi of CCF Charterhouse Corporate Finance acting as the go-between. Obviously it was published knowledge that we had paid around £300,000 per store for the One-Stop acquisition and unfortunately this then became the benchmark for subsequent negotiations. £30 million, therefore, became the asking price, but as the company carried £5 million worth of debt we were only prepared to pay £25 million because we obviously had to take on the debt as well.

As negotiations reached something of a stalemate, I happened to be in London one night when I received a call from Frank Dee. I was in a restaurant with our chief executive, Jim McCarthy, just about to start my meal when the call came through and, anxious for privacy, I locked myself in the disabled toilet and started to discuss the sticking points of the deal with Frank.

I was a smoker in those days and as we got closer and closer to a deal I got through more and more cigarettes without realising that I was in a completely enclosed space and slowly but surely suffocating myself to death. Finally, about two hours and fifteen cigarettes later, I emerged from the toilet with a huge cloud of smoke following me out. I had missed my meal and the restaurant was about to close, so I suggested to Jim that we go to a bar for a drink to celebrate because we had finally reached an agreement. I was never happier than when I was doing deals, and was certainly not in need of yet another meal.

It would never have been so much fun if everything had gone our way, but it rarely did and the cut and thrust of negotiation and the adrenalin rush that went with it was fantastic. I never saw myself as a man manager, I was far too impatient for that and there were elements of the business that bored me to death. Obviously as the company grew I had to get involved with all sorts of things like nomination and remuneration committees, health and safety, pensions, risk analysis and disaster recovery plans, but I tried to delegate as much of the boring stuff as I could. However, I was aware that a lot of the detail came with the territory and by this time I was being paid very well so I couldn't moan too much about having to do a few of the more mundane jobs.

As our main warehouse and office accommodation in Brownhills became stretched, we were fortunate enough to acquire another 50,000-square-foot site directly opposite our existing premises. The site included much-needed office space which then became our dedicated IT and accounts department. With the Day & Nite Stores serviced from a 55,000-square-foot warehouse in Blackburn, we now had balanced distribution facilities in Lancashire, the West Midlands and Hampshire. With spare capacity within the Blackburn warehouse to service an additional 200 C-stores and a similar amount out of the new Brownhills depot, we now had sufficient storage space for the foreseeable future.

Frank Dee was a great retailer with years of experience in the trade and we were very grateful that he agreed to undertake the role of interim group retail operations director when Graham Maguire left us to join the ailing Kwik Save group as managing director in September 2000. Melvin Kenyon, our group IS director, also left at the same time and his role was absorbed into the group finance function headed up by Dean Moore.

In March 2001 we reported our seventh consecutive year of earnings growth and with profit contribution from our C-store estate approaching 90 per cent of the group total, our transformation from a newsagents and discount tobacconist to a national C-store operation was virtually complete. We now operated 890 C-stores of which over 500 had been added in the previous four years with the acquisitions of M&W, One-Stop and Day & Nite. It was now a matter of pausing for breath and improving the quality and efficiency of the retail operations, supply chain and the back office systems, while at the same time reducing our debt levels.

Having rebranded all 890 stores with the One-Stop fascia, we now set about refurbishing some of the older and more tired-looking stores. By analysing sales trends in individual stores we were able to establish which product groups were selling well and use that information to refit the store accordingly. It was not exactly rocket science, but then business decisions rarely are.

Supply chain management took on greater significance and by April 2001 we had completed the integration of the Day & Nite warehousing, distribution and management process. We also rebalanced the distribution network with Darwen. The Darwen depot

News

T&S SWALLOWS ONE STOP

One Stop's fascia is set to dominate the c-store sector in England and Wales after T&S bought the company for £66m.

Hours after the deal T&S chairman Kevin Threlfall told *C-Store* all T&S's Dillons c-stores would be converted over to the One Stop fascia within a year.

This would produce around 800 One Stop stores, reinforcing T&S's position as the biggest operator of company owned c-stores.

Commenting on the decision to sell by One Stop's parent, Portsmouth & Sunderland Newspapers, an elated Threlfall said: "You need a bit of luck in business, and this is where we had it. The timing of this for us was almost perfect."

He explained that while the company's nearest rivals were out of the running – "Alldays is struggling and Forbuoys has its hands full with Martins" – T&S had

recently completed the two-year integration of 180 M&W stores into its business and was primed for growth.

He said the businesses were a perfect fit with only three competing stores, and T&S will be able to service the majority of One Stop's 220 stores from its depot in Nursling, Hampshire, which has excess capacity.

Managing director Jim McCarthy said T&S had proven integration skills and a track record of extracting extra value.

He said M&W's stores were making a one per cent net margin when T&S took them over and this was now 5.4 per cent and the T&S average of 6.3 per cent was attainable.

He said that through economies of scale and greater purchasing power One Stop's three per cent net margin would also be driven up.

He said the business would have an annual turnover in

Threlfall: elated at deal

excess of £800m and more than 80 per cent of its 1,200 stores would be c-stores by the year-end.

McCarthy said the deal represented three years growth in one go, but T&S would not pause for breath.

He forecast T&S would open 50 stores this year, 50 the next and 75 the year after.

One Stop's estate comprises 218 stores, including 97 in-store post offices, mainly in the South of England.

All convenience stores were rebranded to the One-Stop fascia.

came with the acquisition of Day & Nite, servicing the northern One-Stop stores more economically. Sales improved as we started delivering products based on actual store sales that were captured through the EPOS system. Depending on weather forecasts we could flex the algorithm's calculation to take into account potential sales increases on products such as soft drinks and ice cream.

In conjunction with the network rebalancing, we also increased the delivery frequency to the majority of our One-Stop stores. This not only improved product availability for our customers, it also had the effect of reducing stock levels in store, which improved our cash flow and reduced debt levels. With the acquisition of Day & Nite our overall debt had increased to £127 million and interest paid on that debt in the year 2000 amounted to just over £10 million.

This was now a very significant figure, but by lowering stock levels and ensuring careful capital expenditure we managed to reduce our debt level down to £114 million by the end of 2001.

I felt very guilty that we had stopped investing in the Supercigs estate and the legacy Dillons newsagents. Together they were still contributing about £5 million per annum to profits, but we were slowly selling off the smaller newsagents and also for the first time starting to close underperforming Supercigs stores. The relentless increase in tobacco duty was finally having a marked effect on the sale of cigarettes and with fewer customers visiting our stores, our sales of confectionery, for the first time ever, started to decline.

When we had opened our first kiosk in 1975, the number of cigarettes sold in the UK was approximately 125 billion sticks per year. By the year 2000 the market had dropped to about 80 billion sticks and we had effectively lost one third of our customers. For 25 years we had made money out of selling cigarettes but with ever-declining sales and ever-increasing costs of employment, shop rent and rates, there could only be one result.

Retailing doesn't seem to change much on a day-to-day basis but over a period of time different store names come and go. Kwik Save, which had grown rapidly during the 1970s and 1980s, was now in terminal decline and, although it had grown to a national chain of over 800 stores, was soon to disappear from the retail landscape altogether. The Body Shop had also grown quickly but was now going out of fashion and even the mighty and ever-present Woolworths chain was beginning to lose its appeal. In only a few years' time it would also dramatically disappear from the retail scene.

We were aware that it was only a matter of time before One-Stop became our sole retailing brand and we considered changing the name from T&S Stores plc to One-Stop plc. From a stock market perspective it made a lot of sense to change the name because we got fed up with being known as the T&Who Group. In the end we decided that we would change the name, but only after we had finally disposed of Dillons and Supercigs.

I still thoroughly enjoyed visiting the stores, not only to check on our standards but also to talk to our customers and get their views on what we could do better. Talking to customers and learning from them is the most important retail lesson any entrepreneur can ever learn. I have a piece of rock in my office that I obtained on a retail study tour of the United States and it sums up retailing beautifully. It is from the famous Stew Leonard store and it states their store policy. Rule 1: The customer is always right. Rule 2: If the customer is ever wrong, reread Rule 1.

With our stores scattered the length and breadth of the country, we normally stayed overnight and had dinner with the respective area managers to discuss any relevant issues. Paul Mildenstein had joined the company as group retail director and before this we were very grateful to Frank Dee for stepping in while we searched for the right candidate. Paul was like a breath of fresh air; young, ambitious and, in no time at all, he had made his mark on store standards and financial performance. Stuart Ross, on the other hand, had left the business to join Tesco without really being with us long enough to make any impact on our supply chain.

Every year Gill and I took the kids to Blackpool to see the lights around the beginning of November and 2001 was no exception. I had fallen in love with the famous seaside resort as a child because for many years our annual family holiday was spent there and, although I was always travel sick on the long journey before the M6 was built, I had some great memories of the place. For the first few annual holidays we stayed in boarding houses but when we graduated to the Cliffs Hotel, it was like staying in a massive castle. This year I had booked us into the Imperial Hotel and managed to get the suite that Margaret Thatcher stayed in on the annual Conservative party conference. We decided to travel up on the Friday, returning home Sunday afternoon. Day & Nite had owned a few stores in Blackpool and I was anxious to see how the refits to One-Stop had turned out, so I dragged the kids around the stores introducing myself to the managers along the way. Gill was used to me doing this but on this particular day, after such a long journey, she was a little irritated as she just wanted to get the kids settled into the hotel.

The following morning we decided to walk to the famous Pleasure Beach through the town centre. We had a small Supercigs store in a really busy location that we had owned for a number of years and I told Gill that I had to pop in just to make sure everything was OK. As we approached the store I was horrified to see a queue building up outside the store and only one till out of three in operation. There was a busker outside with his dog and I commented to Gill that he was probably making more money than we were.

With people walking away from the queue in frustration I was none too pleased and asked the manageress why there was only one

Day & Nite sold for £25m

Day & Nite: 100 stores to be rebranded One Stop

DAY & NITE, the UK's largest privately-owned chain of convenience stores, has been sold to the T&S Stores group for £25.5m.

The 98 Day & Nite stores, and two others which are under construction, will be rebranded with T&S's One Stop fascia over the next few months.

Frank Dee and Frank Heald, who each owned 40% of Day & Nite, are expected to remain with the business in a consultative role.

Heald described T&S as "the most successful player in the market".

The acquisition, which gives T&S a strong presence in Yorkshire and Lancashire, building on its strengths in the Midlands and southern England, takes the total number of One Stop convenience stores to more than 900.

James McCarthy, chief executive of T&S Stores, said Day & Nite was "very complementary" to the group and would make a significant contribution to its development.

"They are stronger in grocery than we are, and we can learn from that, and their average sales per outlet are also some £2,000-£3,000 a week more than ours," he said.

"On the other hand One Stop is stronger in news, and we can transfer some of that benefit to Day & Nite," he added.

Day & Nite's central warehouse in Blackburn will be integrated with T&S's distribution facilities at Brownhills and Southampton.

Expanding up north with the Day & Nite acquisition.

till in operation. She told me that her two assistants had failed to turn up and she was having to run the shop on her own. Introducing myself I asked her why she hadn't phoned her area manager to get some help, and she replied that she hadn't had a f*****g chance since opening the shop.

With this, she promptly picked up her coat, threw the keys at me and walked out of the shop! There was no way I was going to close the store on a busy Saturday morning and, opening up another till, Gill and I got to work and put the kids in the storeroom. Eventually, after thinning out the queue, I managed to get through to the area manager, who was in our Preston store, and two hours later he arrived with an assistant to relieve us. Gill had worked in Supercigs shops for a time just before we were married and was quite at home working her till.

We laughed about it as I treated everyone to Harry Ramsden's famous fish and chips, but we weren't too happy later in the afternoon when the kids were sick at the Pleasure Beach after eating too many sweets and too many chips.

I know how to treat my family to a great weekend!

– CHAPTER 14 –

Over and Out

2001 turned out to be our eighth record year in succession, with sales exceeding £1 billion for the first time and operating profits approaching £50 million. We were in great shape, but over the Christmas break my mind had started to wander and I was beginning to have a number of negative thoughts. We were not affected by the appalling attack on the Twin Towers in New York in September 2011, though many other businesses were.

On 11 September 2001, which became known as 9/11 (the telephone number used for emergencies in the USA, a coincidence certainly appreciated by the perpetrators of the attacks) the world was stunned when at 9.00am Eastern Standard Time a passenger airliner was flown into one of the Twin Towers in downtown Manhattan, New York. A few may have thought it was an accident but when, 40 minutes later, another airliner was flown into the second tower, no one was under any illusion that these were anything but deliberate attacks. This realisation was reinforced when another aircraft was flown into the Pentagon in Washington, and finally when a fourth aircraft crashed in Pennsylvania, killing all those on board.

Two and a half hours that changed the history of the world:

7.59am   Mohamed Atta departs on AA Flight 11, which under his
           control will crash into the World Trade Center
8.18am   AA Flight 11 is taken over by Mohamed Atta and other
           hijackers
8.46am   American Airlines Flight 11 crashes into the World Trade
           Center north tower
9.03am   United Airlines Flight 175 crashes into the World Trade
           Center south tower
9.37am   American Airlines Flight 77 crashes into the Pentagon
9.59am   South tower of World Trade Center collapses
10.03am   United Airlines Flight 93 crashes into a farm in
           Shanksville, Pennsylvania
10.28am   North tower of World Trade Center collapses

The mighty USA was under attack on its home soil, the first time
since the Japanese attack on Pearl Harbor in December 1941. The
president, George W. Bush, was visiting a school in Florida at the
time, and was quickly bundled into the presidential aircraft and
flown around while it could be ascertained how serious the situation
was and whether any more attacks were likely. Needless to say, all
other aircraft throughout the USA were grounded.

In the very short term, the effects for business were little short of
calamitous. Everyone seemed to freeze. The truth was that there was
a mild recession in place anyway. The so-called dotcom bubble had
burst the previous year, after any company involved with the internet
had seen its shares rise to ridiculous and, with hindsight, clearly
unsustainable heights.

The general economic situation was further damaged when
Enron, the huge energy, commodities and services conglomerate,

became the biggest chapter 11 bankruptcy in American history in December 2001. The knock-on effects were considerable. For example, it virtually caused the collapse of Arthur Andersen, one of the world's leading accountancy firms. The firm was found guilty of obstruction of justice for destroying documents relating to the Enron audit and, as a result, because the US Securities and Exchange Commission could not accept audits from convicted felons, Arthur Andersen was forced to stop auditing public companies.

My major concern was that having acquired our principal competitors, the remaining groups were becoming far too expensive to even consider. Unfortunately we had raised the bar and with prices for individual stores rising all the time, we had become the victims of our own success.

The only other group of substantial size was a company called Alldays, which had 633 stores across the country but was losing money and had debts of almost £200 million. There was absolutely no way we were going to become involved with a company that had so many problems.

Our capital expenditure had risen as a result both of having spent £23 million on modernising internal systems and of a continual demand to improve store standards, and our company debt was now £114 million. While this was manageable, it was going to put pressure on our future plans as we tried to balance expenditure with a desire to bring our debt levels back under £100 million.

I was also concerned that over the next few years we would have to dispose of Supercigs and also Dillons newsagents. While both were still profitable, our future lay in pure C-store retailing and we knew that One-Stop plc would resonate more logically with our shareholders in future. Unfortunately, it also meant that we would have to make up £5–6 million profit from new stores just to stand still.

However, my biggest concern lay in the fact that the major

supermarket companies were now taking the sector very seriously and were all looking at ways to enter the market that was growing every year. In 2002 the British food retailing market was estimated to be worth £100 billion, of which the convenience sector had grown to be worth between £15 and 20 billion. The sheer size of it, coupled with the growth prospects, could no longer be ignored by the big boys.

Tesco had entered the market through its forecourt association with Esso and in 2002 was trading from 75 Tesco Express stores with a further 50 to open in the coming year. Jim McCarthy, our chief executive, and I went to visit a recently opened store in Wednesfield in the West Midlands and were frightened to death by what we saw.

Not only was the store extremely busy, it was way ahead of anything we could offer our customers. We immediately recognised that Tesco as a competitor in neighbourhood markets would be a major challenge, especially with its world-renowned prepared food offer and broader range. In fact, to put it in a nutshell, they would wipe the floor with us.

Although with our newsagents' background we were probably stronger than Tesco in product groups such as news, confectionery and greetings cards, we were way behind them in product groups such as chilled, fresh and ready meals.

These were the real growth areas of the convenience sector and whoever could offer an acceptable range on a consistent basis would lead the way. For years we had experimented with different suppliers but we always ended up losing the battle with either too much stock, which we then had to throw away, or too little stock to satisfy the local demand.

Now suddenly, in all its pomp and splendour, Tesco was doing what we had been trying to do for years and succeeding. It sent a shiver down my spine as I realised it was probably going to take us years, if ever, to achieve the same standards.

Sainsbury's Local also had an estate of about 50 stores located primarily in London and the home counties. The standards were as good as Tesco Express and while we knew that they would probably concentrate on their heartland for the next few years, eventually they could also become serious competitors if and when they expanded their horizons.

Safeway had also entered the convenience market in a joint venture with BP and traded from 51 sites. It also had an additional 179 petrol filling stations, most of which contained convenience outlets.

It was only a matter of time before all the major supermarkets became involved and we would be caught in the crossfire. Timing is everything in business and the more I thought about it, the more I kept thinking the unthinkable: maybe it was time to get out.

We were one of the top 250 PLC companies in the UK with a great track record, thousands of employees and a lot of satisfied shareholders. I did not want to jeopardise everything we had done by just carrying on regardless and trying to ignore what was likely to happen in the future.

We had been a public company for eighteen years and I was immensely proud of what we had achieved for our employees and shareholders alike. We had to do the right thing for them going forward and I could see that a tie-up between Tesco and ourselves had considerable merit for both parties. In fact, the more I thought about it the more convinced I became that it was the right thing to do.

After a long board meeting in January 2002 and agreement from my fellow directors I decided to write to Sir Terry Leahy, chief executive of Tesco. In my letter I hinted at what was on my mind:

> As eating habits have changed, fresh and chilled products have become massive areas of opportunity for the convenience market. There are, however, logistical problems of supplying small

quantities of pre-packed meal solutions, chilled and fresh products on a daily basis. It is this area that will differentiate and determine the success of C-store retailers going forward. For us to achieve a 'Brand' status, we must become a destination store rather than a desperation store. The prize for achieving this goal would be domination of neighbourhood retailing for years to come.

The following month I drove down to Tesco's head office in Cheshunt to meet Sir Terry and we both agreed the idea was worth pursuing. While Tesco analysed our store portfolio, it was vitally important that it remained secret and we decided that any future meetings would not be anywhere near Cheshunt.

The biggest concern that emerged from the potential deal was that it may be referred to the Competition Commission on the basis that the Office of Fair Trading (OFT) would have to decide whether the small-store grocery market should be viewed completely separately from the 'big shop', or whether they were viewed as being part of the same market.

Throughout the summer Tesco continued to review our stores and I had a further meeting with Sir Terry, who had now assembled a team that included group corporate affairs director Lucy Neville-Rolfe to ensure that there were no problems likely to occur with the Competition Commission.

It was remarkable that both sides had managed to keep the whole thing under wraps, but as October approached a few rumours were starting to circulate that our two companies were in talks with each other. Sir Terry finally phoned me and said that provided we could agree on a price that suited both companies, he felt that there was a deal to be done.

I drove down to Hertfordshire, where we met in a hotel and we started off by talking about our respective football clubs. Sir Terry

Billion pound T&S

T&S Stores has affirmed its place in the premier league of c-stores by announcing a year of record growth and sales that stormed through £1bn for the first time.

Like for like sales increased by 5% – up 2% on the first half – with no adverse impact on gross margin. In the year to December 29, pre-tax profits after exceptional costs (primarily integrating Day & Nite into the group), were 12% ahead at £35m. The results were ahead of analysts' predictions and marked the eight successive year of growth for the company.

New in-store concepts are being trialled at One Stop

Chief executive Jim McCarthy told *C-Store* he was very pleased with the results when set against the current trading environment which he described as "very competitive", citing a 'three for a fiver' deal on Easter eggs currently on offer at Tesco and Asda.

"The consumer wants more for less all the time," he said.

In addition to supply chain efficiencies and benefits from the installation of epos across the entire estate, McCarthy attributed growth to stronger consumer deals, better stock turn, range and supplier ratio-nalisation and a stricter adherence to promotions at store level.

One Stop contributed £40m of operating profits through 870 stores, outperforming the market in chilled, alcohol and impulse ranges.

However, McCarthy stressed the group still needed to see better replenishment levels from its direct to store deliveries – currently tracking 10 points behind deliveries from its own RDCs – as a key dynamic in a new three year plan. The plan includes opening "at least" 100 new stores via organic growth and a major store refurbishment programme based on the results of a current trial testing out new product ranges, layouts and pricing architecture.

During the year, the group shed 20 non-core newsagents and high street discount stores and opened 18 One Stop stores. Fifty One Stop outlets were refurbished.

At the results it was announced that group supply chain director Stuart Ross had left the group to become distribution director at Tesco.

Breaking through the £1 billion turnover figure.

---

was a lifelong Everton fan and I was a lifelong Wolverhampton Wanderers fan. Unfortunately although Wolves had been one of the most famous football clubs in the world in the 1950s, we now languished in the division below the Premiership and were no match for the ever-consistent Everton.

We danced around the ring for a while before we got down to the real nitty gritty of discussing the price Tesco were prepared to pay for our business. In most PLC takeovers a 30–40 per cent premium to the share price is the average that is paid. This was complicated by the fact that our share price had enjoyed a good run in the previous few months and this had to be taken into consideration.

In the end we agreed on a deal that represented a premium of 36.3 per cent over the average closing price for the 90 dealing days prior to the announcement. Including debt Tesco was paying around £530 million for our business. It was a fair deal to both sets of shareholders as we had received a good price but by the same token Tesco had not overpaid for a business that slotted in beautifully with its future strategy. As the issue of 2.2414 new Tesco shares was satisfying the purchase for each T&S share, the price they were paying varied with how much the Tesco share price fluctuated from day to day.

It was also good for customers and, importantly for me, was great for all our T&S staff. There were to be no wholesale redundancies as Tesco intended to run our business as a separate entity.

The deal was announced on 30 October 2002 to a snowstorm of press coverage as it came as a big surprise to the City. By and large

Hitting the headlines: front-page news in the *Financial Times*.

the national press thought that it was a good deal for both parties but needless to say there was a lot of coverage that focused on Tesco breaking into another sector previously dominated by independent retailers.

The influential *Financial Times* opened its article as follows:

> Britain's monster food retailer yesterday stormed its way into the neighbourhood market, stealing a march on rivals who had been counting on growth in convenience retailing to revive flagging sales.

I came in for comment as the 'Rags to Riches' story, or as the *Sun* newspaper put it 'Fags to Riches'. The press like nothing better than a tale of a barrow-boy come good, which was fine except for the fact that a hideous picture of me aged 23 had been dug up from somewhere and put into print. When I spoke to Sir Terry on the day of the announcement, with his Liverpool wit he suggested I use some of my money to buy up the negatives!

Amazingly it was the second major deal announced in the convenience sector that week, as on the Monday the Co-operative Group had bought the loss-making 600-store chain of Alldays for £131 million. It was amazing to think that in just one week, the ownership of nearly 2,000 stores had changed hands.

I felt absolutely shattered on the day of the announcement, as I had worked through the night with our financial advisers, Rothschilds, to ensure the deal went through and also to safeguard the interests of my fellow directors and staff.

I had been incredibly lucky to work with some exceptional lawyers in my career: first John Wardle and David Owen at Edge & Ellison and then Chris Rawstron and Russell Orme at DLA. It was John Wardle who had marched me out of the offices of Gallaher's lawyers when we were a signature away from selling out, and it was Chris Rawstron who walked me through all the detail involved when selling out to Tesco.

Chris was a proper Yorkshire lad who called a spade a shovel and was a brilliant lawyer. Whenever we were in meetings I always felt sorry for the other party's lawyer, as Chris always seemed to get the upper hand in terms of presence and charisma. It was like having a Rottweiler by your side, knowing he would only bite if he had to! Russell Orme on the other hand was pure silk and smoothness, but their good cop, bad cop double act made them a formidable force and I was very grateful to them for looking after T&S's interests so well over the years.

Tesco had committed to keep our customer and distribution centre in Brownhills open and retain the 1,000 staff based there on their current employment contracts. They had decided that about half of our 862 C-stores would convert to their Tesco Express format and this would be put into effect over a three- to four-year time span. The remaining C-stores would continue to trade as One-Stop, and this would be set up as a separate company with its head office in Brownhills. It was also decided that as soon as possible the Dillons newsagents chain and the Supercigs discount tobacco shops would be sold.

The only remaining concern was whether any regulatory action, such as referring the bid to the Competition Commission, was required. The proposed takeover would raise Tesco's share of the C-store market from 1.2 per cent to 4.6 per cent by value. The Office of Fair Trading (OFT) invited submissions from the trade about Tesco's bid until 13 November. After that the OFT had a further fortnight to consider whether or not regulatory action was required.

At the end of November I received a phone call from a very excited Lucy Neville-Rolfe at Tesco to tell me that the trade and industry secretary Patricia Hewitt had decided not to refer the purchase of T&S to the Competition Commission and we had now cleared all the necessary regulatory hurdles.

I had a lot of people to thank and December was spent visiting stores and organising parties. We had a wonderful celebration for all the directors of T&S at Le Manoir in Oxford on 10 January 2003, followed by a party at the Savoy on 6 February to thank all our major shareholders, brokers and analysts for their support over the years.

In June 2000 I had been presented with the Central Region National Consumer Products and Services Entrepreneur of the Year Award in a contest run by Ernst & Young. When I got through to the national final in October, a lot of fund managers who owned T&S shares came along to support me. I was staggered to be announced as the winner, especially given the fact that the previous year's winner, Steve Smith of Poundland fame, also came from Wolverhampton!

Those same investors who had supported me that night had owned T&S shares since the 1980s and I thanked the likes of Brian Stillwell, Habib Annous, Iain Scotland and Alan Sippets for sticking with us through thick and thin.

Turning to the analysts I commented that I thought the retail sector was blessed with huge talent and I thanked the likes of Clive Black, Jeremy Hilditch, John Dickinson and David Stoddart for all the articles they had written about T&S over the years, most of which I had to say were very favourable.

I finished my speech as follows:

Well finally, I would like to thank you all for coming. Over these last 18 years I have made some good friends. I've been involved in 10 acquisitions, about 40 analysts' presentations and around 500 institutional one-to-ones, so I think I can honestly say that I have served my time.

Receiving Entrepreneur of the Year Award from Steve Smith of Poundland.

I am sure you will be relieved to know that you have seen the last of me as a lifetime of say 75 years only allows one such story as this. T&S has occupied half my life to date and I just feel so lucky that for the most part, it has been rewarding, a lot of fun and most importantly, successful.

Not many people get the opportunity to start a dream on a market stall and sell their company for over £0.5 billion some 27 years later. I'm sure you will not resent me a moment of pride in saying that we not only built a great company but we also sold it to a great company and I genuinely hope that Tesco can take our business forward and apply their sort of magic to our retail formula.

As for me, well I can assure you that I will not be making a bid

for Safeway at the age of 70. I intend to enjoy every one of my
remaining days. But in my dotage, I shall always look back on the
halcyon days of T&S with great affection. And I shall never forget
that the success was a team event, a success that was not just down
to the people in this room but also down to the thousands of
unsung heroes within the business from the order pickers to the
till operators.

It has been a wonderful journey and I am so glad that we
travelled it together.

On Valentine's Day, at our expense, Gill and I flew our chief
executive, Jim McCarthy, and his wife, Rosemary, to Paris for the
weekend. We had a fabulous time but I have to say not one of us really
understood why the French got so excited about truffles. However, we
did get far too excited about the wine and suffered horribly on the
flight back to Birmingham.

Jim and I had worked together since 1989 and although he had not
been given any assurances about his own future, it did not colour his
view that we had done the right thing for our shareholders. We had
spent thousands of hours together either in meetings, in cars or in
the stores and we had been fortunate enough to agree on most things
along the way. But what I will always remember is how much fun we
had and how much laughing we did.

There were now just two more celebrations and on 19 March we
enjoyed a wonderful evening at the Hotel du Vin in Birmingham
with Robert Leitao and his team at Rothschild. Rothschild had acted
as sole financial advisor to the board and had successfully walked us
through the minefield of completing the deal.

The icing on the cake was an evening hosted by Sir Terry
Leahy and his team at Claridges in London on 31 March. It was a
wonderful night and a stylish end to what had started over a year

before when I had driven down to Cheshunt to meet Sir Terry for the first time.

Colin Holmes, one of the young rising stars at Tesco, had taken over as chief executive and I decided it was time for me to move aside and let him do his job. I could not stand the thought of saying goodbye to everyone at T&S and knew that it would be better to go quietly. So, without telling anyone, I set my last date as Thursday, 3 April.

I had just one more thing to do.

As I prepared to leave I called Rita down to the car park. She had been with me for eighteen years and deserved something special for

Business partner and lifelong friend Dave, the 'S' in T&S.

putting up with me for so long. I put my arms around her and gave her the keys to a new Peugeot, a car she had always wanted. It was a very emotional end to a relationship that had stood the test of time and had made my life a lot easier.

As I drove away for the last time I looked in my driver's mirror and saw the two massive aluminium letters of T&S on the side of the building. As they slowly drifted away I reflected on how the business had started as a friendship between two ordinary lads in the pub called Threlfall and Smith.

Although Dave had been retired from the business for many years we had remained great friends. I felt immensely proud of those

Dave, Lorraine, Gill and I enjoying a drink together.

two letters because they represented not only what we had achieved as a business but, equally important, what we had achieved as a friendship.

– CHAPTER 15 –

Up the Creek Without a Paddle

I am often asked how I came to be involved in narrowboats, a question to which there is no short or simple answer. However, the origins of my involvement go back decades. It should be recognised that the 1970s had been a period of political and economic upheaval, the governments of both main parties having experimented with various ill-thought-out policies that fuelled a decade of rampant inflation and penal taxation rates. By the mid-1980s the taxation system had received a radical overhaul that, among many things, dispensed with surtax and the investment income surcharge that could, for some taxpayers, result in a rate of tax on top-slice income that was greater than 100 per cent. By the late 1980s the higher rate of income tax was down to 60 per cent, but capital gains tax had been introduced at 30 per cent.

Our accountants back in those days were a Birmingham firm called Farmiloe & Co, the senior partner of which was a wonderful gentleman called Stan Farmiloe, who had been a Spitfire fighter pilot in the Second World War. It was quite difficult to deal with him on the phone as he was as deaf as a post like so many fighter pilots after the war, because of the continual atmospheric pressure changes that had to be suffered from rapid climbing and descending during aerial dogfights.

Stan had a long-held belief that he should work to minimise his clients' tax bills and in fact he hated the taxman so much that he spent hour after hour, day after day trying to dream up schemes that would reduce the payment of tax and it became an obsession with him. In conjunction with a friend of his, a partner in a Birmingham law practice, they devised a scheme that allowed their clients to invest in various businesses and, by taking advantage of prevailing tax legislation, mitigate or defer their tax liabilities. In reality I didn't want anything to do with it at first because I liked to keep everything as simple as possible and these schemes sounded far too fancy and complex for me.

The business model for the scheme was a narrowboat company, Boats Centres Ltd, that owned three inland marinas plus a boat-manufacturing subsidiary. The clients would register as a new business and then acquire a number of narrowboats funded by leases or bank borrowings. Boat Centres would build the boats, manage them and hire them out for holidays for a percentage of the income generated. The accountant and lawyer retained a captive audience of clients for whom they could now also charge fees for helping to operate the scheme. The costs of buying the boats were allowable against tax using whatever reliefs were currently available; these would change over time. The short-term result would be tax losses, generated in the trade, that the client could offset against their earlier years' higher rate tax paid. The main benefit, however, was that after a few years the boats would be sold and new replacements bought. The way the tax system worked meant that the sale would generate a capital profit. The result was that trading losses received relief at 60 per cent and the capital gain was charged at 30 per cent.

This seemed a magical system of converting income into capital while at the same time halving one's tax bill and also deferring the payment for a few years. In the end the logic of what Stan was saying was too good to ignore and after I heard that my own bank manager had bought a couple of boats that was good enough for me. So I, along with a number of my colleagues, became involved as well and I bought three boats.

But as we all know, perpetual motion does not exist. Boat Centres was majority-owned by the accountant and lawyer but, because their interest was the tax scheme, they failed to pay enough attention to the day-to-day operations. The managers of the Boat Centres were all 'lifestyle entrepreneurs' who loved everything about canals and barges and had little concern for efficiency or profit. Further complications were introduced when it was decided to use the boat-building subsidiary as a property development vehicle to take advantage of the redevelopment of the west side of Birmingham city centre. The directors bought a large, derelict Victorian warehouse, in the middle of the redevelopment zone, with the hope of making a large resale profit because it sat where the two phases of development met.

Then the economic collapse of 1993 arrived! Building work in Birmingham stopped either side of the warehouse; clients found they could not fund new boats, hirers decided to stay at home. Nevertheless, boat-building continued apace even without buyers. Borrowings at the Boat Centres increased, backed by ever-inflated valuations on the Victorian warehouse, until the cash ran out and administrators were called in. The only option was to acquire the assets of the operating company but leave the subsidiary, along with the warehouse, to the tender mercies of the administrators.

Now I, along with my colleagues who had also bought boats, didn't fancy having redundant narrowboats lying on our front

lawns so Stephe Boddice, Dave Smith, myself and a friend of
ours called Chris Davies decided to buy the operating assets and
management rights to the hire company to protect the tax losses
that we had claimed.

An interesting sideshow to all of this took place a few years later.
An aircraft leasing company, based in Northern Ireland, had been
using similar tax relief schemes to defer liabilities to the Inland
Revenue. The Revenue had calculated that this company was
costing the Treasury several hundred million pounds a year but
decided direct confrontation would be expensive. A series of court
cases were brought against two boat scheme clients at random
and, would you believe, it just happened to be my bank manager
and me.

I nearly died when I saw the announcement in glorious pink
and black splashed all over a whole page of the *Financial Times*
– 'Inland Revenue versus Gallagher & Threlfall'. The Court of
Appeal threw out the Revenue's case but, the Treasury cost being so
great, we were effectively blackmailed into accepting a compromise
settlement. Failure to do so would have meant a House of Lords
case and the threat, if the Revenue failed here, to introduce
retrospective legislation to obtain the desired result. Who said
the law is fair? This case resulted in a fundamental change in the
accounting treatment of wasting assets and in how the Inland
Revenue was allowed to interpret the wording of taxation statutes.

I never wanted to get involved in the first place and while Stan
may have been deaf, I must have seemed blind because now not
only was I famous in the *Financial Times* for all the wrong reasons
but along with Stephe, Chris and Dave, from November 1993 also
owned a narrowboat company which I had no idea how to run.

The company was called Alvechurch Boat Centres Ltd and the
head office was based in the marina at Alvechurch, a small village

just outside Birmingham. We owned two more marinas, one in Anderton near Northwich in Cheshire and the other in Gayton near Northampton.

Between the three bases we operated approximately 100 narrowboats selling holidays on the canal system between March and October. The narrowboat owners, or sponsors as they are called, normally own up to half a dozen boats each, which are operated on their behalf and receive about a 10–12 per cent return per annum on their investment over a period of ten years. At that point the boats are normally sold out of the fleet having become too old and tired for the holiday market. As each narrowboat costs in the region of £50,000 it was essential to find outside investors to fund the capital expenditure of building the boats, which, with 100 in the fleet, could never have been financed out of company resources.

In addition to the holiday sales, other streams of income came from building boats, brokerage, moorings, private work, shop, chandlery and yard sales that included such things as fuel, Calor gas and pump-outs. Tony Stockwell and Al Harris were running Alvechurch when we bought it and for the first five years we muddled along making small profits in good years and losses in bad years. In 1997 we bought a fourth marina in Wrenbury, Cheshire, that served the popular Llangollen holiday route. However, as Tony and Al were starting to think about retirement it became apparent that we needed some fresh blood in the company.

In 1998 we were incredibly fortunate to employ someone who was to take the business forward in a way that we had never dreamt possible. Edward Helps had been manager of business services for the AA for a number of years and was now looking for a new challenge. Like myself, he had started commercial life as a market trader and we immediately had something in common. I knew that Ed was the right man for us but unbelievably just as he was about to join us, he received a better job offer and I was mortified. We offered him an equity stake in the business, which fortunately tipped the balance in our favour and in 1998 Ed joined us as managing director just as Tony Stockwell and Al Harris announced their retirement.

The number of boats we operated did not significantly increase above the 100 mark but we slowly started to sell more and more holidays per boat. With the holiday season running from March to October the maximum number of hire weeks would in theory be about 35, but in reality we had never exceeded 26 weeks per boat. But as we came into the new millennium our average weekly rental increased from 18.7 weeks per boat to 25.7 weeks per boat over a four-year period, and profits increased from nothing to £300,000 per annum. In 2003 we acquired another base in Hilperton near Trowbridge, which added another holiday route for people who wanted to cruise the Kennet and Avon canal, and then in 2004 we made a real step change in size when we acquired the substantial business of Viking Afloat.

Viking Afloat was a well-established and respected brand with 70 boats operating out of Worcester, Whitchurch, Rugby and Gailey, and the addition of these bases once again increased the number of cruising routes we were offering to our customers. In 2006 we acquired Red Line Boats at Goytre Wharf, which operated in the Brecon Beacons National Park, and with the fleet size growing to 185 boats and ten different cruising routes to choose from, we had become the largest narrowboat operator in the UK.

Even with the large increase in boat numbers we still managed to average 25 holiday weeks per boat, and in 2006 we made just over £500,000 pre-tax profit on a turnover of £6.2 million.

In 2008 we extended our operation by acquiring the timeshare interests of 70 Canaltime boats and also the management of 20 further boats operated by different syndicates. Having the boats at our marinas ensures us mooring income as well as all the work in repairing the boats and ensuring they are maintained at a high standard for the timeshare owners. With the timeshare business we also acquired Blackwater Meadow, a marina based just outside Ellesmere in Shropshire.

Our most recent acquisitions included the addition in 2009 of a franchise operation at Union Wharf, Market Harborough and in 2010 the purchase of Reading Marine at Aldermaston Wharf, which allows access to the Thames as well as cruising on the Kennet and Avon canal. With our diverse portfolio of canal-related activities we decided to rename the parent company ABC Leisure Group, under which all the brands and activities now operate.

It was sensible to operate the hire fleets under the original brand names to ensure they maintained their original uniqueness and culture, and today we operate Alvechurch, Viking Afloat, Red Line Boats and Wessex Narrowboats from ten company-owned marinas and four franchises, all under the umbrella of ABC Boat Hire.

The business today is very different from the one we acquired just over twenty years ago. Having bought out the other partners, Ed, Stephe and me are now its equal owners and, in reality, the success we have enjoyed has in most part been down to the employment decision we took back in 1998 with the appointment of Ed as managing director.

So what have I learnt from my twenty years' involvement with narrowboats?

First, I have to say that it is a unique industry with a lot of barriers to entry through its sheer complexity, where scale counts for very little. I will explain.

When we were building our retail business, size really mattered. If we bought out a competitor, the first thing we did was close their head office and warehouse, integrating them both into ours. There was also a lot of duplication in management, so savings were made there. Obviously with higher turnover our buying terms improved with nearly all our suppliers.

Reduction in overheads and improved buying power became a virtuous circle as we continued through 1,000 stores and £1 billion turnover. Eventually our size gave Tesco the opportunity to become the number one convenience store operator overnight, and in turn also improved their buying power.

In the narrowboat industry, there is little benefit from scale. We do not get a better licensing deal just because we operate nearly 200 boats. As most of our small marina shops are serviced from wholesalers, we gain little or no advantage from owning ten marinas. We may buy chandlery at slightly better rates than other operators, but turnover is low and the benefits are minimal.

Another anomaly within this industry is that all the marinas around the country are unique in every aspect. By this I mean that there is no set template you can apply to managing all the bases in the same way. Most of our convenience stores were laid out with the same basic ranges and this similarity allowed our area managers to identify quickly if there were problems in a particular location. Because of that we were able to open stores quickly and it became like a pastry-cutting exercise.

There is no such luxury when trying to run a marina! No two marinas are the same and no two days are the same.

The skill set required by a marina manager is very varied. They must have people skills, be able to delegate, be customer-focused, work flexible hours, have some knowledge of engineering, be sales-orientated and so on. In other words, finding a really good base manager is about as difficult as enjoying watching Wolverhampton Wanderers playing football.

When something goes wrong or a manager leaves it is extremely difficult to replace like with like, as the job advert has to apply to someone with all the attributes just mentioned. It is a little more difficult than replacing a shelf-stacker.

Apart from the difficulties of running marinas, they are also extremely expensive to maintain. Dredging, pontooning, tree, lawn and hedge maintenance all carry a significant cost and, with so much competition around from new marinas, standards have to improve continually in order to keep existing moorers, let alone attract new ones. So, while Stephe, Ed and I have enjoyed building up ABC Leisure over these last twenty years, it has not exactly been a breeze.

When we were expanding the business I visited most of the marinas around the country. It was fascinating to see the variety that existed across the spectrum of canal, river and coastal locations. We were almost tempted to become involved with the Norfolk Broads when I flew Edward to Beccles International Airport (open about 50 days a year) near Cromer in my light aircraft. After flying around and searching for the airfield for fifteen minutes, he considered himself lucky to survive the first trip so we never returned.

We thought the optimal total number of routes was about eighteen and although we have not achieved this, there are still other locations where we would like to base a hire fleet.

Unfortunately our ambitious plans came to a grinding halt when the banking crisis of 2008 ushered in a recession from which the country is still trying to recover. Holiday booking patterns tend to lag the economy by a couple of years and it was not until 2012 that we really felt the downturn of consumer spending. Weeks booked per boat fell by 20 per cent, from 24.4 weeks in 2011 down to 20.2 weeks in 2012, and even this didn't tell the whole story as we had discounted a lot of prices to achieve this result.

Hiring a narrowboat is not a cheap holiday and the average cost throughout the year is around £1,000 per week. If you break it down over a couple of families and a dog it is not too bad, but nevertheless there is a perception in the real world that what we sell is expensive.

There are approximately 33,000 boats on the canal system. Of this total around 1,000 are hired out to the public, with the largest three companies enjoying a market share of around 50 per cent. At the last count we are the biggest with 195 boats, Anglo Welsh are second with 137 boats and Black Prince are the third-largest operator with 103 boats. Of the other players there are 25 operators with 10 or more boats.

Other boating holiday locations have suffered more, with Broads boat numbers declining from 1,400 down to 700 before recovering slightly over the last few years, but the worst affected has been the Thames, where numbers have fallen from 800 to 100 and are still going down.

Another factor that has affected the industry has been the number of marinas that have been built over the last ten years. Every farmer with a field next to the canal network saw it as an opportunity to develop a marina and a better way of getting rich than buying a weekly lottery ticket. Because of this the total number of boats on the system remains fairly constant at 33,000, while the number of marinas being built continues to increase. At this moment in time there are nineteen marinas with a total of 3,000 berths that have planning permission but as yet remain unbuilt. In addition to this there are currently nine applications providing 825 berths that have applied for planning permission and are awaiting a decision.

In 2012 the government-owned British Waterways was transferred to the ownership of the Canal and River Trust, a charity that had been set up to look after the waterways of England and Wales. It is responsible for 2,000 miles of canals, rivers, docks and reservoirs along with museums, archives and the country's third-largest collection of protected historic buildings. As it happens it also employs about 2,000 people and enjoys the benefit of 2,000 volunteers.

To secure the finances of the new charity, the waterways were underwritten with a £500 million property endowment from which it will receive substantial annual income. It is also thought that volunteers and donors will be more inclined to contribute to a charity rather than a government quango.

Whatever happens I am sure that this has been the right move. For years our canals and rivers have suffered from underinvestment, and the recent flooding has proved how much dredging work needs to be done to minimise flood damage in future years.

I still get a great kick out of being part of the industry but I recognise that if the narrowboat holiday experience is to prosper, things must change. We must listen to our customers and ensure that we get the basics right. Far too often we receive complaints about television reception, toilets and heating not working properly and while being on a narrowboat will never be five-star luxury, we have to try to meet our customers' needs. We are now considering satellite TV, mobile phone signal boosters and Wi-Fi to meet the increasing needs of an in-touch society.

I work with some fabulous people who spend their time working hard to improve the business. Fortunately I don't have to be at the coalface every day, but I get a lot of pleasure from being involved in it.

We haven't, as yet, quite figured out how to build an 'infinity pool' on the end of our boats, but we are working on it!

– CHAPTER 16 –

Jack in the Box

In the 1950s my hometown of Wolverhampton was famous for three things: the Goodyear tyre factory, smog (being part of the Black Country) and the local football team, Wolverhampton Wanderers.

Wolves, as the club is affectionately known, was formed in 1877 and was one of the founder members of the Football League. Its stadium, called Molineux, is situated just on the edge of the city and has been its home since 1889. The stadium name originates from the Molineux House which was built in the area by Benjamin Molineux, a local merchant, in the 18th century and whose grounds were later developed to include numerous public leisure facilities.

The club's traditional colours of gold and black allude to the city council's motto 'Out of darkness cometh light', with the two colours representing light and darkness respectively.

The first ever official game was staged on 7 September 1889 before a crowd of 4,000. The ground was capable of hosting 20,000 spectators, although English football crowds rarely reached that number in the 19th century. Wolves bought the freehold in 1923 and then followed a series of ground improvements culminating in 1934 with four complete stands that would form its basis for the next half-century.

In the days before seating regulations, the ground could hold more than 60,000 spectators, with the record attendance being 61,315 for a first division match against Liverpool on 11 February 1939. The 1940s and the 1950s saw average attendances for seasons regularly exceed 40,000, coinciding with the club's peak on the field.

During this time Molineux became one of the first British grounds to install floodlights, enabling it to host a series of midweek friendlies against teams from across the globe. In the days prior to the formation of the European Cup and international club competitions, these games were highly prestigious and attracted huge crowds and interest, often being televised by the BBC.

It was to one of these midweek matches that my father first took me to watch the Wolves in 1955 when I was six years old. We had to be there at least an hour and a half before the kick-off and I can remember thousands of people funnelling down to the turnstiles for the South Bank stand.

The atmosphere in the ground was fantastic, and just before kick-off all the young boys like me were passed down to the edge of the ground so that we would be able to see the match. The thought of allowing that today would send shivers down most mothers' spines, but in those days it was just accepted as the normal thing to do.

I will never forget that first match under the floodlights and from that day forward I became a Wolves fan. There must be something genetically tribal about being a football fan, because once you have fallen in love with a particular team there is no going back. It would have been impossible for me to change loyalty to another Midlands club like West Bromwich Albion or Aston Villa.

It is hard to believe that the passion for a particular football club can make grown men fight, but the fact that it does proves there is something very deep-rooted in our tribal loyalty. I have known friends who are the most placid of individuals turn into completely different characters once they enter the football stadium. They rant and rave, scream and shout for the duration of the match but as soon as they leave the ground they revert back to their normal demeanour.

Having won the FA Cup twice before the outbreak of the First World War, in 1893 and 1908, Wolves developed into one of England's leading clubs under the management of ex-player Stan Cullis after the Second World War, going on to win the league three times and the FA Cup twice more between 1949 and 1960.

This really was a golden age for the Wolves, who were captained by the famous Billy Wright, who also captained England a record 90 times and was the first player to win a century of international caps. In total, 34 players have won full England caps during their time with Wolves, including the club's record goalscorer, Steve Bull, who notched up an incredible 306 goals in all competitions.

I watched them as often as I could and, when I was away at boarding school, my ears would be glued to the radio at 4.45pm on a Saturday to hear how they had got on. In fact, in the football season, wherever I have been in the world, I have never been able to settle until I have found out the Wolves result.

Although the decade opened with a fourth FA Cup victory and almost the first double of the 20th century, the 1960s saw Wolves begin to decline. Stan Cullis was sacked in September 1964, in a season that ended with relegation and the club's first spell outside the top division in more than 30 years.

Fortunately the exile lasted only two seasons and they were promoted in 1967 as runners-up in the second division. The club's return to the top flight heralded another period of relative success and they won the League Cup in 1974 and 1980. I have been incredibly fortunate to have been to Wembley three times to watch the Wolves and see them win on every occasion.

Wolves then went through a dreadful time in the 1980s and were acquired by the infamous Bhatti brothers, who did not invest in the club. Three consecutive relegations saw a financially moribund Wolves slide into the fourth division for the first time in the club's history.

By 1986 the club's existence was hanging by a thread, but the Bhattis finally relinquished ownership of the club and a long and painful rehabilitation started. Wolverhampton city council purchased the club's stadium and surrounding land, while a local developer paid off the club's outstanding debts in return for planning permission to develop an Asda superstore on the adjacent land.

Finally, in 1990 lifelong fan Sir Jack Hayward purchased the club and immediately funded the extensive redevelopment of the by-now-dilapidated Molineux into a modern all-seater stadium. Sir Jack then funded the playing side in an attempt to win promotion to the newly formed Premier League.

Sir Jack was born a quarter of a mile from the ground and went on to make his fortune from developing the Port Authority in Grand Bahama. He became famous for his philanthropy that included buying Lundy Island for the National Trust, bankrolling the restoration of Brunel's ship SS Great Britain, funding the restoration of the Memorial Hospital in the Falkland Islands and many other projects.

Unfortunately it was not until 2003 that we were finally promoted to end a nineteen-year absence from the top level. The stay proved short-lived as we were immediately relegated back to the newly retitled Championship. After former England manager Glenn Hoddle failed to return us to the top level, he famously resigned and Mick McCarthy was appointed as manager on 21 July 2006.

Mick was born in Barnsley and had a distinguished footballing career, playing for Barnsley, Manchester City and Celtic. As his father was Irish, he was eligible to play for the national team and represented the Republic of Ireland 57 times. He then also managed the team, guiding them to the second leg of the 2002 World Cup.

He was the perfect fit for Wolves and as a lifelong fan I knew that he would be able to work well with our chairman and owner, Sir Jack.

However, there was a major problem brewing in the boardroom with Sir Jack having become disillusioned not only with the club's lack of success on the football pitch but also with the criticism he was receiving from the fan base. He had injected somewhere in the region of £80 million into the club, building a new stadium and investing heavily in players who had kept us in the Premiership for only one season during his seventeen years at the helm. From seeing him as the saviour of Wolves, fans had started to doubt Sir Jack's commitment by actually criticising him for not spending enough on quality players capable of keeping us in the top flight.

It became Sir Jack's fault that we had been relegated and in a famous quote he said that he was no longer prepared to be the 'Golden Tit' where everyone came to drink from his wealth. He was absolutely right and I was appalled that a man who had given so much to the club in both money and time was being treated in such a hostile and unfair way.

Out of the blue, at the end of July I received a telephone call inviting me to a meeting with the great man.

I had never met Sir Jack before but he immediately put me at ease and explained to me that the following day his son Rick and also co-director Paul Manduca were both resigning from the board. He asked me if I was interested in becoming chairman and along with another Wolverhampton businessman, John Gough, helping him to sell the club!

It was a lot to take in, but he thought it was vitally important that the new board should be made up of local businessmen who were not only capable of making the right sort of commercial decisions but who were also lifelong fans and would be there for the duration.

He asked me whether I had any interest in buying the club myself but I assured him that not only was it way beyond my finances, but also I would never have wanted one of my most pleasurable pastimes to become a business venture. Wolves were far too important to me for that!

After giving it some thought I told Sir Jack that becoming chairman would be too big a responsibility, but I was happy to form a board and help set in motion a strategy that would eventually lead to us finding the right sort of buyer for the club. John Gough had been a friend of mine for a number of years and we regularly played golf together at our club, South Staffordshire, a couple of miles from the ground. John was also a lifelong Wolves fan and I relished the thought of us working together to try to find the right sort of person who could take the club forward.

To complete the board, we needed a finance director and we approached John Bowater, who was delighted to join us as he too had supported the Wolves all his life.

The announcement of the new board at Wolves hit the headlines of our local evening newspaper, the *Express and Star*, and I made it clear in my statement that I was not investing any money in the club and that my only reason for becoming involved was to bring some commercial expertise to the table and help find a new owner for the club. I also went on to say that being lifelong fans we would put the interests of Wolverhampton Wanderers Football Club ahead of any financial considerations.

The only problem with all of this was that, unbeknown to me, Sir Jack had not discussed the changes with his chief executive, Jez Moxey, who happened to be away on holiday. Sir Jack was known to be a bit of a maverick and once he had made his mind up about something, he generally went ahead and did it.

Needless to say, I was not welcomed with open arms and a big friendly hug on my first meeting with Jez on the Monday after he got

Welcome to the Wolves board from Sir Jack Hayward.

back from holiday. In fact his opening words to me were 'What the … do you know about running a football club?', to which I answered: 'About the same as you know about running a chain of convenience stores.'

I completely understood where Jez was coming from and knew he had every right to be furious about what had happened, but assured him that the board would support him 100 per cent and that hopefully we could all work together to find the right solution.

In fairness to Jez, he was an excellent chief executive who had done a great job under difficult circumstances and at times he had come in for a lot of stick from the fans that was completely unwarranted. By now Sir Jack had returned home, so we were left to get on with the job of trying to find a new buyer. He had made it clear that he would sell the club for £10 but that whoever ended up buying it would have to inject a further £30 million into the club's finances.

In selling T&S to Tesco, I had become involved with Robert Leitao, one of the senior partners at Rothschild who had acted for the Glazer family in their takeover of Manchester United and had also been involved in Randy Lerner's £62.6 million purchase of Aston Villa. I phoned Robert and made an appointment to see him along with Jez Moxey to ascertain how we should go about marketing the sale, but before the meeting I felt I had to know what the club was really worth.

Doug Ellis had been the chairman and major shareholder of Aston Villa for a number of years before it was sold, and John Gough and I took him out to lunch to ascertain what how much he considered the Wolves to be worth. Amazingly he came up with the same figure as Sir Jack and thought that £30 million was about the right figure, which at least gave us some confidence that we were in the right sort of financial parish.

The 2006/2007 football season started well and we had a couple of meetings with potential interested parties, but nobody was banging down our door with a cheque in their hands. We did meet a couple of shady Indonesian businessmen who were going to finance the deal through a trust fund in Kazakhstan. Needless to say we didn't take that any further.

Our board meetings were quite unremarkable in that we would go through the numbers comparing them with the budget and discuss all the things concerned with running the club like catering contracts, season ticket prices, policing costs etc. We would then invite Mick McCarthy into the meeting to discuss how we were doing as a team, what injuries we had, why we weren't scoring enough goals, all the normal things you would expect to be discussed.

The problem was that Mick was such a charismatic and powerful figure, he just filled the boardroom and we were frightened to ask any searching questions in case it made us look stupid. There was absolutely no link between the boardroom, the training ground and how we performed on the pitch. All the important decisions on whom we bought, length of contracts and wages were all made by Mick and Jez; the rest of the board were just informed rather than involved in the decision-making processes.

I was beginning to realize that Jez was absolutely right in that I knew nothing about running a football club and the way it was going, I never would. It seemed OK that we were allowed into the debate on how much we should sell a pasty for, but when it came down to spending a few million pounds on players we were not to be trusted.

I was perfectly happy that we had the right man for the job in Mick, I just felt that there was not enough due diligence and detail going into the decision-making process. When we were talking about spending £2 million on a player I just didn't feel that enough research went into the discussion. If we were spending £2 million at T&S I used to want to see a detailed breakdown and also how we were going to get a return on our money. In a football club, decisions on spending £2 million didn't seem to get the same sort of focused analysis as they did in the real world.

Since coming off the board, I have discussed with Jez what the 'model' board structure for a football club should be. The problem is that no two football clubs are alike and no two board structures are alike. Some clubs have high-profile and hands-on owners/chairmen with low-profile managers, and other clubs have high-profile and hands-on managers with low-profile owners/chairmen; and lots of clubs have a mixture of the two. There are also clubs that have a lot of members on the board who may or may not own shares, and there are clubs that have very few members on the board.

So football clubs do not tend to have the same sort of structure as a typical PLC may have, with a definitive line between executive and non-executive functions. However, I do believe that there are certain rules that should apply to any football club, regardless of status or ownership.

There should be a rolling two- to three-year plan that is updated at the end of each season, which includes financial targets as well as league aspirations. There should definitely be financial budgets for player transfers, capital expenditure, player wages, academy costs, medical staff, scouting and all the other cost centres that exist within a football club.

I also passionately believe that there should be a separate board appointment for a director of football who is responsible for all mainstream football activities except the players. This would include the academy, recruitment, scouting, medical and sports sciences. The head coach would then also be a board appointment, but he would only have to worry about the players rather than all the other detail.

You could then either have a structure whereby both the head coach and the director of football report to the chief executive, or have a structure whereby they are on an equal footing to the chief executive, who is in charge of running all non-football activities within the club. The board would then be completed with the chairman and maybe a couple of non-executives and the secretary.

Back in 2006 our season was going better than expected and we started to move up the league. Steve Morgan had made his fortune from building houses and he was a major shareholder in Redrow plc. He also happened to be a friend of Delia Smith, the famous cook, television presenter and football director, so when Wolves were playing Norwich, Steve came along and joined us for lunch in the boardroom. He had been a lifelong fan of Liverpool and at one time had been mooted as a potential buyer of the club, but in the end the £150 million price tag was too much of a stretch even for Steve.

John Gough and I suggested to Steve that Wolves would be a great alternative for him as cumulatively we were the ninth most successful club in English domestic football history, behind Manchester City, with thirteen major trophy wins. We said it would be a great challenge for Steve to take us back to the glory days of the 1950s when the name Wolverhampton Wanderers was known throughout the world.

He started coming to a few more home matches and slowly but surely he seemed to warm to the idea that maybe, just maybe, it was the thing to do. He met and got on with Sir Jack and eventually agreed a deal to buy the club in August 2007 for the nominal sum of £10, with the proviso that £30 million was injected into the club. It was not a straightforward contract, however, as Sir Jack was to find out later when his grandchildren, who were shareholders, sued him for selling the club for next to nothing.

The season finished well but unfortunately we lost in the play-offs to our arch-rivals West Bromwich Albion. In the 2007/2008 season we finished within a single place of a successive play-off, losing out by a goal difference of only one.

Announcing to the fans that Steve Morgan has bought the Wolves.

With Steve having settled into his chairman's role, I felt it was time for me to leave the board and although I would have liked to see us win promotion to the Premiership, it was the right thing to do. Steve certainly didn't need me to tell him how to spend his money and in any case I had fulfilled my promise to Sir Jack to find a buyer for the club.

I was delighted Steve had bought the club. He was exactly the sort of person we wanted and I knew that he would be there for the long haul; and given his great success in business, who was going to bet against him succeeding at Wolves?

I was also quite relieved to get back into the Billy Wright stand with my mates as, contrary to public opinion, being a director of a football club is not as glamorous as it sounds. While you can enjoy the kudos of sitting in the director's box, you also have to be at the ground a good two hours before kick-off to welcome the away team directors and entertain them during lunch as you await the 3.00pm kick-off. This involves wearing a suit and tie and being involved in small talk for a couple of hours, to people who are only really interested in watching their football team.

After the match you then have to entertain them again until the crowds have dispersed and Gill and I would finally get home around 7.00pm. Also being a director you were expected to go to as many away games as possible, and depending upon the fixture you could well be out all day long.

It was a great relief to me to get back to my old routine of arriving ten minutes before the start of the match, having a quarter-pound beefburger with extra cheese and burnt onions and escaping two minutes before the end of the match to avoid getting stuck in traffic.

I also had the added benefit of being able to shout at the director's box if the team was playing badly!

We were top of the league for most of the following season and Mick McCarthy won the Championship Manager of the Season Award at the conclusion of the campaign, with our team winning the league, having led the table for 42 of the 46 games played.

For the following three seasons, like most newly promoted clubs, we struggled to stay away from the relegation zone and eventually, after a drubbing at home by arch-rivals West Bromwich Albion, Mick McCarthy was sacked. At the time of his dismissal he was the seventh longest serving manager in English league football, having spent just over five years at Wolves.

While I understood the decision, I felt really sorry for Mick because he was one of the most honest people you could ever wish to meet. He was arguably the best manager to take a club from the Championship division to the Premiership, but then he appeared to struggle at the higher level.

In fairness, he was probably never given sufficient funds at Sunderland, where he had been manager before joining Wolves, to build the sort of team he wanted but that argument certainly did not apply at Wolves. Mick spent a lot of money on a lot of players but they just never seemed to gel together the way he wanted them to. I think probably he will always be thought of as being too good a manager for Championship teams but not good enough for the Premiership. He may well look back on his career and say that he would have been better off being a specialist manager and never taking the risk of failing at the top level. Whatever happens, I wish him all the best at Ipswich and the Wolves fans certainly have a lot to thank him for.

After Mick had gone Wolves went into a nosedive. Even Steve Morgan would admit that a couple of ill-thought-out management decisions cost us dearly as we dropped down two divisions in two seasons. Fortunately we appeared to get the third management decision correct and Kenny Jackett has taken the club back into the Championship at the first attempt.

The rollercoaster ride of being a Wolves fan continues to be one of the most exciting rides around!

Jez Moxey was probably dead right when he said that I knew nothing about running a football club, but the one thing I have learnt is that the fans are never happy. Last season, the Wolves fans probably got more pleasure out of seeing their team win week after week than the Manchester United fans did out of seeing their team slowly disintegrate over the course of the season.

The only time the Wolves fans would be happy is if we won the Premiership title, the FA Cup, the Football League Cup and the Champions League Cup all in the same season but knowing them as I do, they would still probably be calling for the manager's head!

– CHAPTER 17 –

Well Done, Beef!

I was brought up with a cricket bat in my hand, as my father was more in love with cricket than he was with my mother. It was a passion that had grown up with him from his early days watching Accrington in the Lancashire League and he merely existed through the winter months, only really coming alive when the cricket season started in May. Most of our family photos are of my sister and me down at the cricket club rather than on holiday in Blackpool or Bournemouth. After moving down to the Midlands for work, and getting married in Wolverhampton, he joined the local cricket club to get to know people and of course play the sport. Fordhouses Cricket Club (FCC) was one of the top teams in the Staffordshire League and from May to September most weekends were spent down at the ground.

Dad was an excellent opening bat and captained the 1st XI for a number of years, but he was also very heavily involved in the running of the club and seemed to spend most of his spare time doing the secretarial work. As we lived in a small semi-detached house in a small cul-de-sac, I loved the open space of the cricket ground and spent many an hour playing there, while my Dad was on the tractor mowing the outfield or helping to prepare the pitch for the weekend match. My mother was on the ladies' committee and always helped to prepare the teas. My sister Sharron was allowed in the kitchen with her, but I was banned because I stole the cakes and biscuits.

I always carried my trainspotting book with me and as soon as I heard a train coming would race into the field just in time to spot the number. I used to love watching my father bat and would count the runs, getting very excited as he approached the landmark 50. Once he had reached the target everyone would clap and I can remember feeling so proud of him. When he was finally out, I would run on to the pitch and carry his bat back to the pavilion as everyone applauded his innings. After the match my parents used to stay on and have a drink with everyone and, as Sharron and I grew older, we were allowed to stay up with them and enjoy a bottle of lemonade and a packet of crisps.

They were fantastic days and the atmosphere of being part of a cricket club family is very difficult to explain to anyone who has never experienced it. After my father started working on the markets he had to give up playing on a Saturday but still continued to turn out on a Sunday. As he got older he dropped into the second team but was still playing for the third team well into his sixties.

I was never a good batsman as my eyesight was poor and I just could not pick up the flight of the ball as it left the bowler's hand. As a bowler I was reasonably quick but never good enough for the first team, which was a huge disappointment to me at school as I loved the game so much. After going away to boarding school and becoming a teenager I started to find other interests in life rather than cricket and slowly drifted away from the club altogether. My father became president of FCC and in 1975 managed a tour to Australia with a team assembled from the Midland Cricket Club Conference, for which he had been elected cricketer of the year in 1964.

For some years he had corresponded with Sir Donald Bradman who, without a shadow of a doubt, was the best batsman of all time. As the touring side was playing a match in Adelaide, where Bradman lived, my father asked whether it was possible for them to meet up for lunch. Bradman was quite a reclusive man and my father did not think there was a chance he would accept his invitation, but unbelievably received a reply inviting him not only to lunch but also to his house for the whole day. I never heard my father talking about his wedding day, but lost count of the number of people he told about his day with the great 'Don'.

It is against this background of association with FCC that I became involved with it again at the age of 42. My father had never asked me to do him a favour in his life until just before he died in 1991, and this one favour concerned the future of his beloved cricket club.

It had been formed in 1928 and for a number of years the land had been leased from Bradburn & Wedge, a local car distributor, at a peppercorn rent of £80 per annum. Jack Bradburn, one of the family directors, was a keen cricketer and a good friend of my father and had been happy to grant FCC a new 25-year lease as a favour to the club back in 1983. The problem was that in the intervening period Bradburn & Wedge had gone into receivership and the land was now owned by the liquidators of the company acting on behalf of the creditors. As the receiver looked through the remaining assets of the company trying to find something of value, he came across this lease for a four-acre greenfield site at a rent of £80 per annum, right in the middle of a modern housing estate. He nearly fell off his chair when he realised the potential value of this site if planning permission for housing development could be obtained.

Obviously he could do nothing about our tenure until the end of the lease, then we would have to vacate, but in the interim there was a deal to be done if we could find somewhere else quickly.

My father was naturally devastated by the thought of losing his beloved cricket club and begged me to try to help them find an alternative location; I promised him I would. The following day at the age of 78 he took his own life and I was left with a promise that somehow I had to honour. Two months earlier, at Christmas lunch, he had hinted to me that he didn't plan to be around much longer and asked me if when he was gone I would scatter his ashes on the square at the cricket club, but I thought it was just the port talking. When the time came I duly took his ashes to the ground and in trying to remember from which end he opened the batting didn't take too much notice of the howling wind.

Unfortunately most of my father's ashes ended up in my hair rather than on the cricket square. When I got home and showered the rest of Dad's remains down the plughole I reflected that he would have found it highly amusing and I can just imagine him saying to me, 'You can't even get that right!'

Most of the people attending his funeral had some connection with FCC as he had been a member for over 50 years and president of the club for the last 21 years. The chairman Ron Smith asked me if I would take his place as president and considering the promise I had made, I had little choice but to accept.

This started a 22-year battle to fulfil a promise that I just had to keep.

Ron and I arranged a meeting with the receiver to discuss the options and try to open a friendly dialogue. As we only had twelve years left on the lease, our negotiating stance was fairly weak in relation to dictating terms and he seemed in no hurry to do any sort of deal. The only way we were ever going to have a share of the action was to find a new ground so that we could give vacant possession back to the receiver. In truth our ground had become far too small for the modern game and with cricket balls regularly crashing through people's windows, it was only a matter of time before someone was

Club's own 'Mr Cricket' dies, aged 78

One of Wolverhampton cricket's best-known figures has died after a lifetime dedicated to the sport. Jack Threlfall's ashes will be scattered on the ground at Fordhouses Cricket Club, where he was known as "Mr Cricket".

Mr Threlfall died aged 78, after being associated with the club for many years.

His passion for the game led to the foundation of one of the West Midlands' fastest-growing companies, T and S Stores, his son Kevin said today.

"He worked as a salesman for a time in the area and was told by his manager that he couldn't play cricket one Whit Tuesday.

"He said that since cricket was his first love and business second then he would leave and set up on his own."

He went on to run a market-stall in Wellington, which later inspired his son to launch T and S Stores, now a multi-million pound company with more than 500 shops selling cigarettes, confectionery and soft drinks throughout England and Wales.

The company was set up by Kevin Threlfall in the 1970s and expanded rapidly, taking over the newsagent chains, Alfred Preedy and Dillons in 1989.

Jack Threlfall

Fan

Kevin Threlfall said: "He always said that he wanted his ashes to be scattered at the end where he used to open the batting and we will be respecting his wishes."

Born in Lancashire, Jack Threlfall was a lifelong fan of the county side. He lived in his final years at Cranmere Avenue, Tettenhall.

He played for some time for a Lancashire League club before moving to the Wolverhampton area, where he joined Fordhouses Cricket Club.

Mr Threlfall scored thousands of runs for them as an opening batsman, playing until his mid-60s. He was secretary, captain and president during his long service.

He was also a Midlands Cricket Club Conference Cricketer of the Year and president in 1979-80, and helped arrange tours of West Midland teams abroad.

Mr Threlfall also leaves a widow, Edna, and daughter Sharron. His funeral will be held at St Michael and All Angels Church, Tettenhall on Friday.

Father dies,
February 1991.

seriously hurt. Obviously for the club to still remain FCC we had to find somewhere suitable in the same area, which was not going to be an easy job. The receiver for his part agreed to discuss with the planners what the chances were of obtaining planning permission for a housing development.

We viewed a number of potential sites over the coming years but nothing really fitted the bill. Finally, after nine years' searching, we found our ideal solution. We had heard through the grapevine that the local Dowty Sports and Social club lease was about to be sold and we would have to move very quickly to secure a deal. It was a perfect location as it was a ten-acre site which included a bowling green and enough space for us to play two simultaneous cricket matches. The clubhouse left a lot to be desired as it was built of wood and needed a lot of renovation to meet the required standards.

Fortunately it was a very well-supported club, with over 500 members and a profitable bar, which was very important as this would give us revenue with which to develop the cricket club. I lent the club the necessary funds with which to do the deal, but it was still going to take a couple of years before the cricket square was of sufficient quality for match standards. Running two clubs at the same time was expensive but also time-consuming, as everyone on the committee had other commitments as well. Eventually everything fell into place and in 2001, after 73 years, we finally left the old ground for our new home just half a mile away.

It was very sad for me to have to say goodbye to a place where I had spent hundreds of hours growing up but I had some great memories to hold on to and, as the saying goes, nothing lasts forever. The committee decided to call our new ground the Jack Threlfall Memorial Ground in honour of my father's immense contribution to the club spanning 50 years.

The receiver was delighted that we had managed to find a new home and could now relinquish the lease at the old ground. We were not the only party involved, however, as two brothers lived in a cottage at the entrance to the ground with an acre of land, the lease of which ran for many more years to come. The next couple of years were wasted in negotiation for what became known as the famous tripartite agreement. If the brothers were to relinquish the lease on the cottage, they obviously wanted sufficient funds out of the deal to buy and fit out another property. Numerous meetings were held with the receiver until eventually we were all happy with the details. The brothers got what they wanted and we agreed on a percentage of the proceeds depending on how many years were left on our lease at the point of sale, with a minimum of 20 per cent and a maximum of 25 per cent. The really frustrating part of the deal was that the receiver was allowed to recoup all of his costs out of the proceeds before the balance was paid out to the creditors, the brothers and us. Therefore, he was never really bothered how long the meetings went on for or how much work he did, as all the hours were booked to the costs. The creditors had long given up expecting to receive any proceeds from the liquidation, so any amount of distribution was to be a bonus, no matter how small.

At one time the value of the land was estimated to be around £3 million but, with the country now in recession, the price had probably halved. Bellway, a national house builder, had been very interested at one point but had eventually walked away due to the length of time it took to agree the tripartite deal. To frustrate matters further, the council had indicated that planning permission for a housing development would not be given easily as it would mean the loss of a leisure facility to the area. In fairness to the residents living around the cricket ground, who had initially opposed the scheme, they now backed it as the vacant land had become a meeting place for undesirable youths.

Again a further seven years passed by and nothing happened; our lease expired, the receiver's costs increased but at least we had the guarantee of 20 per cent of the proceeds if and when the land was eventually sold. Finally, in late 2008, planning permission was granted but again the process was painfully slow and protracted as all manner of pre-commencement issues had to be satisfied. Bellway did eventually buy the site for £1.5 million, nothing like the £3 million it had been worth several years before. After expenses had been deducted and my loan repaid we received a cheque from the receiver for £100,000, which was way short of what we had hoped for but, equally, better than nothing.

However, there was a bonus ball to the prize that came our way in the form of an unusual type of payment. When developers discuss a proposition with the council they have to enter into what is known as a Section 106 agreement, which entitles the council to write the rules when it comes to open space areas, affordable housing and, in our case, the loss of a sporting activity. Bellway had to pay the council £325,000 for the loss of the sporting activity and we now had to fight the council for all of that money to be paid back to us.

Our argument had some logic because the only reason the council had received the Section 106 money from Bellway was because we had vacated the ground in the first place. However, we had relocated to a facility still in the same area of Fordhouses that, as it happened, was leased from the council and we wanted the money to spend on the renovation of their freehold. It is notoriously difficult to get money from councils and a very compelling argument has to be put forward to stand any chance of success. Ron Smith had retired from the club and his successor as chairman, Peter Jones, had considerable experience in dealing with councils. He put together a sustainable development plan which we had to present to twelve members of Wolverhampton council. The proposals went into great detail about how we were going to spend the money, how we planned to develop a youth programme and, above all, how we would improve cricket substantially enough to justify the investment.

Another year went by but we finally got the full £325,000 and entered into another agreement, this time with the council, for a new 99-year lease on the ten-acre site coupled with a development plan detailing how the money was to be spent. Together with the money we had obtained from the receiver our funds totalled over £425,000. Therefore we could be fairly ambitious with our development plans. We allowed ourselves a budget of £375,000, with £50,000 put into a sinking fund for any future potential repairs. My son-in-law, James Colton, project managed the works in conjunction with our architect, Peter Bromley, and we allowed twelve months for everything to be completed. Fortunately the project came in on time and also on budget and by the end of 2012 we had a wonderful new facility that bore comparison with any of the top cricket clubs in the West Midlands.

The whole complex included four new changing rooms and shower facilities, an upstairs viewing area and committee room, a new kitchen, two snooker tables, a members' lounge and a separate function room that could hold 200 people and which we could let out. In addition to this, we installed new state-of-the-art cricket net facilities, a dance studio and a crown green bowling square with its own pavilion. I was immensely proud of what we had achieved and I now had to find someone for an official opening, whose stature in the game matched the quality of our new complex.

I knew just the man.

Back in 2001, I had received an invitation from Phil Collins and Paul Monk, two of the directors of Golden Wonder Crisps, to play golf in Scotland for a couple of days. Paul Monk had formed a charity called Caravan, which raised money for people from the grocery trade who had fallen on hard times, and he asked me to go along as one of his guests. Sir Ian Botham and some of the Sky Sports cricket pundits were the celebrities invited on the three-day golf event to attract members of the trade to go along. The first day I would be playing with Ian Botham against Phil Collins and Ivan Lendl at a course called Monifieth, and the second day at Carnoustie. I was absolutely over the moon as Ian Botham had been my cricketing hero for years and Ivan Lendl was one of the finest tennis players ever to grace Wimbledon. They also happened to be very talented golfers. Ivan Lendl was a scratch golfer and Sir Ian played off a handicap of 5. I was playing off a handicap of 11 and felt as nervous as a kitten standing on the first tee with these two sporting icons who were far better at golf than I was. In the end we had a great match and I played as well as I ever have, probably because I was terrified of letting down my partner. We had a memorable lunch together and Sir Ian talked about the walks he was doing to help raise money for leukaemia research. As it happened, one of his walks was passing through Shrewsbury fairly soon and, as it was near to where I lived, I agreed to go along and support his cause.

My wife Gill and I had dinner with Sir Ian and his lovely wife, Lady Kath. After that I got to know Beefy, as he is affectionately known, fairly well as we met quite frequently at charity events.

The Caravan charity event was an amazing success and has been repeated for the last ten years in either Spain or Portugal and grown to be probably the best golfing charity weekend on the grocery calendar. It has raised well over £1 million and now boasts probably the largest gathering of sporting celebrities of any annual charitable event.

I asked Beefy if he would do me the honour of opening our cricket club officially and was delighted when he agreed to do it. Normally a fee would be charged for such an occasion but Beefy did it as a

Receiving the 'Monkey Classic' golf trophy from Beefy at Valderrama.

favour to me and I shall be eternally grateful for his generosity. It says something about the class of the man.

The appointed day duly arrived and it poured down all morning, threatening to ruin an occasion that so many people were looking forward to. Fortunately, the very moment Beefy arrived at my house the rain stopped and as we pulled into the cricket club the sun started shining. Over 500 people turned out to see the great man and I don't think I have seen so many autographs given and so many photographs taken in my life. Beefy stayed all afternoon and a great day was had by everyone. When he finally cut the ribbon to open the club officially, I thought of my father and wondered how the sun had started to shine at just the right time. It was quite ironic that one of my Dad's greatest days was spent with the best batsman ever to grace the game of cricket, and in the same way one of my greatest days was spent with arguably the greatest all-rounder the game has ever known.

Beefy opens Fordhouses Cricket Club, 8 May 2013.

The club is now financially sound and, with the new facilities in place, bar takings continue to grow. We run four senior teams in the Staffordshire and Birmingham leagues and in addition have four youth sides with some really promising youngsters coming through the ranks. We are a very happy team and I work with a really great group of people on the committee who give their time unselfishly to make sure the club runs smoothly. The official opening date was 8 May 2013 and it had taken 22 years and three months to make good the promise I had made to my father, but I have to say it was well worth the time and effort. The club now has a lease that will ensure that cricket can be played at the same venue for the next hundred years and I am also hopeful that at some time in the future we shall be one of the top clubs in the premier division of the Birmingham league.

– CHAPTER 18 –

Going Back to School

When you have been on a treadmill for 25 years you have to be careful that when jumping off you don't hit a brick wall. I was fortunate that I had a number of outside interests that would keep me busy over the coming years. In preparation for my semi-retirement I had built an office above my double garage at home and it was wonderful only having to walk a few steps rather than the horrible 40-minute journey to Brownhills.

Having been looked after so well by Rita meant that I had to learn some basic secretarial functions like doing my own typing and getting up to speed with such things as emails and spreadsheets. I bought a computer and started having lessons once a week, but it did not come naturally to me and I wasted a lot of time just trying to catch up with the most basic skills.

I was still employed by Tesco as a consultant, involved in the narrowboat business, president of the local cricket club and also chairman of my old preparatory school. In addition to this I was still flying my aeroplane and playing golf at least twice a week, so I can't say that I was exactly bored.

I had become involved with Birchfield, my old preparatory school,

Learning to live without Rita: my office above the garage in Wolverhampton.

some eight years earlier when the chairman invited me onto the governing body. As a pupil I had never really enjoyed my time at the school because it was such a huge culture shock for me, at the age of eleven, to go from a state school with 42 pupils in an average class, to a private school with a maximum of 20.

I don't think it helped that my Dad sometimes took me to school in his van and it soon got around that my parents were traders rather than professional people. After that I didn't get invited to as many birthday parties as the other boys.

So it was probably a bit of inverted snobbery that took me back to Birchfield, because I felt deep down that I had failed there and I now had an opportunity to prove myself.

Birchfield had been founded in 1935 and had moved to its existing site in the early 1960s just after I had left to go to Denstone. As an all-boys preparatory school it had averaged around 150 pupils per year until the 1990s, when numbers just exploded from 165 in 1989 to 266 in 1999. This was down to a combination of birth rates, the economy and an exceptional headmaster.

Unfortunately after the tragic death of the young headmaster, Mr Benwell, numbers started to decline and when I took over as chairman in 2004 they were in freefall. By 2006 pupil numbers were back to around 160 and it was staggering to think that in just ten years they had increased by 100, only to see all that growth disappear in the next seven years.

I had become chairman purely and simply because nobody else wanted the job. It was very difficult for me to turn down the appointment when my fellow governors knew that I had recently semi-retired and also the school was running into financial problems and we needed a solution.

However, I knew there was a lot of work to be done and I made it clear that I was only going to stay in the role for three years. I had been on the board for seven years so another three would take my total involvement up to ten years, which I thought was quite long enough. I was incredibly fortunate that my deputy chairman, Barry Frankling, had agreed to take over from me after the three years.

Too many governors sit on school boards for far too long and end up contributing very little. I am a great believer in having a constant churn of governors with, if possible, at least one governor leaving and one new one joining every year. It is also important to get the right balance of skills and ensure that the board does not end up full of accountants and lawyers, not that I have anything against accountants and lawyers!

Schools are a lot easier to run when numbers are increasing, but when the numbers are declining it is exceptionally difficult knowing where to make the necessary cuts and which teachers can be made redundant.

As pupil numbers declined so did our trading surplus, and that meant we had no money to spend on repairs and maintenance. As a charity we didn't need to make a profit because we did not have shareholders and therefore any surplus was ploughed back into the school. But as you can imagine, with 150 boys running around a school every day, there is an immense amount of wear and tear happening that at some stage has to be dealt with.

We could not allow standards to drop as that just exacerbates the problem of declining pupil numbers; and if you are not careful, word gets around that you are in financial trouble and that can turn into a death spiral for the school.

Fortunately the bank was extremely supportive and allowed our overdraft to rise as we continued to spend more than was coming in from school fees. We had recently commissioned a valuation of the whole school that showed substantial headroom over what we were borrowing, but nevertheless as the overdraft grew so did the interest payments and at some stage in the future that debt would have to be repaid.

As the numbers looked increasingly bleak, I began to wonder why I had taken the job on in the first place. T&S with all its problems had never seemed as difficult as running Birchfield. We needed a plan and we needed it quickly.

We were not alone in our dilemma, as prep schools around the country had been caught in a pincer movement that had been engineered by the senior schools. As private education became more and more expensive in the 1990s there was a financial squeeze on the public schools as pupil numbers declined and also boarding became less popular.

To combat this reduction in income the public schools all started to lower the age limit of entry from thirteen down to eleven and this caused a massive blow to the prep schools, which were suddenly faced with losing two years' income at the senior end of the school. There was a mixed reaction from parents, with some wanting their children to get the benefit of the senior status at their prep school while others saw it as an opportunity to get their children settled into senior school at an earlier age.

Birchfield was also a boys-only school, which meant that our marketing could only be targeted at 50 per cent of potential pupils. The more we looked at the numbers, the more we realised that staying as we were was not an option. We had to introduce girls and become co-educational.

This was easier said than done as we had absolutely no track record and there was competition from at least three schools, all of which were far better options than we were. It was also going to involve considerable capital expenditure, as we would have to build separate changing rooms and lavatories to accommodate the girls.

Then we had a stroke of luck.

A gentleman called Richard Phillips approached us with a view to running a nursery from the school. It was a perfect location, being situated in the countryside but within travelling distance of Telford and Wolverhampton. With school numbers having declined, we had adequate classroom space to accommodate the new nursery and Richard agreed to finance whatever capital projects were needed. This principally involved a play area, a separate entrance and new changing rooms and lavatories.

Of course there was no guarantee that the new nursery would be commercially viable but in reality, as far as the future of the school was concerned, it was the last throw of the dice. It gave us a logical reason to introduce girls into the school and become co-educational. The nursery would become the feeder for the main school and as it took boys and girls in fairly even numbers, it was hoped that we would soon have classes evenly split between the two sexes.

The problem now was how we were going to market the idea to the parents to ensure that we got the idea off the ground. We knew that whatever we did was going to have to be fairly dramatic because the competition around us was so strong.

I wrote to the parents, knowing that the letter would provoke a very mixed reaction:

Dear Parents

The exciting decision for Birchfield to evolve into a fully co-educational establishment was taken almost a year ago. As you are aware much has happened in terms of fabric and the cultural move towards the arrival of girls in September 2006.

To further celebrate this historic change and to invest in Birchfield's exciting new future, the governors have decided to financially support girls by offering a golden opportunity to the first six girls registered for September 2006: a 50 per cent fee remission for the entirety of their school life at Birchfield. Historically as an all-boys' school we have had an excellent academic and all-round reputation; as a co-educational school we are unknown. My belief is that girls will only enhance this highly held esteem.

We sat back and waited for the backlash.

It did not take long for parents to voice their opinions and we decided to call a parents' evening and face the music. It was an evening I could have done without, as we were lambasted for subsidising the fees so dramatically just to get the first girls into the school. We tried to justify our actions by saying that we had no choice, but the parents were having none of it.

One parent stood up and said that I used to sell cut-price cigarettes, but now I was selling cut-price education. Nobody laughed, but deep down even I thought it was quite funny.

However, we got through the evening and I explained to the parents that this really was the last throw of the dice and unless we could attract a minimum of six girls into the reception form, they could all start looking for another school.

Miraculously we got our six girls; not five, not seven but exactly six! This, coupled with the twelve boys who were already signed up for the September intake, gave us eighteen pupils in total, a third of whom were girls.

Just as pleasing to me was the fact that not one of the boys' parents pulled out of the September admission, because it must have been a lot to stomach that all the girls' parents in the form were going to be paying half the fees that they were having to dish out.

The Prepcare nursery was a huge success from day one and has been brilliantly managed from the outset by Penny Shevyn, who, together with her team, has built up a reputation that is second to none. They now look after over 100 little youngsters, aged from just six weeks to five years old.

I thoroughly enjoyed working with the headmaster, Richard Merriman, who oversaw all the changes that we had to put into place. While I could get away from the school, he lived above the shop and had to cope with meeting extremely tight budgets that demanded very tight cost controls.

Richard had come to us as a headmaster and I like to think that he left us as a businessman and a headmaster. He went on to get the top preparatory school job in the Midlands as headmaster of Foremarke Hall at Repton. When I left the board of governors I had the distinction of either having been taught by or worked with every headmaster we ever had at Birchfield.

Today Birchfield continues to thrive as a co-educational preparatory school with numbers maintaining the long-term average of around 150 and with a pupil split of roughly two- thirds boys and one-third girls.

For a number of years I had not been in contact with anyone at my old senior school, Denstone College, except annual Christmas cards to my old housemaster, Mike Swales. However, in 2006 I was organising a reunion of our all-conquering 1966/1967 rugby side in order to celebrate 40 years since our wonderful achievement.

It was incredibly difficult to find everyone after such a long period of time, but with people coming from France, Ibiza and Canada I managed to find ten of the original team and we all got together for a wonderful night and a celebration dinner back at Denstone.

We all stayed at the nearby Alton Towers hotel and arranged to meet in the bar before taking a bus up to the college so that we could all drink. Standing at the bar was an experience I will never forget, as some of us had not seen each other since leaving Denstone 40 years earlier.

Most of us had put on more than a few kilos in weight and also lost most if not all of our hair. To begin with, it was difficult to identify with each other but after about half an hour, it was like we had never been apart, and by the time we got on the bus to go to Denstone we were half-cut and making far too much noise.

It was a night to remember and as we were still the only rugby team to win every match in the school's 148-year history, the teachers and the staff treated us like royalty. We somehow managed to get back to Alton Towers and carried on drinking through most of the night. I have absolutely no recollection of crashing out, but I woke up with two of the lads in a bunk bed and a thumping headache!

The following year I was invited to be president of the Old Denstonian Club, which involved attending a few regional dinners and playing in a couple of golf events. The first event was in London and Gill and I were delighted to meet the headmaster, David Derbyshire, and his wife Viv.

David had joined Denstone in 1997 when the school was really struggling. As part of the Woodard Corporation its future was in the balance and there was actually a threat of closure hanging over the school.

David set about reviving the school's reputation and finances and in just ten years managed to turn Denstone around into being one of Woodard's flagship schools. It was a remarkable achievement and from the word go we seemed to hit it off together. Eventually he asked me if I would like to join the board of governors.

Having put so much time and effort into Birchfield my immediate reaction was that I wanted to have a few years off, but at least at Denstone I would not have to be as involved as I had at Birchfield.

Denstone is about an hour and twenty minutes' drive from where I live just outside Wolverhampton, so it is not as though I could just pop in when I felt like it. I also wondered whether returning so often would remind me of how unhappy I had been in the first two years or how happy I had been in the last two.

In the end I felt that it had been a large part of my life and if I could help in any way then I should. To watch a school grow in terms of academic achievements, facilities and just sheer enjoyment of the experience by the pupils is very rewarding.

When I was at Denstone, apart from sport, it was just a matter of getting through the days, the weeks and the terms. I don't think pleasure or enjoyment were words ever associated with the early years of our education, where bullying and vindictiveness was commonplace. It was also an all-boys' school, so we were never going to be prepared for the real world that included getting on with and hopefully marrying the opposite sex.

Nowadays most of the pupils seem to actually enjoy the experience of going to school. They have choice in what they can study, choice in games, music, the arts and even a choice of food. They can decide whether they go as day pupils or as boarders and whether they board weekly or termly, and they can even mix with the opposite sex.

In private education these changes have been brought about purely and simply because parents are paying for and demanding more and more for their money. Over the years, as fees have continued to grow more than inflation, so have the requirements of parents seeking the best possible choices for their children.

As the school numbers started to swell from the year 2000 onwards, so did the finances of the school and soon a brand new sports hall was built, followed by a new music school. As the reputation of the school improved, pupil numbers improved again, the finances improved again and yet another classroom block was added.

And so this virtuous circle continued, providing ever-improving modern facilities and, more importantly, engendering a feeling of pride in the school from pupils and teachers alike.

Over the last ten years pupil numbers have almost doubled from 320 to over 600, which proves that the school's reputation has improved dramatically over a short period of time.

My main job within the council is being chairman of the foundation, which involves trying to get as many Old Denstonians back to the school as possible, and the most tangible aim is to raise funds for scholarships and bursaries to help educate children whose parents struggle to pay the normal school fees.

The opening of the Threlfall Library at Denstone College with wife Gill, sister Sharron and children Nicholas and Jade.

Over the last three years we have created the Alistair Hignell Sports Scholarship, the Lionel Lethbridge Music Scholarship and the Mike Swales Science Scholarship. As we become more financially successful it also allows us to award a greater percentage of our fee income to help support those parents who are desperate to educate their children privately, but struggle financially.

I continue to enjoy my role on the governing body and most recently we completed the building of a brand new library, which is outstanding in every way. After agreeing to support the project I was humbled to find out that it was to be named the Threlfall Library, and taking my family along to its opening on 12 March 2014 will always remain one of my proudest moments.

CHAPTER 19

Stick to Your Knitting

By definition entrepreneurs take risks and it is virtually impossible to go through your business life without making a few wrong turns and more than a few bad decisions, and I have certainly made my share of both. As you get older, for some reason decisions tend to get more difficult to make than when you are young. I suppose a lot of it has to do with a blend of youthful energy and innate confidence that comes more naturally when you have less to lose and have made fewer mistakes. If anything, it should probably be the other way around because as we get older we gain experience, become wiser and should be able to sort out the wheat from the chaff with a far more reasoned and considered approach.

One of the great rules of business is to stick to what you know, because danger lurks in making decisions about things you know little or nothing about. I have been involved in retailing for over 50 years and therefore it is my area of expertise, and I should know that any business venture I choose to consider should be in or allied to that field. I know nothing about house building and I should have known better than to get involved with an investment in which I was a lamb to the slaughter but unfortunately, to my great cost, I didn't follow my own advice.

After selling out to Tesco and having time on my hands, I had been approached by a builder who had a good reputation and had done some work for me on one of the properties I owned. Money was tight and he was finding it difficult to get any development financed by the bank, so he approached me with an idea that seemed to make sense. He would find the development opportunities, build them at cost and I would finance the venture and we would share the profits. For each house we built, there would be a detailed analysis of all potential costs and then a contingency of 10 per cent would be added to cover any overruns. It would then be entirely up to me whether we proceeded with the project, and if so I would make stage payments along the way and we could compare the actual costs with those forecast at the outset.

It all sounded very feasible and I looked forward with excitement at becoming not only a successful retailer but now a property tycoon. The first project that we embarked upon was to buy an old police station and convert it into two semi-detached houses. The building costs were reasonably within budget and I have to say the quality of the build and the finished product looked excellent, so I looked forward to a quick sale and a profit of £30,000 to be shared equally between us. Unfortunately it didn't work out exactly as planned because by the time we had finished building them, the property market had taken a downturn and we could not sell the houses at the prices we were asking. Each house had to be sold for £20,000 less than we had originally planned and the project eventually lost £10,000 instead of making £30,000.

That was the first mistake. We had only talked about sharing the profits equally but there had been no discussions on sharing the losses equally, so I had learnt my first lesson. Unfortunately it was too late because I had already embarked upon another project that was to cost me a lot more.

For £250,000 we had secured an option on a piece of land that currently served as overflow parking for a pub/restaurant just outside Dudley in the West Midlands. Having secured planning permission for a mini development of six small terraced houses, I went ahead and bought the land. The scheme, together with building costs, was estimated to total no more than £600,000, including a contingency this time of 15 per cent. We were confident that the location was excellent and the houses would sell quite quickly at £125,000 each, giving rise to a handsome profit of £150,000 out of which I would receive the £10,000 that I had lost on the police station project, and then we would split the remaining balance. The deal was structured in the same way as before, with me paying the building company the stage payments as they became due.

All started well until one day I received a call from the builder saying that he would like to see me, and I immediately started to feel that something might be wrong. He produced a spreadsheet and told me that unfortunately all the groundwork costs had increased enormously, as the well that existed below the property had cost far more to fill in than originally anticipated. On top of this the cost of building materials had risen well above the contingency figure, the result being that our anticipated profit of £150,000 had all but disappeared. I was stunned and asked to see all the working papers behind the figures, but he could have told me anything because I really didn't understand the building trade.

That was lesson number two. No matter how much you trust someone to invoice you for work at cost, it will never work out in your favour because it is human nature and plain common sense that the person will look after their own interests before yours. I was absolutely stupid to put myself in a position whereby I was totally relying on someone else to protect my interests, and it is amazing how greed can confuse your judgement.

As if all this wasn't bad enough, things were about to get a whole lot worse.

The houses were finally built, looked really smart and I have to say there was little wrong with the quality of the finished product. Three houses sat on either side of a courtyard and there was adequate parking for at least one car per household. The development looked really good, but unfortunately once again we had been too ambitious with our projected sale prices. Instead of selling for £125,000 each, we were now told that we would be lucky to get much over £100,000 each as the market had become extremely difficult for first-time buyers. The projected profit of £150,000 had suddenly become a projected loss of £150,000, but once again I was about to receive a bombshell that would make a £150,000 loss look like chicken feed.

The phone rang and the builder said he needed to see me urgently and could he come around straight away; within minutes he was at my house. He looked deathly pale and proceeded to tell me that a receiver had been appointed and that his company was in liquidation. As his whole family worked in and relied on the business for their income it was devastating news and I felt genuinely sorry for them all.

Later that morning it slowly started to dawn on me that I may have a problem with regard to ownership of the completed development, and I phoned my solicitor to discuss the issue. The more we talked about it the more dread I felt, as I realised that the only security I had was the tenure of the land which I had bought directly from the vendor. The stage payments had been paid directly to the builder and I asked my solicitor where I stood with regard to this. Surely I had security of ownership? He went very quiet and said that he would get back to me shortly. An hour or so later he confirmed my worst fears that no such agreement existed; the money I had paid out to the builders as stage payments had effectively become theirs and the development was now owned lock, stock and barrel by the receiver. My blood started to run cold as the full extent of what I had done, or more accurately not done, began to sink in.

I tell this story not to make myself look stupid, which I patently was, but to point out to people that when handing money over to third parties you have to be very careful with ownership rights. I had used a small firm of solicitors to act for me in order to avoid high costs and had paid the price for not getting the best advice, which led to a lot of bitterness and litigation, but that is another story. The truth of the matter is that I should have been advised of the pitfalls of what I was getting into concerning the relationship with the builder.

This was lesson number three. If you want the best legal advice make sure you use a reputable firm and be prepared to pay their prices.

In the end I had to buy my own development back from the receiver, so you can imagine how that made me feel, and I learnt a very expensive lesson. Fortunately I managed to do a good deal with the receiver and then, by holding on to the houses until the property market turned and then selling them, I didn't lose as much as I had originally feared. Nevertheless the whole sorry episode cost me in the region of £250,000, a red face and an experience that I will never forget.

The really annoying thing is that one of my best friends, John Gough, is an experienced and noted builder and if only I had sought his advice in the first place, I would probably have avoided the disaster. Needless to say I have never been invited to join the board of a property development company and I just cannot understand why!

Another venture which was out of my comfort zone of business involved the purchase of a pub/restaurant business which neither made me a fortune nor lost me one. Dave Smith, my partner at T&S until 1989, had a brother-in-law called Malcolm Stark who had been in the restaurant business for most of his working life and was

looking to start up a venture on his own. He had a located a pub/
restaurant that was for sale on the main Shifnal to Wolverhampton
road called The Horns of Boningale, which had an excellent
reputation and good development potential. Needing finance,
Malcolm approached David and me and we eventually agreed to
finance the venture, with the three of us holding equal shares.

We built a large extension on to the restaurant, increased
the dining capacity from 30 to 100, built a brand new kitchen
and significantly improved the bar area. The total cost of the
improvements, together with the purchase of the premises, added up
to a sizeable investment of £500,000, but the resulting development
looked excellent and was in a great location.

Before the additional investment the pub had been taking about
£4,000 per week and now needed to take double that amount to
cover the costs of the extra expenditure and increased staff numbers.
Within three months we were taking £10,000 per week, making good
profits and were fully booked for most of December.

I found the business absolutely fascinating as we grappled with
the challenges of menu selection and price points. The pub trade
in Britain has dramatically changed since the introduction of
drink-driving laws and a move to more families eating out. When I
was young, pubs were for drinking in and rarely served food, there
were few restaurants to choose from and family occasions were
usually held in local hotels. Today most successful pub/restaurants
take more money on food than they do on drink. The dry/wet
split, as it is known in the trade, favours a sales split of 60 per cent
on food and 40 per cent on drink, giving an overall gross profit
margin of somewhere above 50 per cent, depending on competition
and location.

The really interesting part of the equation is how to maximise
sales and margin because every day of the week has a differing sales

pattern. It is almost impossible to sell food on a Monday night as very few people eat out. On Tuesday, Wednesday and Thursday it becomes a little easier, then Friday and Saturday are your busiest nights with Sunday trade being almost exclusively confined to lunchtime.

You have to vary your menu approach, therefore, on a day by day basis. For example, on Monday night we introduced fish and chips at a price which barely covered the cost, believing that we would fill the place and make money on the drinks side. Unfortunately it did not work out like that because although we filled the place, most people asked for water to go with their meal and even had the cheek to keep ordering more and more bread and butter.

The Horns at Boningale, a wonderful pub/restaurant.

On Tuesday, Wednesday and Thursday nights, we offered midweek specials with two eating for the price of one, and I have to say that worked very well. On Friday and Saturday nights we were normally fully booked and in addition to our regular menu we offered blackboard specials at premium prices. Sunday tended to look after itself with an offering of two roast options or a fish dish, and we were normally fully booked and enjoyed an excellent reputation for our roast potatoes.

So the formula was set and we were making money on the last £2,000 of our weekly take. However, the kitchen was so busy that we needed to employ another chef to cover for illness, holidays and busy nights. In addition to this, we needed a front of house person to take bookings, seat people at the tables and take orders for the kitchen. We also needed someone else to work at the bar. Lo and behold, all the extra costs took away the profit we were making and once again we had to increase turnover in order to stand still.

We increased our prices where we could but there is a point at which people realise what you are doing and, if you are not careful, they will take their trade elsewhere. We had a great reputation for fair prices combined with reasonable food and excellent service, and our lunchtime trade increased to such an extent that people would queue in the car park waiting for the opening time of 12.00pm. Year by year we edged up our margins but there were always exceptional costs to knock back our profits, and we never seemed to make the money that we should out of such a successful business.

It was difficult for me to enjoy a meal there because I was permanently looking around to see if people were being kept waiting for their food. One year we held our T&S director's Christmas meal in the main restaurant, and I spent half the evening helping out in the kitchen because one of the waitresses had failed to turn up for work.

After seven years of what I have to say was great fun and a great challenge, Malcolm became ill and we had little option but to sell out. We had a lot of interest and sold the freehold business for a better price than we had expected.

Looking back over the years, we never made a lot of money out of running the business on a year by year basis, but by the same token we never lost money either. However, we did sell out for a good price and enjoyed a good capital return on our investment. I learned a lot about a trade that is fascinating because of all the different strands that have to be brought together to make it commercially viable. It is also extremely demanding in terms of hours, and requires a lifestyle approach in order to succeed that would not suit most people.

My only other business involvement outside retailing occurred in 1999 when I was invited to join the Staffordshire Building Society (SBS) as a non-executive director. Geoff Gallagher, who had been our Barclays Bank manager during our rapid expansion, had approached me as he also sat on the board as a non-executive. Although I knew very little about the industry, it was a great opportunity for me to broaden my commercial experience in a completely different field and also take on a new challenge.

I have to say that in many ways the SBS was probably typical of most building societies of its time and was rooted in the past rather than the future. The board was largely made up of former executives who had retired from the day job, and it was all a little bit cosy and hail-fellow, well-met. Because of this the average age of board members tended to be over 60, and decisions made by the acting executives were rarely challenged in a constructive manner. However, I was fortunate to work there with Lord Hodgson, who was deputy chairman of the Conservative Party between 1997 and 2000. He was a breath of fresh air and extremely bright, and I like to think that between him, Geoff Gallagher and me, we made a difference in a positive way.

The SBS was well run and profitable but at the turn of the last century there were just too many building societies in existence, and with the banks entering the market business became incredibly competitive. Most societies survived through the inertia of the customer base, meaning it was just too difficult and costly to move to another mortgage provider, so customers just stayed put. It really annoyed me that most societies offered a better deal to potential new customers than to their existing ones, and at regional society conferences I would stand up and ask the conference chairman why this was so.

I rarely got a straight answer, but everyone knew that it was standard practice and was the best way of protecting profitability. Nowadays, with the advent of the internet there is far more transparency and I think customers get a better deal.

Needless to say, the SBS as a regional player got hoovered up in the ensuing consolidation of the industry and in 2003 merged with the Portman Building Society, who in turn got hoovered up in 2007 by the Nationwide Building Society. Over the last twenty years the consolidation of the building society movement has been phenomenal but was also long overdue.

I cannot say that being on the board of the SBS was the most thrilling commercial experience I have ever enjoyed and at times the rhetoric and financial detail was beyond me, but I got the gist of what was going on and our members at least enjoyed a financial windfall when the business was merged with the Portman. However, I did meet some very nice people; though in truth, the highlight of the day for me was always the lunch served in the boardroom!

– CHAPTER 20 –

Life After Death

My local golf club is South Staffs, just outside Wolverhampton, and for a number of years I have captained the A team, which plays in friendly annual fixtures with our local clubs, normally on a home and away basis. On 23 April 2014 we were playing our first match of the season at home to Moseley; I was looking forward to a good competitive match and hoping that the weather would be kind to us.

The matches involve eight players per team going out in fourballs and we normally start about 3.00pm, which gives us time to get around the golf course, shower and sit down for dinner about 8.00pm. We then discuss all the bad shots and the simple putts we had missed and, like most groups of men, spend the rest of the evening putting the world to rights and talking rubbish. We normally play about twelve matches a year and it is a great way of playing other golf courses and meeting old friends.

23 April started like any other day; I spent the morning in my office, had a quick sandwich with Gill at lunchtime and then set off to the golf club around 2.00pm.

I met Moseley's captain, Martin Knowles, whom I had known for a couple of years. We decided to go off first and I chose to play with a good friend of mine called John Mumford.

On the third hole I managed to hole a ridiculous 30ft snaking putt and commented that if I lived for another 300 years, I would never make that putt again. By the sixth hole the match was all square and as I played my shot to the short par three, I apparently dropped down dead.

I say apparently, because I have absolutely no recollection of what happened to me and to this day I still have no memory of getting up that fateful morning, going to the golf club and playing the first five holes.

As I collapsed at apparently 4.05pm, the first miracle happened in that Martin, who was a retired policeman, just happened to be fully trained in CPR (cardiopulmonary resuscitation) and got me into the recovery position. My playing partner, John Mumford, phoned 999 and while Martin was giving me CPR, his partner ran back to the clubhouse to get the defibrillator.

Playing in the group directly behind us was another retired police officer, Steve Woodward, who also happened to be trained in CPR. Steve and Martin continued to work on me until Ian Guest, our golf shop manager, arrived with the defibrillator and proceeded to shock me.

By the time the ambulance arrived at 4.20pm there was still no sign of life, in spite of me having received four shocks from the defibrillator. The ambulance people then took over and the air ambulance arrived minutes later; then the two teams worked together on me.

At 4.45pm Gill arrived from our house and was told to be prepared for the worst, as I had been out of it for 40 minutes and they could still not get a pulse. I was then put into the ambulance and driven off to hospital.

They managed to get my heart going in the ambulance but Gill was told that it would be touch and go whether or not I survived, and the next few hours would be vital. They were also worried about brain damage, which happens very quickly if the brain is starved of oxygen.

Our two children, Nick and Jade, together with Gill and some close family friends, began a vigil but were sent home at about 10.00pm by which time my condition had stabilised.

Miracle number two happened when Gill was phoned at 7.00am the next morning to be told that I was sitting up in bed talking to the nurses; nobody could understand how I could possibly have recovered so quickly. Even the doctors were completely bemused.

Tests showed that there was very little damage to my heart and the CPR that had been administered to me was so good that my brain was still in good working order. (Well, as good as it ever was.)

My first recollection of anything was when I opened my eyes an hour later to see Gill, Nick and Jade sitting at the end of my bed. I looked around me and said, 'I guess I've had a heart attack,' but had no memory of how or when, as I could not remember a single thing about the previous day.

As I sat there with tubes inserted everywhere, I began to take in the enormity of what had happened and how lucky I had been. I had been spending a lot of time in my office writing my book; nobody would have found me there until it was too late. It had been the only time I was playing golf that week and had I been anywhere else but on the golf course, I almost certainly would have died.

There are two main reasons for heart attacks, with the majority caused by plumbing problems or furring up of the arteries and veins. These are normally dealt with by the insertion of stents or, in more serious cases, bypass operations.

Less common is heart failure due to electrical problems, when the heart goes into rapid fibrillation and cannot pump the blood around the body. In layman's terms it is a fuse board problem and can be caused by a number of genetic predispositions. In my case the heart just stopped beating due to an electrical problem and I became unconscious within seconds.

For many years I had been aware of an occasional irregular heartbeat, especially if I drank too much coffee or was under stress at work. It felt as though the heart was missing a beat, whereas in fact the feeling was due to extra, or ectopic, beats.

When I turned 65 years old, I decided to have a full medical and address any health issues that I may have had. For one of the tests I was put on a treadmill and wired up to an ECG (electrocardiogram) machine, and then the pace was slowly increased from walking to jogging and then running fast.

As my heart rate increased to 130 beats per minute, the test was suddenly stopped, as the supervisor was not at all happy with the way my heart was coping with the increased rate. The test results so far were then analysed in detail and a decision was taken to send me to a heart specialist for further investigation.

Detailed tests and an MRI (magnetic resonance imaging) scan indicated that I could have a condition commonly known as hocum, or HOCM (hypertrophic obstructive cardiomyopathy), the same condition that affected the footballer Fabrice Muamba when he collapsed playing football.

As it is a rare condition I was then advised to see a professor in London for his assessment. Further tests were conducted and in the end he concluded that I did not have hocum. His parting words advised me to just get on with my life.

As I 'died' some nine months later, there was patently something wrong with me, which remains undiagnosed to this day, showing that not all eventualities can be foreseen no matter how many specialists you see.

The team that saved my life.

I have now been fitted with an ICD (internal cardioverter defibrillator) that should act as a back-up generator if I ever experience the same problem again. It basically gives an electric shock to the heart that starts it beating again.

No one ever thinks that anything unusual is ever going to happen to them personally. Things we read about in the paper such as acute illness, murder, horrific car accidents and burglary are all things that happen to other people. I had gone along assuming that I would hopefully live into my eighties without incident and then suddenly bang, I wake up in hospital only to find out that I had died for 40 minutes!

I had not factored into my life that any of the above might happen and had planned my retirement around being able to carry on with all the things that gave me pleasure. With our holidays and other little trips, Gill and I tended to be away for about ten weeks of the year.

In addition to this I still had a business interest with my shareholding in the narrowboat holiday company, and golf tended to get me out of the house two or three times a week. My involvement with the cricket club and my old school also made sure that I had a fairly full diary.

At least once a year Tony Reed, chief executive of One-Stop, takes me out around the stores and I find it fascinating to see how things have moved on from my day. I really appreciate the involvement, as so many of the colleagues that I employed are still with One-Stop and it is great to go back and see them. I was extremely touched to learn that the new boardroom had been named after me – it was a wonderful gesture from Tony and much appreciated.

Some businessmen cannot cope with the thought of retirement and I can remember Malcolm Walker, who built up the highly

The 'Threlfall' boardroom at One-Stop Brownhills.

successful Iceland frozen foods chain, telling me that he would not know what to do if he could not go into work. As he approaches the age of 70 he still does a full week's work and I am sure that one day they will find him keeled over in one of his deep freezers. Mind you, if that happens they can keep him frozen until they find a solution to eternal life and then he can come back and run the company forever!

I started to reminisce about my life, and it's only when you look back that you realise how many stupid things you do when you are young. I can remember saying to my mother, when I was about ten years old, that I was going across to the cricket club for a game with a few friends but I would be back by teatime. I would then get on a bus to the town centre with my trainspotting book and pencil in my back pocket, walk to the railway station, and jump on a train to Crewe having bought only a platform ticket.

The Crewe sheds were known as North and South and were two of the largest holding points for trains in the country. They were fantastic locations for spotting trains, but to get around them without being seen and evicted by the workmen was an art in itself.

Each shed would hold over 100 trains at any one time but with engines being constantly shunted from one location to another, they were incredibly dangerous places to be around. If health and safety officers had existed in those days they would have had nervous breakdowns because they were life-threatening enough locations for responsible grown men, let alone ten-year-old boys dodging between the engines to avoid being caught.

On one occasion I was hiding under some goods trucks in a siding just waiting to pick my moment to make a dash into the sheds when no one was around. Unbeknown to me a train had been hooked up to the trucks and with a sudden jolt they started to move. Crouched under the trucks I started to walk quickly to keep up with the speed at which they were moving. I couldn't just lie down and wait for the trucks to pass overhead, as I didn't know what the guard's van at the end of the train had beneath it.

In the end I panicked and just dived between the wheels as the train started to pick up speed, ripping my trousers as I landed on the stones. I was more concerned with what my mother would say about my trousers than I was about nearly being killed.

I decided that was probably enough excitement for one day and walked back to Crewe station, only to find that the next train back to Wolverhampton had been cancelled. This meant that I would not be back until at least 7.30pm and I would be in big trouble, especially if she came to find me.

In the end I walked through the front door of the house at 7.45pm, having picked up my cricket bat out of the garage and before she could start, I told her the other boys were still playing but I thought I had better come home just in case she was getting worried!

However, I did get a clip around the ears for ripping my trousers.

Strangely enough, in my fifteen years as a pilot and flying light aircraft there were probably fewer dangerous moments than in my trainspotting days. The only time for genuine concern came one winter's day when I had taken the plane up for a short trip in beautiful clear skies.

The plane had been in the hangar for a couple of weeks but the weather had been exceptionally cold, so I thought it was a good idea to take it up for an hour and get everything de-iced. I took off to the north-west but as I retracted the wheels I heard a crunching sound as they locked into the undercarriage.

Not liking the sound of what I had heard, I immediately tried to lower the wheels but nothing happened. I realised that the wheels were jammed and it was probably ice that was keeping them in. I tried disconnecting the power to the wheels, hoping that they would fall down under their own weight, but that didn't work either.

I then had a brainwave – well, it seemed like a brainwave at the time – and that was to fly above the cooling towers of Ironbridge power station just to the west of Halfpenny Green airfield. I thought that if I flew very slowly just above them, then the heat rising from the towers would melt any ice that had gathered in the undercarriage. In principle it was a great idea but in practice it just didn't work.

After an hour of flying around I decided that enough was enough and as it was starting to get dark, I had to return to the airfield and declare an emergency. I radioed in to the field and in preparation for my emergency landing the fire engine was readied and an ambulance called from Wolverhampton just in case anything went horribly wrong.

Obviously as a plane travels through the air at over 100 mph and the air pressure on the wheels helps to keep them retracted, the hope was that if I landed with two stages of flap at almost the stalling speed of 60 mph, they might just drop under their own weight.

If the wheels did not come down, it just meant that the propeller would be ruined and the underside of the plane would be badly scratched. It would have been incredibly unlucky for anything life-threatening to happen.

As I brought her down towards the runway, the control tower wished me luck and I could see the fire engine and the ambulance waiting to follow me down the runway. In the event, about 50ft above the ground both wheels dropped from the undercarriage and locked into place.

I made a perfect landing and felt really stupid as the ambulance and the fire engine followed me towards the hangar. In fairness, everyone was delighted that nothing serious had happened and I was just relieved that no damage had been caused to my plane.

At the age of 60 and after 674 hours spent in the air, I finally decided to stop flying. Strangely enough, instead of gaining in confidence every time I took to the air, I started to think that sooner or later something dreadful must happen.

For my 60th birthday Gill had bought me a one-hour aerobatic flight in a jet, to be flown with a fighter pilot who had served for a number of years in the French air force. With two friends, Gill and I flew to Le Touquet in my single-engine Trinidad TB20 and then on to Abbeville, where I was to meet the pilot.

Although an old plane, the Fouga Magister was still a force to be reckoned with. Originally built as a jet-powered two-seater trainer, it had a maximum speed of 450 mph and could climb at over 3,000ft a minute. As it came in to land it made a deafening sound and within minutes I was airborne with Claude, my pilot, over the French coast and climbing to an altitude of 20,000ft.

I had no idea what aerobatics he had in mind but he seemed to think I was twenty years old, not 60. He dropped out of the sky and started performing barrel rolls and then loop-the-loops. I learned later that at one point we were pulling 2.5 G, which is about five times the pressure felt on any ride at Alton Towers.

After about five minutes I had to ask him to stop, as I was a hair's breadth away from being violently sick. He then let me fly the plane myself, which was an incredible experience as everything is controlled from a single joystick which is amazingly sensitive to the slightest movement, left, right, up or down.

After landing back at Abbeville, the flight back home to the airfield at Halfpenny Green in my small TB20 seemed incredibly slow, even though it still rattled along at about 160 mph. We arrived home exhausted but also thrilled at a wonderful day's flying.

I knew then that enough was enough and my flying days were over. I had enjoyed over fifteen years of great fun and as I pulled my plane into the hangar for the last time, I thanked it for looking after me so well and on the following day put it up for sale.

A wonderful flying day at Compton Abbas with my Trinidad TB20.

In one way or another, the grocery trade has formed a massive part of my life and it has changed dramatically since the end of the Second World War. It is amazing to think that grocery rationing still existed 60 years ago, and the development of food retailing over that time span has been phenomenal.

The choice, variety and quality that exist today bear absolutely no comparison with what was available in post-war Britain. I was lucky enough to see people queuing for Typhoo Tea when retail price maintenance was abolished. My father sold hundreds of cases by being one of the first people in the West Midlands to take just 1d off per packet.

In the 1960s the supermarkets came into fashion as self-service stores took over from the traditional grocers. Then the discounters, such as my own chain Lo-Cost and Kwik Save, started to dominate in the 1970s with a limited range of goods at considerably lower prices.

As affluence increased through the 1980s, the discounters went out of fashion as the supermarkets fought back with quality fresh food and ever-improving ranges of meal solutions. The discounters could not offer a complete grocery solution for the average housewife who was slowly becoming money-rich but time-poor.

Over the last ten years Tesco won the race for space with their Extra format stores, sometimes of 100,000 square feet, helping them to grow to a market share of just under a third of all grocery sold in Britain, a truly remarkable achievement under the brilliant leadership of Sir Terry Leahy.

But over the last few years the competition has caught up and grocery retailing is now fought out at the top end between Waitrose, M&S and Sainsbury's and at the lower end between Morrisons, Asda and the newly revived discounters from Germany, Lidl and Aldi.

Tesco has been caught having to fight the middle ground and its market dominance, while still huge, is being threatened by some smart retailers. The number of shoppers visiting supermarkets is also declining as more and more people shop online and have home deliveries.

In addition to this the ever-improving convenience stores are also taking more and more market share away from the supermarkets. The store numbers are growing, but yet again Tesco have the upper hand and a growing market share with their Tesco Express and One-Stop formats.

There is no doubt in my mind that retailing is going to get even tougher and although I have loved every minute of being involved, I am truly glad to be out of a battlefield that is going to see a lot of bloodshed over the coming years.

It is tempting to witter on about the things I have learnt along the way, but there are any number of books about management that can offer far better advice to would-be entrepreneurs than I ever could.

In some ways the fear of failure is a better incentive to succeed than sheer ability, and I happen to believe that self-confidence is more an innate trait than something that develops along the way. Obviously success strengthens resolve and confidence, but nevertheless some people seem to have it in spades and others seem to lack it.

Money in itself should never be the sole goal of any person and I can remember my father telling me that if I ever got as much pleasure out of spending money as he had out of making it, I would be a very rich man!

After selling T&S to Tesco, Gill and I spent a lot more time travelling and visiting our villa in Portugal. There is a happy medium to be achieved in balancing work and leisure and we never went away for long periods, as we wanted holidays to remain special and not become some sort of boring routine.

However, we did spend enough time in Portugal to fall in love with two stray dogs that we eventually brought back to England with us.

The first little Heinz 57 terrier had been abandoned in the Pingo Doce supermarket car park near our villa in the Algarve and every time we went there to shop the poor little thing looked hungrier and sadder, until eventually she went in the back of the car with us and then back to England. With great imagination we named her Pingo!

The following year a scruffy, pathetic-looking small Portuguese biscuit-coloured hunting dog called a Podango appeared on the golf course just below our villa and I started feeding him every day. He was petrified and would only go to the food when I had retired a safe distance.

Over the course of the next ten days he became my friend and I fell in love with him. He looked so lost and helpless and was barely a

Grandkids: Jack, Mia, Sam and Oliver with our wonderful dogs Biscuit, Molly and Pingo.

year old, and I was fascinated to know how he had ended up on the golf course. Sometimes Portuguese people abandon their dogs near villas in the hope that idiots like me will take them in.

Well it worked and, as the end of our holiday approached, Gill and I resolved to take him home with us, but how were we going to catch him? In the end I went to see a local vet who happened to own a tranquilizer gun and he agreed to come along, shoot the dog and then, as the tranquilizer drug took effect, grab hold of him. Carlos parked his car by the roadside and, walking past bemused golfers with his rifle in his hand, proceeded to get under cover in a bush and await the arrival of the dog.

The next thing that happened was two police cars arriving with sirens blaring; Carlos had been reported by the golfers as some madman hiding in the bushes shooting at golfers as they went past!

Carlos explained to the policemen his real reason for being there and fortunately they saw the funny side of the story and drove off. With Carlos back in position we waited and waited and waited, but the dog did not arrive so we had to abandon the idea until the following evening.

We reconvened and this time the dog came running down the fairway towards me but instinctively seemed to know something was different. Whether he could smell Carlos in the bushes or not we didn't know, but he was certainly more cautious. Eventually there was a loud bang, but the tranquilizer dart had missed the dog and gone straight into a tree. Round one to the dog as he disappeared up the fairway with his food in his mouth.

The following evening Carlos tried again but this time the dart went into the sand bunker by the side of the green, never to be seen again. Round two to the dog.

The following day Gill and I had to fly home, but we had become friendly with two ladies who run an organisation called

SOS Algarve Animals, which takes in and rehomes stray dogs that are abandoned in the Algarve region. It is a terrible problem in Portugal and Ginny and Laura do a wonderful job, finding homes for up to 200 strays a year.

They promised to keep feeding our dog until it was caught. Five weeks later I got a call from a very excited Ginny to tell me that finally the capture had happened. He spent five weeks in quarantine and Gill and I flew back to Faro just before Christmas to pick him up.

Carlos, Ginny, Laura, Gill and I enjoyed a fantastic celebration dinner and the following day we flew him home to England. To keep up our tradition of wonderfully imaginative names we called him Biscuit, and as we sat on the plane on Christmas Eve in Faro airport the captain announced:

Good morning ladies, gentlemen, boys and girls, we have 185 souls on board and a very lucky dog in the hold called Biscuit.

For some reason everyone cheered, and for Gill and me it was the best Christmas present we could have wished for.

Apart from holidays to Portugal we have visited some wonderful places over the last ten years. While younger people are on the ski slopes in January and February Gill and I prefer to go on a nice cruise, preferably somewhere warm.

Picking the right cruise line is essential and as we get older we prefer the more sedate cruises that could easily pass as posh floating nursing homes. Gone are the days of camps in the Maasai Mara or safaris through the Okavango Delta in Botswana which, although wonderful at the time, seem far too energetic now.

Last year we were thrilled to see Antarctica and the Falkland Islands and this year was a completely different experience, visiting Vietnam and Cambodia. For me, travelling the world has been one of the great thrills of life, but I have always returned to England thinking how lucky I was to be born here and that I would never want to live anywhere else.

Lying in my hospital bed recovering, I drifted in and out of sleep and time seemed to pass very slowly as nurses went about their nightly duties and the occasional patient called out in pain. I thought about how lucky I had been to get this far; from leaping through train wheels, waking up while having my appendix removed, flying around in my plane and finally surviving death, I realised that I had probably used up more than my share of luck.

The care I had received from the ambulance service, the air ambulance service and the NHS had been fantastic. The heart and lung department in the Wolverhampton New Cross Hospital is comparatively new and reputed to be one of the finest in the country. I know the NHS comes in for a lot of criticism but there is a school of thought that suggests the more serious your condition, the better treatment you receive. This was certainly true in my case.

Yet another holiday – Gill and I cruising in 2011.

I started to think how far the NHS had come since its inception in 1948. I also thought how lucky I had been, to be born in Britain into a fantastic period of post-war hope and change. Husbands returning home from battlefields started families with their loved ones and we became the hopeful generation that tried to make sense out of a war-torn world.

The hippy, flower-power, give-peace-a-chance 1960s cleared the way for a new kind of politics and laid the foundations for an entrepreneurial spirit to break through and flourish.

I'm so glad that I lived through those times when rewards had to be worked for rather than gifted on a plate. As I built up my business through the 1980s and 1990s I probably didn't see enough of my kids, but it seemed to be the more natural thing to do with Gill bringing up the family and me going out to work. She did a far better job than I would have done, and had I been more involved I would have probably just got in the way.

When you have a young family and a busy life, the weekdays seem to revolve around getting the kids to bed so that you can enjoy a little bit of peace and quiet. The problem is that the weeks just seem to fly by, with life becoming a blur, and if you are not careful you can meet yourself coming backwards before you have even set off. As you get older and your final years become more precious, it is the one race you want to slow down in as you approach the finishing line.

When I collapsed on the golf course, but for a miracle, my race would have been run. I would have been furious as I still had two chapters of the book to write! But I now appreciate and enjoy every day as if it is my last, and my family and friends have been a fantastic support to me.

This book was never about money; yes, it happened to be a by-product of what I was doing, but it is a book about my life as I lived it, the luck that I enjoyed along the way and the wonderful people I became involved with.

My final words are reserved for one very, very special person. Gill has supported and loved me for over 40 years and my thanks go out to her because she has made my life richer than any amount of money could ever have done.

– APPENDIX –

LIST OF CURRENT UK SUPERMARKET CHAINS

Supermarket	Founded/came to UK	Owned by
Aldi	1989	Aldi Süd GmbH
Asda	1949	Wal-Mart through subsidiary Corinth Services Ltd
Booths	1847	Owned by the original founding family
Budgens	1872	Musgrave Group
Co-op, and The Co-operative Food		Various Co-op societies
Costcutter	1986	Bibby Line Group
CK's Supermarkets	1988	
Farmfoods	1955	
Filco Foods	1956	
Heron Foods	1979	UK private company
Iceland	1970	
Lidl	1994	Lidl Stiftung & Co. KG
Londis	1959	Musgrave Group
Mace		Palmer and Harvey
Marks & Spencer	1884	Publicly traded on the London Stock Exchange
Morrisons	1899	Publicly traded on the London Stock Exchange
Nisa-Today's	1977	UK private company
Ocado	2002	Publicly traded on the London Stock Exchange
Sainsbury's	1869	Publicly traded on the London Stock Exchange
Spar	1957	Owned by Independent Retailers
Tesco	1919	Publicly traded on the London Stock Exchange
Waitrose	1904	John Lewis Partnership
Whole Foods Market	2004	Publicly traded on NASDAQ

Current market share (%)	2007 market share (%)	Notes
4.6	2.6	No-frills supermarket
17.4	16.6	Founded by a group of Yorkshire farmers
		North-west of England and Yorkshire
		Found in England and Wales, with stores up to 10,000 square feet (930 m2)
6.1	4.4	Identities shared by about 20 retail co-operatives including:
		• The Co-operative Group (the largest, with 5.4% market share)
		• East of England Co-operative Society
		• Midcounties Co-operative
		• Central England Co-operative
		• Scotmid
		Symbol group and convenience store
		Welsh-based supermarket founded in Llandeilo
0.8	0.5	
		Welsh-based supermarket founded in Llantwit Major
		Primarily frozen foods; operates 170 stores throughout the Midlands and the North
2.1	1.6	First store opened at Oswestry, Shropshire in 1970
3.4	2.2	No-frills supermarket
		Symbol group and a convenience store
		Irish-owned franchise symbol group and a convenience store founded by Jonny Lingiah
3.8 (separate measure)		Clothing and food retailer
11.1	11.2	Fourth biggest supermarket in the UK, over 450 stores
		Retailers' co-operative and symbol group
		Online only, partnership with Waitrose and Morrisons
16.5	16.2	Superstores as well as 'Local' and 'Central' sites
		Symbol group
28.6	31.6	Including 'Extra', 'Superstores', 'Metro', 'Express' and 'Homeplus' outlets. UK's largest non-food retailer
5.0	3.9	Waitrose has a variety of store styles, including:
		'Waitrose Stores', 'Waitrose Convenience Stores and Little Waitrose', 'John Lewis Foodhall', 'Waitrose Food, Fashion & Home', 'Waitrose Food & Home' , 'Welcome Break outlets' (motorway services outlets)
		Which? Best Supermarket 2013
		Entered the UK with the acquisition of seven Fresh & Wild stores

LIST OF DEFUNCT UK SUPERMARKET CHAINS

Supermarket	Founded/came to UK	Fate
Aberness		Bought by Somerfield
Alldays		Bought by the Co-operative Group
All 'Ours		Merged with Premier Stores
Bejam	1968	Bought by Iceland
Bells Stores		Bought by Sainsbury's, branded as Sainsbury's at Bells before being converted to Sainsbury's Local
Bishops		Bought by Budgens
BP Safeway	1962	Dissolved following Safeway takeover by Morrisons
Carrefour	1970s	UK business sold to Gateway/Somerfield, then later to Asda
Capital Freezer Centres		Now owned by Farmfoods
Circle K		Merged with Alldays
County Stores		Sold to Gateway, converted to Somerfield
Crazy Prices		Bought by Tesco
Healds Day & Nite		Bought by Tesco
David Greig		Bought by Somerfield
Europa		Bought by Tesco
Fairway		Bought by Gateway
Fine Fare	1956	Bought by Gateway
Food Giant		Originally part of Somerfield Group, all stores converted to Kwik Save following the Somerfield/Kwik Save merger
FreshXpress	2007	Administration in 2008, liquidated in 2009
Galbraith Supermarkets	1894	Bought by Allied Suppliers, then Argyll Group
Gateway Foodmarkets	1950	Rebranded as Somerfield
Select & Save		Bought by Costcutter
Grandways		Some stores sold to Argyll Group for their Presto chain and Kwik Save, remainder renamed Jacksons
GT Smith		Bought by Co-operative Group
Haldanes	2009	(including UGO stores)
Hillards		Bought by Tesco
Hintons		Bought by Argyll Foods to become part of Presto
Irwin's Stores		Bought by Tesco
International		Bought by Gateway
Jackson's		Bought by Sainsbury's, branded as Sainsbury's at Jackson's before being converted to Sainsbury's Local
Key Markets		Bought by Gateway
Kwik Save	1959	Bought by Somerfield Group 1998. Smaller stores sold to BTTF, after administration smaller stores became FreshXpress
Laws		Bought by Wm Low for £7.1 million
Lennons		Bought by Dee Group
Liptons	1871	Bought by Allied Suppliers

Closed	Notes
2000	Scottish convenience chain
	Symbol group within the Moffat company
1989	Frozen Foods
2004	Small chain of 54 convenience stores in the north-east of England
1984	63 stores in south-east England
1990	Partnership between BP plc and Safeway, listed as Equinox retailing. Some stores now Tesco Express
1990	
	ABF-owned Northern Ireland group
	Presence in central London
1986	
2009	Smaller stores of former Kwik Save chain. Bought out by management team led by Brendan Murtagh
1992	Scottish chain
1992/3	Regional in Yorkshire
2002	Regional in West Yorkshire
2011	Went into administration 2011
	Mainly in north-east England and Yorkshire
2004	Regional in Yorkshire and north Midlands
2007	Smaller stores sold to BTTF and converted to FreshXpress, larger converted to Somerfield or leased to others by Somerfield
	Chain of supermarkets focused on north-east England
	Part of Key Market. Rebranded part of Gateway chain when Dee took over Gateway
	Converted to Presto or Lo-Cost stores

Supermarket	Founded/came to UK	Fate
Lo-Cost		Converted to Safeway
Local Plus		Bought by the Co-operative Group
Mac Fisheries		Bought by Dee Group
Mace		
Mainstop		Acquired by Morrisons
Morning, Noon & Night		Bought by Scotmid
Netto	1990	Bought by Asda in 2010 for £778m from Dansk Supermarked Group. 147 stores were rebranded in 2011 as Asda local stores. The remaining 47 stores have been sold off to other companies such as Morrisons and new convenience store UGO and other retailers due to competition laws
Normans supermarkets		Bought by Plymco
Normid		Rebranded Co-op
Norco		Rebranded Co-op
One Stop		Bought by Tesco, still exists today
Premier Supermarkets		Bought by Mac Fisheries
Presto	1977	After buying out Safeway, all stores were converted to Safeway
PriceRite		
Quality Fare		Bought by the Co-operative Group
Rainbow		Discontinued, rebranded as parent Co-op
Richway Supermarkets		
Safeway (UK)	1962	Bought by Morrisons
Sainsbury's Savacentre	1977	Discontinued, rebranded Sainsbury's
7-Eleven		Taken over by Budgens
Shop Rite	1972	Bought by Kwik Save, still trades as ShopRite in the Isle of Man, stocking a range of Waitrose and Iceland products as well as locally produced goods
Somerfield	1865	Purchase agreed by the Co-operative Group on 16 July 2008 for £1.56bn; from 2009 many larger stores were sold off and smaller stores rebranded to The Co-operative Food
Stewarts Supermarket Limited		Bought by Tesco
Supernational		Bought by Gateway
Templeton Supermarkets	1880	Bought by Allied Suppliers then Argyll Group
VG		Bought by Alldays
Victor Value		Bought by Tesco
Wallis	1955	Bought by Somerfield
Walter Wilson		
Wm Low		Bought by Tesco

These supermarkets are either no longer trading, have been renamed, or have been taken over and rebranded.

Closed	Notes
1978	Wet fish shops closed
1981	
2011	Was a no frills supermarket. On 30 September 2011, Netto UK ceased trading
	Was owned by United Co-operatives
	Aberdeen-based co-operative society
1965	Subsidiary of Express Dairies, opened UK's first supermarket in Streatham, south London in 1951. Sold after losing out on purchase of Irwin's stores to Tesco
1998	
	Retail chain operating in south of England and the Isle of Wight
2005	Safeway Compact stores sold to Somerfield. Was still trading under Safeway in Channel Islands until becoming Waitrose in 2010
2005	
	Convenience Store chain
1994	Discount supermarket chain
2011	
	ABF-owned Northern Ireland group
	Scottish chain, rebranded as Presto
1968/1986	Independent chain. Larger stores were rebranded as Tesco, remaining sold to Bejam in 1986
2003	Founded by Francis J. Wallis of Rainham, Essex in 1955. By 1968 there were 38 stores. In 1977 100 of 380 stores were sold to International stores for £21 million. Taken over by Somerfield sometime around 1999, the larger stores were rebranded while the smaller stores were sold to Co-Op. FJ Wallis Ltd was dissolved by voluntary strike-off in 2003
	Presence in Scotland and northern England

GROUP ACQUISITIONS

Group acquisitions	Group acquisitions store numbers	STORE NUMBERS			Year
		Opened	Closed	Balance	
					1978
					1979
					1980
					1981
					1982
					1983
USM					1984
					1985
					1986
Buy-wise	89				1987
					1988
Dillons & Preedy	398		20	550	1989
		33	38	545	1990
JCR	22	54	16	583	1991
		14	16	581	1992
		32	15	598	1993
Gibbs; Macs	101	134	28	704	1994
		42	32	714	1995
Paper Chain	109	127	37	804	1996
M&W	179	257	74	987	1997
		36	56	967	1998
One Stop	218	275	42	1200	1999
Day & Nite	100	128	55	1273	2000
		18	56	1235	2001

Amounts paid for acquisitions	£ million
Dillions/Preedy	54.1
JCR	4.0
Gibbs/Macs	15.1
Paper Chain	10.1
M&W	42.8
One Stop	67.0
Day & Nite	25.0
	218.1

Turnover £ million	Pre-tax profit £ million	Continuing EPS per pence	Dividend per pence	C-Store like-for-like sales increase year/year
2.1	0.0			
3.6	0.0			
6.2	0.1			
11.6	0.3			
15.6	0.3			
25.7	0.4			
36.4	0.8	3.05	0.79	
50.6	1.2	4.65	1.50	
67.9	1.8	7.05	1.75	
95.9	2.4	8.90	2.10	
129.6	3.0	9.89	2.63	
197.1	6.6	10.50	4.00	
283.1	12.1	13.67	5.00	
314.0	13.4	15.71	5.50	
345.3	12.5	15.17	5.90	
352.1	12.6	13.44	6.10	
411.7	13.9	14.53	6.50	7%
445.2	15.5	16.13	7.10	7%
500.2	17.7	17.36	7.75	4%
549.1	20.0	19.70	8.50	6%
648.4	22.0	22.30	9.35	3%
773.8	26.1	26.25	10.25	6%
886.3	31.2	29.68	11.25	2%
933.3	35.0	31.96	12.00	4%

TOTAL CIGARETTE CONSUMPTION

Year	Billions of cigarettes		Date	RRP £	Specific duty £
1960	110.9		01/01/1979	0.58	0.18
1961	113.4		18/06/1979	0.64	0.18
1962	109.9		**17/09/1979**	**0.67**	**0.24**
1963	115.2		13/03/1980	0.69	0.24
1964	114.4		**31/03/1980**	**0.74**	**0.27**
1965	112		04/02/1981	0.78	0.27
1966	117.6		**16/03/1981**	**0.92**	**0.36**
1967	119.1		12/08/1981	0.95	0.38
1968	121.8		14/09/1981	0.97	0.38
1969	124.9		08/02/1982	0.99	0.38
			09/04/1982	**1.04**	**0.41**
1970	127.9		08/09/1982	1.06	0.41
1971	122.4		24/01/1983	1.08	0.41
1972	130.5		**18/03/1983**	**1.11**	**0.43**
1973	137.4		27/10/1983	1.13	0.43
1974	137		25/01/1984	1.15	0.43
1975	132.6		**16/03/1984**	**1.25**	**0.50**
1976	130.6		01/10/1984	1.27	0.50
1977	125.9		23/01/1985	1.29	0.50
1978	125.2		**22/03/1985**	**1.35**	**0.54**
1979	124.3		25/09/1985	1.37	0.54
			22/01/1986	1.39	0.54
1980	121.5		**21/03/1986**	**1.5**	**0.61**
1981	110.3		24/09/1986	1.52	0.61
1982	102		01/10/1987	1.55	0.61
1983	101.6		**18/03/1988**	**1.58**	**0.63**
1984	99		03/10/1988	1.61	0.63
1985	97.8		02/10/1989	1.65	0.63
1986	95		**23/03/1990**	**1.75**	**0.70**
1987	96		01/10/1990	1.8	0.70
1988	97		**20/03/1991**	**1.96**	**0.80**
1989	98		02/04/1991	2.02	0.80
			01/11/1991	2.08	0.80
1990	102.5		**11/03/1992**	**2.21**	**0.89**
1991	97.9		02/11/1992	2.27	0.89
1992	92.8		**17/03/1993**	**2.37**	**0.98**
1993	88.9		02/08/1993	2.41	0.98
1994	88.3		**01/12/1993**	**2.52**	**1.05**
1995	88		01/04/1994	2.54	1.05
1996	87.2		**01/12/1994**	**2.64**	**1.11**
1997	84		**01/01/1995**	**2.7**	**1.15**
1998	84		03/04/1995	2.74	1.15
1999	84		**28/11/1995**	**2.89**	**1.25**
			01/04/1996	2.93	1.25

Total annual cigarette consumption from 1960 to 2012 (left column); recommended retail price and duty on a packet of 20 Benson & Hedges Special Filter/Gold from 1979 to 2014 (right column).

Year	Billions of cigarettes	Date	RRP £	Specific duty £
2000	81.5	**26/11/1996**	**3.08**	**1.32**
2001	79	18/03/1997	3.12	1.32
2002	76	28/07/1997	3.17	1.32
2003	74	**01/12/1997**	**3.36**	**1.44**
2004	72	31/03/1998	3.42	1.44
2005	70	**01/12/1998**	**3.64**	**1.54**
2006	67.5	**09/03/1999**	**3.82**	**1.65**
2007	64.5	01/07/1999	3.88	1.65
2008	61.5	01/02/2000	3.92	1.65
2009	58.5	**21/03/2000**	**4.17**	**1.81**
		08/08/2000	4.22	1.81
2010	52.5	13/02/2001	4.27	1.81
2011	50.3	**08/03/2001**	**4.33**	**1.85**
2012	51.5	11/09/2001	4.39	1.85
		17/04/2002	**4.45**	**1.88**
		25/06/2002	4.51	1.88
		09/04/2003	**4.59**	**1.94**
		01/07/2003	4.65	1.94
		17/03/2004	**4.74**	**2.00**
		29/06/2004	4.82	2.00
		18/01/2005	4.89	2.00
		17/03/2005	**4.98**	**2.05**
		11/10/2005	5.05	2.05
		23/03/2006	**5.14**	**2.10**
		16/05/2006	5.23	2.10
		16/01/2007	5.33	2.10
		22/03/2007	**5.44**	**2.17**
		22/01/2008	5.55	2.17
		12/03/2008	**5.66**	**2.24**
		01/12/2008	**5.67**	**2.24**
		17/02/2009	5.78	2.24
		22/04/2009	**5.85**	**2.29**
		25/11/2009	5.95	2.29
		01/01/2010	**6.13**	**2.29**
		24/03/2010	**6.29**	**2.38**
		23/11/2010	6.43	2.38
		04/01/2011	**6.62**	**2.38**
		23/03/2011	**6.95**	**3.10**
		07/09/2011	7.09	3.10
		21/03/2012	**7.47**	**3.35**
		07/07/2012	7.72	3.35
		20/03/2013	**7.98**	**3.52**
		01/09/2013	8.23	3.52
		19/03/2014	**8.47**	**3.68**

T&S STORES – TURNOVER AND PBT

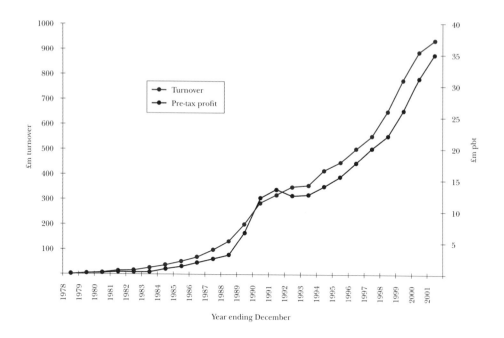

T&S STORES PLC – SHARE PRICE PERFORMANCE

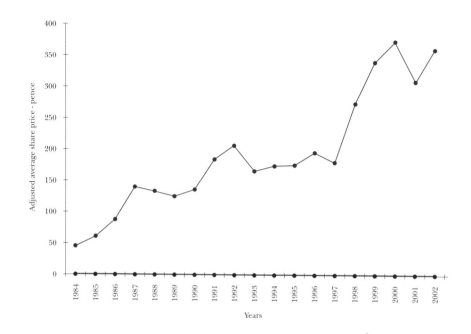

– INDEX –

7-Eleven 140–1, 170

9/11 207–8

Abbeville 292

ABC Leisure 229–34

Accrington 249

Actado 100

Adelaide 251

aerobatics 292

Aldermaston Wharf 229

Aldi 65, 294

Alfred Preedy & Sons *see* Preedy

Alldays 184, 209, 215

Alliance & Leicester 180

Alternative Investment Market (AIM) 108

Alvechurch 226–7

Alvechurch Boat Centres 226–9

analysts 217

Anderton 227

Anglo Welsh 232

Anne (waitress) 22

Annous, Habib 217

Antarctica 298

Arthur Andersen 209

Asda 183, 238, 294

Associated British Foods 30

Aston, Keith 147–8

Aston Villa 242

ATMs 180

Atta, Mohamed 208

Austria 42

'baby shark' method 65

'back to basics' 162

bakeries, in-store 180

Bank of England 90, 162–3

banks 78–9

Barber, Anthony 76

Barclays 101

Barclays Merchant Bank 107, 109

Barrow-in-Furness 190

The Beatles 52, 53

Beccles International Airport 231

Beckett, Terence 105

Bellway 255, 256

Bennett, Derek 71–2, 74, 75, 89, 91

Benwell, Mr 263

Bhatti brothers 238

Birchfield Preparatory School 20–4, 261–8

Birkenhead 113–14

Birmingham

   Cash & Carrys 43, 46–7, 63–4

   redevelopment 225

Birmingham Post & Mail 123

Black, Clive 172, 217

Black Monday 136–7

Black Prince 232

Black Wednesday 161–2

Blackburn 199

Blackpool 203

Blackwater Meadow 229

Blair, Tony 162

Bloom, John 52

Blundell's School 37

Boat Centre 224–5

Boddice, Stephe
    as accountant 93, 95, 98
    and computerisation 111–12, 130
    and Dillons/Preedy acquisition 124–5, 127
    and narrowboats 226, 229–31
    and results announcements 175
    retirement 153
    and USM listing 110

Body Shop 202

books 155–6

Botham, Ian 258–60

Botham, Kath 258

Bowater, John 240

Bowdler, Tim 185

BP 183, 211

Bradburn, Jack 251

Bradburn & Wedge 251

Bradman, Donald 251

break-ins 112–13, 147

Brear, Mr 25

British American Tobacco (BAT) 94

British Waterways 233

Britton, Rita 195–6, 220–1, 261

Bromley, Peter 257

Brown, Gordon 162–3

Brownhills
    after Tesco take-over 216

Brownhills (*continued*)
    distribution functions 157
    expansion of premises 199
    office functions 129
    warehouse 111, 118–19
Brownsword, Andrew 195–6
building societies 281–2
Bull, Steve 237
Burntwood 75
Bush, George W. 208
Buy-Wise Supermarkets 71, 117–20

C-stores *see* convenience stores
Callaghan, James 103
Cambodia 298
Canal and River Trust 233
Canaltime 229
Cannock market stall 40–1, 43–58, 64, 69
Caravan 257–8
caravans 59–61, 69
cardiopulmonary resuscitation (CPR) 284, 285
Carlos (vet) 297, 298
Carter, Peter 107, 110
carton flow racking 119
Carver, Mr 21
Cash & Carrys 43, 46–7, 49, 63–4
CBI 105
Cheshunt 212
Christine (first girlfriend) 22, 25, 27
Christmas crackers 50–1
cigarette kiosks 81–2, 83
cigarettes
    own-label brands 154–5
    sales in UK 201

Circle K 140–1, 170

Claude (pilot) 292

Clegg Commission 107

click and collect 124

Co-operative movement 183, 184, 215

Cohen, Jack 29, 89

Collins, Phil 257–8

Colton, James 257

Combined Cadet Force (CCF) 34–5

Competition Commission 212, 216–17

computerisation 111, 130

confectionery 96–8, 114–15

convenience retailing 140, 163, 169–70, 180–3, 210, 294

convenience stores (C-stores)

    24-hour trading 154

    acquisitions 143, 148–9, 152, 164, 179

    customer services 180

    development of identity 142–3, 158–9

    launch team 159

    rebranding to One-Stop 189, 199–200

    types 141–2

Cook, Vick 80, 99, 112

Costcutter 184

costs, cutting 145–6

Cradley Heath shop 95, 97, 132

Crellin, David 153, 189

Crewe 289–90

cricket 19–20, 249–60

cruises 298

CTN stores 124, 148, 150

Cullis, Stan 237

customers, talking to 202

Cut Price Cigarettes 82, 108

Darwen 200–1

Davies, Bob 167–8

Davies, Chris 226

Davies, Deanne 32–3

Davies, George 123–4

Davies, Jim 30, 32–3

Day & Nite 184, 197–200, 203, 204

Dee, Frank 197–8, 199, 202, 204

Dee Discount 197

Denstone College 24, 25–8, 30–41, 268–72

Derbyshire, David 269

Derbyshire, Viv 269

Dewhurst 44

Dickinson, John 217

Dillons

    acquisition 123–4, 127–31

    branding of newsagent stores as 189

    C-stores 142, 180

    disposal 209, 216

    trading hours 131–2

discotheques 61, 69

Discount Foods 86

distribution 119

dividend payment 187, 188

DLA 215

dogs 295–8

door-to-door sales 54–5

dotcom bubble 208

Douglas-Home, Alec 52

Dowty Sports and Social club 254

DTC 131

Dudley 275

Durnall, Fred 95, 111–12, 113, 120

earnings per share 187, 188

Edge & Ellison 90, 116, 215

Edinburgh 173

Ellesmere College 37

Ellis, Doug 242

Elston Hall Primary School 16–17

Enderby 124

Enron 208–9

Entrepreneur of the Year Award 217, 218

EPOS 153–4, 160, 164, 168, 196, 201

Esso 163, 210

Everton 213

Exchange Rate Mechanism (ERM) 161

Express and Star 240

fagging 30, 34

Falkland Islands 298

Fantasia pick and mix 119, 120, 131, 143–4

Farmiloe, Stan 223–5, 226

Farmiloe & Co. 223

Feeney, Ralph

   and Buy-Wise 71

   and J&F Cash & Carry 46–7, 63–4

   and Lo-Cost 66–8, 69, 75, 79, 80, 91

   and Oriel Foods acquisition 89

Financial Times 214–15, 226

Fine Fare, history 30

Flello, Doug 152

flying 194, 231, 290–3

food retailing 180–1, 183–4, 210

football clubs, structure 244–5

Forbuoys 116

Fordhouses

   move to 22

   shop 94–5

Fordhouses Cricket Club (FCC) 249–60

Foremarke Hall 267

Frankling, Barry 263

fund managers 166, 169, 173–8, 217

F.W. Woolworth 44, 202

Gallagher, Geoff 100–1, 281

Gallagher, Peter 102, 112, 152

Gallaher 94, 116

garage forecourt retailing 141, 183–4

Gayton 227

GBL Wholesale 62–3

Gibbs News 148–9, 152

Ginny (Algarve) 298

Glasgow 173

Glazer family 242

golf 114–15, 193–4, 257–8, 283–4

Goodyear 235

Gordon, Tim 119, 129, 197

Gough, John 239–40, 242, 245, 277

Grand Bahama 238

Grassi, Jonathan 197

Green, Nigel ('Nipper') 39

Green Shield stamps 88–9

Greenspan, Alan 137

greetings cards 97, 130–1

grocery trade 141, 293–4

gross domestic product (GDP) 163

growth stocks 187–8

Gubay, Albert 65

Guest, Ian 284

Halfpenny Green Airport 193, 291, 292

Harris, Al 227–8

Hawthorne, Andy 43, 46–7, 64, 69

Hayward, Jack 238–42, 245–6

Hayward, John 129, 143

Hayward, Rick 239

Heald, Frank 197, 204

Healey, Denis 79

heart attacks 285–6

Heath, Edward 76, 78, 103–4, 105

Helps, Edward 227–8, 229–31

Hewitt, Patricia 217

Hilditch, Jeremy 172, 217

Hilperton 228

HOCM (hypertrophic obstructive cardiomyopathy) 286

Hoddle, Glenn 238

Hodgson, Lord 281

Holmes, Colin 220

Homfray, Miss 80

The Horns of Boningale 278–81

Hoskyns, John 106–7

house prices 138–40, 163

Howe, Geoffrey 106

Howe, Ian 86

ICD (internal cardioverter defibrillator) 287

Iceland 289

ICI 105

Imperial Tobacco 94

impulse purchase 96

income stocks 188

inflation

    1970s 64, 75–9, 81, 85

    1980s 105–7, 139

    1990s 161

Inland Revenue 226

Ipswich Town 248

Iran 105, 107

Ironbridge power station 291

J&F Cash & Carry 46–7, 63–4

Jack Threlfall Memorial Ground 254

Jackett, Kenny 248

Japan 140

JCR convenience stores 143

John Menzies 95, 131, 132

Johnson, Robin 101, 112

Johnston Press 185

Jones, David 124–6

Jones, Peter 256–7

Joseph, Keith 104

Kennet and Avon Canal 228, 229

Kenyon, Melvin 153–4, 199

Kings Heath 75

Kinnock, Neil 162

Kirby, Lorna 130

Knowles, Martin 283–4

KVIs (known-value items) 45

Kwik Save 65, 71, 85–6, 134, 199, 202

Laker, Freddie 163

Latham, John 40

Laura (Algarve) 298

Lawrence, Chas 189

Lawson, Nigel 138–40, 161

lawyers 215–16

Leahy, Terry 211–15, 219–20, 294

Lee (friend) 22, 25, 35–6, 58

legal advice 277

Leitao, Robert 219, 242

Lendl, Ivan 258

Lerner, Randy 242

Lever, William 44

Levin, Bernard 53

Lidl 294

Liverpool 52, 102, 112–14, 245

Liverpool Football Club 245

Llangollen 227

Lloyd, Alan 189

Lo-Cost Discount Stores 66–70, 72–5, 79–92

    disappearance 134

    expansion 84

    fascia 92

    merger with Buy-Wise 75

    sale 89–91

    Wolverhampton 66–70, 72–4

Lo-Cost label 84–5

Lomas, Peter 124–5

Londis 184

'loss leaders' 45

lottery sales 154

lottery terminals 150, 151

Low Hill 16–18

Luton 121

Lyons, John 152

Lyons Tetley 86–7

M&S 294

M&W 164–8

Maasai Mara 298

Mac Fisheries 44

Mac's 149

Maguire, Graham 166–7, 199

Major, John 140, 161

Manchester 102

Manchester City 245

Manchester United 242

Manduca, Paul 239

Marbella 69, 81, 168

marinas 230–2

Market Harborough 229

Mars Corporation 55

McAndrew, Kevin 152

McCarthy, Jim

    at Dillons 129

    chief executive 171, 188

    and Day & Nite acquisition 198, 204

    group retail director 129, 130, 142, 167

    and M&W acquisition 165

    and results announcements 171–3

    Tesco Express visit 210

McCarthy, Mick 238–9, 243, 247–8

Merriman, Richard 267

mice 56–7

Midland Cricket Club Conference 250

Mildenstein, Paul 202–3

Models and Hobbies shop 22–3

Molineux, Benjamin 235

Molineux 235–6

money, not sole goal 295, 300–1

money-off coupons 49–50

Monk, Paul 257–8

Monkhouse, Bob 117, 168

Montgomerie, Colin ('Monty') 194

Moore, Dean 189, 199

Moreton Country Club 22, 23, 58, 61

Morgan, Steve 245–8

Morrisons 183, 294

Moseley Golf Club 283

Moxey, Jez 240–4, 248

Muamba, Fabrice 286

Mumford, John 284

narrowboats 223–34

National Union of Mineworkers (NUM) 78

Nationwide Building Society 282

neighbourhood retail chains 184

Nescafé coffee 85

Net Book Agreement 155–6

Neville-Rolfe, Lucy 212, 216–17

news and magazines 131, 132

newsagents 95–6, 131–2

    first acquisition 95

newspaper distribution 151

Next 123–8

NHS 299–300

Norfolk Broads 231, 232

Norman, Greg 114, 115

Norwich 157

Nursling 164

oil crisis (1970s) 77–8

Okavango Delta 298

One-Stop

    acquisition 184–7, 200

    rebranding of C-stores to 189, 199–200

    under Tesco 216, 288, 294

online lottery 154, 180

Operation Check-Out 89

Oriel Foods 86, 89–91

Orme, Russell 215, 216

Owen, David 215

ownership rights 276–7

Page, John 89–90

Paperchain 156–8

Pareto's principle 65

Pay Point 180

Pedigree Petfoods 55

pet food 54–8, 69

Pets At Home 57–8

Phelan, John 136

Phillips, Richard 265

Picton Jones 101

portfolio insurance 137

Portman Building Society 282

Portugal, villa in 193, 295

Post Offices, in-store 143, 159, 180

Poundland 217

Preedy 82, 114, 123–4, 127–30, 131, 185

prep schools, pincer movement on 264–5

Prepcare nursery 267

Preston 197

property development 274–7

pruning 145–7

pub/restaurant venture 277–81

pub trade 278, 281

purchase tax 62–3

Purdy, Geoff 152, 195

Radox bath salts 62–3

Ratray, Mr 21

Rawstron, Chris 215–16

RCA Corporation 86

Reading Marine 229

recessions
    1990s 162
    2000s 208, 231
Red Line Boats 228, 229
Red Shops 116
Redrow 245
Reed, Tony 288
resale price maintenance 28–9
Retail Information Technology 153
Ridgley, Ray
    and Buy-Wise 71, 74–5, 117–18
    and cut-price tobacco 82
    departure 127–8
    and gauging of likely sales 97
    and Lo-Cost 79, 80, 89, 91
robberies 112–13, 147–8
Rocester 35
Rolls Razor 53
Ross, Mike 69
Ross, Stuart 197, 203
Rothschild 215, 219, 242
Rowlandson Organisation 149
Rubery 75
rugby
    injury 32
    school team 36–9
Ruston Cash & Carry 47

Safeway 183, 211
Sainsbury, John James 29–30
Sainsbury's 181, 294
    history 29–30
Sainsbury's Local 183, 211
Sanders, Dave 99

Sanders, Dawn 98–9, 112

school governors 263

Scotland, Iain 217

Section 106 agreement 256

self-confidence 295

Seymour, Andy 36

Shevyn, Penny 267

Shirley, Darren 172

shopfitting 99–100, 112, 115

Short, Bob 30, 36, 41–2

Sippets, Alan 218

site development 101–2

Smith, Dave

    as best man 86

    dog 98

    early ventures 59–61, 69

    friendship with 59, 127–8, 193, 220–2

    Marbella 69, 81

    marriage 99

    and narrowboats 226

    and pub/restaurant venture 277–8

    retirement 124, 127

    and T&S Stores 110, 112, 123, 124

    and T&S Tobacco 82, 93, 102

Smith, Delia 245

Smith, Dot 60

Smith, John 162

Smith, Lorraine 99, 193, 221

Smith, Ron 252, 256

Smith, Steve 217, 218

smokers' sundries 120

smoking, at Denstone 33–4

Smout, Clive 146

SOS Algarve Animals 298

South Staffordshire Golf Club 240, 283

Spar 184

Spar Landmark 152

Sperry & Hutchinson 88–9

Spillers 55

squint 16, 18

Staffordshire Building Society (SBS) 281–2

stand-alone brands 85

Stark, Malcolm 277–81

Stew Leonard 202

Stillwell, Brian 217

stock control, computerised 111

stock market crash (1987) 135–8

stock relief 79

Stockport 117

Stocks, Lynton 39

Stockwell, Tony 227–8

Stoddart, David 217

store visits 113–14

Sun 215

Sunday trading laws 149–50, 151

Sunderland (football club) 248

Supercigs

    Blackpool 203–5

    decline 158, 168–9, 201

    as discount operation 130

    disposal 209, 216

    name choice 108

    newspapers and magazines 152

supermarkets 132–4, 293–4

supply chain management 200–1

Supreme cigarette brand 154–5

Swales, Elizabeth 32

Swales, Mike 32, 268

symbol groups 141, 183, 184

T&S Stores
    board photo (1998) 177
    celebrations after sale 217–21
    disposals of stores 159–60, 179
    expansion
        to 100 stores 117, 118
        to 200 stores 117, 121
        to 340 CTN stores 148
        to 500 C-stores 165
        to 600 stores 123–4, 129
        to 704 stores 153
        to 800 stores 157
        to 890 C-stores 199
        to 1,000 stores 168–9
        to 1,200 stores 188–9
    name change to 108
    reorganisation (1992) 145
    results communication 170–6
    sale to Tesco 211–16
    shareholders 171, 173–4
    Stock Market listing 117
    USM listing 108–10
    see also convenience stores
T&S Tobacco
    expansion
        to 25 stores 99
        to 49 stores 102
    first shop 94–5
    formation 82
    name change 108
    recruitment of team 93–9

Tarbuck, Jimmy 194

tax cuts 104

tax relief schemes 223–6

Taylor, Basil 165, 168

Tennant, Brian 102

Tesco 87–9, 133–4, 203, 294

    acquisition of T&S 211–16

    consultancy 261

    history 29

Tesco Express 163, 183, 210, 216, 294

Tettenhall 22

Texas 140

Thames 232

Thatcher, Margaret 103–7, 135, 140, 203

Thorne, Willie 168, 169

Threlfall, Edna (mother) 16–20, 22

    and caravan 60

    and cricket 250

    and Denstone College 25, 27

Threlfall, Gill

    and aerobatic flight 292

    Blackpool 203, 205

    and children 300

    courtship 83–4

    and Denstone College 269, 271

    and football 247

    friendships 33, 221, 258

    holidays 298

    and Kevin heart failure 283, 284–5

    overseas trips 91

    Portugal 193, 295–8

    tribute to 301

    wedding 86–8

Threlfall, Jack (father)
  business 20, 40, 293
  and caravans 60
  and cricket 19–20, 249–53, 259
  death 252–3
  and Denstone College 25
  early years 16–19
  Kevin to school by van 20, 262
  and Kevin's engagement 68
  on money 295
Threlfall, Jade 271, 285
Threlfall, Kevin
  appendix removal 189–92
  birth 16
  broken engagement 68–9
  childhood 16–24
  courtship 83–4
  heart failure 283–7
  wedding 86–8
  youth 25–42
Threlfall, Nicholas 271, 285
Threlfall, Sharron 16, 20, 28, 31, 250, 271
Threlfall Library 271–2
The Times 155
tobacco duty 94, 118–19, 123
tobacco suppliers 94
Tompkins, Richard 89
trading stamps 88–9
trainspotting 19, 250, 289–90
Traves, Sean 80, 93
Trinidad TB20 aircraft 292–3
Triumph cigarette brand 154–5
Turner, David 143
Typhoo Tea 293

unemployment 105
Unilever 44
Union Wharf 229
Unlisted Securities Market (USM) 108

Value Foods 65
Vaseline 85
VAT 105–6, 107
vehicle insurance 146
Vickerey, Ian 143
Victoria Wine Company 167
Vietnam 298
Viking Afloat 228, 229

Waitrose 294
Walker, Malcolm 288–9
Wallasey 112
Walters, Alan 106–7
Wardle, John 90, 116, 215–16
warehouses 79–80, 111, 118–19, 129–30, 145, 164
Warwick cigarette brand 155
washing machines 44, 52–3
wastage, managing 182
Wednesfield 210
Weeks, Michael 86
Wellington market 28
Wentworth 114
Wessex Narrowboats 229
West Bromwich Albion 245, 247
Weston, Michael 165–6, 167
WH Smith 95, 131, 132
Wheelers 116
Whitgift School 37–8
Wilson, Harold 78

Winalot 55, 56
Wolverhampton
early years in 16–24
Lo-Cost store 66–70, 72–4
West Indian community 74
see also Fordhouses; Low Hill; Tettenhall
Wolverhampton New Cross Hospital 299
Wolverhampton Wanderers (Wolves) 213, 235–48
boardroom changes 239–42
club history 235–8
recent years 245–8
sale 239–43, 245
Woodard Corporation 269
Woodward, Steve 284
Woolworth, Frank Winfield 44
Woolworths 44, 202
Worksop College 37
Wrekin College 37
Wrenbury 227
Wright, Billy 237

Yom Kippur War 77